Reprinted 1984 from the 1890 edition.
Cover design © 1981 Time-Life Books Inc.
Library of Congress CIP data following page 354.

PICKETT'S CHARGE AT GETTYSBURG.   Page 214.

RECOLLECTIONS OF A PRIVATE.

A STORY OF THE ARMY OF THE POTOMAC.

BY

WARREN LEE GOSS,

AUTHOR OF "THE SOLDIER'S STORY OF HIS CAPTIVITY AT ANDERSONVILLE
AND OTHER PRISONS"; "JED: A BOY'S ADVENTURES IN
THE ARMY OF '61-'65."

NEW YORK:

THOMAS Y. CROWELL & CO.,

46 EAST FOURTEENTH STREET.

TYPOGRAPHY BY J. S. CUSHING & CO., BOSTON.
PRESSWORK BY BERWICK & SMITH, BOSTON.

PREFACE.

THE first few chapters of this book were published under the title of "Recollections of a Private" in the *Century Magazine.* Herein I have endeavored to speak for my many comrades in the ranks. Could their voices have been heard mine would have been silent.. The general of an army, in his reports, gives the anatomy of army movements and of battle. A description of the many incidents of the private soldier's experience shows its living soul.

The importance of the views of a private soldier has lately been expressed by Lord Wolseley, adjutant-general of the British army, in his "English View of the Civil War," published in the *North American Review.*[1] After pointing out the dangers resulting from popular clamor, "when in the middle of a war, they (the journalists) take it upon themselves, to drive or to force those whom they influence, to decide what the naval or military commander should do," the distinguished author says, "If these *Century* articles could be as widely read among us as they have been in America, we might possibly be saved in the future from disasters such as were entailed on us in the Crimea by very similar action. In particular, I should like those articles by Mr. Warren Lee Goss, 'The Recollections of a Private,' duly studied. For, after all, questions of strategy and of tactics, and of the importance of organization of all kinds, turn upon the effect which is ultimately produced on the spirit, and well-being, and fighting efficiency of the private soldier."

[1] July, 1889.

The "Army of the Potomac" was the people in arms. It mirrored the diversified opinions and occupations of a free and intelligent democracy. The force that called it together was the spirit that made a government of the people possible. Its ranks were largely filled with youth, who had no love for war, but who had left their pleasant homes, and the pursuits of peace, that the government they loved might not perish. To the large numbers of patriotic young men in the ranks is to be attributed much of its hopeful spirit. Thus it was that, though baffled by bloody and disheartening reverses, though it changed its commanders often, it never lost its discipline, its heroic spirit, or its confidence in final success. Its private soldiers were often as intelligent critics of military movements as were their superiors.

In every other conquering army its commander has been its life and soul. Napoleon, in substance, once declared, that it was not great armies that won triumphs, but great commanders. Again he said, "It is not men who make armies, but a man," thus deifying great generals. The reverse of this might be said of the "Army of the Potomac." Its final triumph over the army of Northern Virginia, commanded by the genius of Lee, was won by constant hammering and attrition, during which the blood of our common soldiers paid the greater tribute. In our great army, the private soldier who carried forty rounds of cartridges and a brave heart, who fought without expectation of reward or promotion, was its truest hero and the fittest representative of its conquering spirit. His unselfish sacrifices, and heroic confidence in final victory, saved the nation and preserved the union of states.

The title of these papers, "Recollections of a Private," must not be read literally. In them the writer has availed himself of the reminiscences of many comrades known by him to be trustworthy. For convenience and to give a greater sense of reality to the descriptions, he has often made use of the first person in chronicling the recollections of his comrades.

The author desires to express obligations to Dr. Thomas H. Mann, of Milford, Mass., formerly a private in the 18th Massachusetts Volunteers, for suggestions. Several incidents in the book are also, by his permission, drawn from his memoranda.

He is also indebted to Josiah N. Jones, of the Sixth New Hampshire, and to William J. Mantanye, of the Seventy-sixth New York, for invaluable material contained in diaries kept by them during the many stirring scenes of their army service.

To Captain J. F. Huntington, of Boston, for the use of a valuable manuscript, and to many others of whom space does not permit mention, thanks are due.

W. L. G.

Norwich, Conn.

CONTENTS.

CONTENTS.

LIST OF ILLUSTRATIONS.

Drawn by J. R. Chapin and W. H. Shelton. Engraved by George T. Andrew.

ix

RECOLLECTIONS OF A PRIVATE.

A STORY OF THE ARMY OF THE POTOMAC.

CHAPTER I.

THE YOUNG RECRUIT.

BEFORE the war had really begun I enlisted. I had read the papers, and attended flag-raisings, and heard orators declaim of "undying devotion to the Union." One speaker to whom I listened declared that "human life must be cheapened," but I never learned that he helped on the work experimentally. When men by the hundred walked soberly and deliberately to the front and signed the enlistment papers, he didn't show any inclination that way. As I came out of the hall with conflicting emotions, feeling as though I should have to go finally or forfeit my birthright as an American citizen, one of the orators who stood at the door, glowing with enthusiasm and patriotism, and shaking hands effusively with those who enlisted, said to me :

"Did you enlist ? "

"No," I said. "Did you ? "

"No ; they wont take me. I have got a lame leg and a widowed mother to take care of."

Another enthusiast I remember, who was eager to enlist — others. He declared the family of no man who went to the front should suffer. After the war he was prominent among those in our town who at town-meeting voted to refund the money to such as had expended it to procure substitutes during the war. He has, moreover, been fierce and uncompromising toward the ex-Confederates since the war closed, and I have heard him repeatedly express the wish that all the civil and general officers of the late Confederacy might be court-martialled and shot.

I was young, but not unobserving, and did not believe, from the first, in a sixty days' war; nor did I consider ten dollars a month, and the promised glory, large pay for the services of an able-bodied young man. Enlistment scenes are usually pictured as entirely heroic, but truth compels me to acknowledge that my feelings were mixed. At this

Leaving for the Front.

moment I cannot repress a smile of amusement and pity for that young recruit — myself.

It was the news that the Sixth Massachusetts Regiment had been mobbed by roughs on their passage through Baltimore which gave me the war fever. When I read Governor Andrew's pathetic telegram to have the hero martyrs "preserved in ice and tenderly sent forward," somehow, though I felt the pathos of it, I could not reconcile myself to the ice. Ice in connection with patriotism did not give me agreeable impressions of

war, and when I came to think of it, the stoning of the heroic
"Sixth" didn't suit me; it detracted from my desire to die a soldier's
death. I lay awake all night thinking it over, with the "ice" and
"brickbats" before my mind. However, the fever culminated that
night, and I resolved to enlist.

"Cold chills" ran up and down my back as I got out of bed after
the sleepless night, and shaved, preparatory to other desperate deeds
of valor. I was twenty years of age, and when anything unusual
was to be done, like fighting or courting, I shaved. With a nervous
tremor convulsing my whole system, and my heart thumping like
muffled drum-beats, I stood before the door of the recruiting-office,
and, before turning the knob to enter, read and re-read the adver-
tisement for recruits posted thereon, until I knew all its peculiarities.
The promised chances for "travel and promotion" seemed good, and
I thought I might have made a mistake in considering war so serious,
after all. "Chances for travel!" I must confess now, after four
years of soldiering, that the "chances for travel" were no myth.
But "promotion" was a little uncertain and slow.

I was in no hurry to open the door. Though determined to enlist,
I was half inclined to put it off awhile; I had a fluctuation of desires;
I was faint-hearted and brave; I wanted to enlist, and yet ——.
Here I turned the knob, and was relieved. I had been more prompt,
with all my hesitation, than the officer in his duty; he wasn't in.

Finally he came, and said: "What do you want, my boy?"

"I want to enlist," I responded, blushing deeply with upwelling
patriotism and bashfulness. Then the surgeon came to strip and
examine me. In justice to myself, it must be stated that I signed
the rolls without a tremor. It is common to the most of humanity,
I believe, that, when confronted with actual danger, men have less
fear than in its contemplation. I will, however, make one exception
in favor of the first shell I heard uttering its hoarse anathema and its
blood-curdling hisses, as though a steam locomotive were travelling
the air. With this exception, I have found danger always less terrible
face to face than on the night before the battle.

My first uniform was a bad fit: my trousers were too long by
three or four inches; the flannel shirt was coarse and unpleasant, too
large at the neck and too short elsewhere. The forage cap was an
ungainly bag with pasteboard top and leather visor; the blouse was

the only part which seemed decent; while the overcoat made me feel like a little nib of corn amid a preponderance of husk. Nothing except "Virginia mud" ever took down my ideas of military pomp quite so low.

After enlisting I didn't seem of so much consequence as I ex-pected. There was not so much excitement on account of my military appearance as I deemed justly my due. I was taught my facings, and at the time I thought the drill-master needlessly fussy about shouldering, ordering, and presenting arms. At this time men were often drilled in company and regimental evolutions long before they learned the manual of arms, because of the difficulty of obtaining muskets. These we obtained at an early day, but we would willingly have resigned them after carrying them for a few hours. The musket, after an hour's drill, seemed heavier and less ornamental than it had looked to be. The first day I went out to drill, getting tired of doing the same things over and over, I said to the drill-sergeant : "Let's stop this fooling and go over to the grocery."

His only reply was addressed to a corporal : "Corporal, take this man out and drill him like h—l"; and the corporal did. I found that suggestions were not as well appreciated in the army as in private life, and that no wisdom was equal to a drill-master's "Right face," "Left wheel," and "Right, oblique, march."

It takes a raw recruit some time to learn that he is not to think or suggest, but obey. Some never do learn. I acquired it at last, in humility and mud, but it was tough. Yet I doubt if my patriotism, during my first three weeks' drill, was quite knee high. Drilling looks easy to a spectator, but it isn't. Old soldiers who read this will remember their green recruithood and smile assent. After a time I had cut down my uniform so that I could see out of it, and had conquered the drill sufficiently to see through it. Then the word came : On to Washington !

Our company was quartered at a large hotel near the railway sta-tion in the town in which it was recruited. Bunks had been fitted up within a part of the hotel but little used. We took our meals at the regular hotel table, and found fault with the style. Six months later we should have considered ourselves aristocratic to have slept in the hotel stables with the meal-bin for a dining-table.

There was great excitement one morning at the report that we were going to be sent to the front. Most of us obtained a limited pass and went to see our friends for the last time, returning the same night. All our schoolmates and home acquaintances "came slobbering around camp," as one of the boys ungraciously expressed it.

We bade adieu to our friends with heavy hearts, for lightly as I may here seem to treat the subject, it was no light thing for a boy of twenty to start out for three years into the unknown dangers of a civil war. Our mothers — God bless them! — had brought us something good to eat, — pies, cakes, doughnuts, and jellies. It was one way in which a mother's heart found utterance. Our young ladies, (sisters, of course) brought an invention, generally made of leather or cloth, containing needles, pins, thread, buttons, and scissors, so that nearly every recruit had an embryo tailor's shop — with the goose outside. One old lady, in the innocence of her heart, brought her son an umbrella. We did not see anything particularly laughable about it at the time, but our old drill-sergeant did.

Finally we were ready to move; our tears were wiped away, our buttons were polished, and our muskets were as bright as emery-paper could make them. How our buttons and muskets did shine! We were brilliant there, if nowhere else.

"Wad" Rider, a member of our company, had come from a neighboring State to enlist with us. He was about eighteen years of age, red-headed, freckle-faced, good-natured, and rough, with a wonderful aptitude for crying or laughing from sympathy. Another comrade, whom I will call Jack, was honored with a call from his mother, a little woman, hardly reaching up to Jack's shoulder, with a sweet, motherly, careworn face. At the last moment, though she had tried hard to preserve her composure, as is the habit of New England people, she threw her arms around her boy's neck, and with an outburst of sobbing and crying, said : "My dear boy, my dear boy, what will your poor old mother do without you? You are going to fight for your country. Don't forget your mother, Jack; God bless you, God bless you!" We felt as if the mother's tears and blessing were a benediction over us all. There was a touch of nature in her homely sorrow and solicitude over her big boy, which drew tears of sympathy from my eyes as I thought of my own sorrowing mother at home. The sympathetic Wad Rider burst into tears and sobs. His eyes refused, as he expressed it, to "dry up," until, as we were moving off,

Jack's mother, rushing toward him with a bundle tied like a wheat-sheaf, called out, in a most pathetic voice, "Jack! Jack! you've forgotten to take your pennyroyal."

We all laughed, and so did Jack, and I think the laugh helped him more than the cry did.

Everybody had said his last word; we were on the cars and off. Handkerchiefs were waved at us from all the houses we passed, and we cheered till we were hoarse, and then settled back and swung our handkerchiefs. Handkerchiefs did double duty that day.

Just here let me name over the contents of my knapsack, as its contents were a fair sample of what all the volunteers started with. There were in it a pair of trousers, two pairs of drawers, a pair of thick boots, four pairs of stockings, four flannel shirts, a blouse, a looking-glass, a can of peaches, a bottle of cough-mixture, a button-stick, chalk, razor and strop, the "tailor's shop" spoken of above, a Bible, a small volume of Shakspere, and writing utensils. To its top was strapped a double woollen blanket and a rubber one. It was boiling over, like a ripe cotton-pod. I remember, too, many other things left behind because of lack of room in or about the knapsack. We would have packed in a portable cooking-stove each had there been room.

On our arrival in Boston we were marched through the streets — the first march of any consequence we had taken with our knapsacks and equipments on. Our dress consisted of a belt about the body, which held a cartridge-box and bayonet, a cross-belt, also a haversack and tin drinking-cup, a canteen, and, last but not least, the knapsack strapped to the back. The straps ran over, around, and about one, in confusion most perplexing to our unsophisticated shoulders; the knapsack giving one constantly the feeling that he was being pulled over backward. We marched along the streets, my canteen banging against my bayonet, both the tin cup and bayonet badly interfering with the butt of my musket, while my cartridge-box and haversack were constantly flopping up and down — the whole jangling like loose harness and chains on a runaway horse. I felt like old Atlas, with the world on his shoulders and the planetary system suspended around him.

We marched into Boston Common, and I involuntarily cast my eye about for a bench. But for a former experience in offering advice, I should have proposed to the captain to "chip in" and hire a team to carry our equipments. Such was my first experience in war harness. Afterward, with hardened muscles, rendered athletic by long marches and invigorated by hardships, I could look back upon those days and smile, while carrying a knapsack as lightly as my heart. That morning my heart was as heavy as my knapsack. At last the welcome orders came: "Prepare to open ranks! Rear, open order, march! Right dress! Front! Order arms! Fix bayonets! Stack arms! Unsling knapsacks! In place, rest!"

The tendency of raw soldiers is to overload themselves on their first march. Experience only can teach them its disadvantages, and the picture I have attempted to draw is not exaggerated. On the first long march the reaction sets in, and the recruit goes to the opposite extreme, not carrying enough of the absolutely necessary baggage, and thereby becoming dependent upon his obliging comrades when a camp is reached. Old soldiers preserve a happy medium. I have seen a new regiment start out with all the indescribable material carried by raw troops, sometimes including sheet-iron stoves, and come back after a long march covered with more mud than baggage, stripped of everything except their blankets, haversacks, canteens, muskets, and cartridge-boxes. These were the times when the baggage of the new recruits was often worth more than their services.

During that afternoon in Boston, after marching and countermarching, or, as one of our farmer-boy recruits expressed it, after "hawing and geeing" around the streets, we were sent to Fort Independence for the night for safe-keeping. A company of regulars held the fort; guards walked their post with a stiffness and uprightness that was astonishing. They acted more like pieces of mechanism than men. Our first impression of these old regulars was that there was a needless amount of "wheel about and turn about, and walk just so," and of saluting, and presenting arms.

We were all marched to our quarters within the fort, where we unslung our knapsacks. The first day's struggle with a knapsack over, the general verdict was "got too much of it." At supper-time we were marched to the dining-barracks, where our bill of fare was beefsteak, coffee, wheat bread, and potatoes, but not a sign of milk or butter. It struck me as queer when I heard that the army was never provided with butter and milk.

The next day we were started for Washington, by rail and boat.
We marched through New York's crowded streets without awakening
the enthusiasm we thought our due ; for we had read of the exciting
scenes attending the departure of the New York Seventh for Washington on the day the Sixth Massachusetts was mobbed in Baltimore,
and also of the march of the Twelfth Massachusetts down Broadway
on the 24th of July, when the regiment sang the new and thrilling
lyric "John Brown's Body."

The following morning we took breakfast in Philadelphia, where
we were attended by matrons and maidens, who waited upon us with
thoughtful tenderness, as if they had been our own mothers and
sweethearts instead of strangers. They feasted us and then filled
our haversacks. God bless them ! If we did not quite appreciate
them then, we did afterward. After embarking on the cars at Philadelphia, the waving of handkerchiefs was less and less noticeable
along the route. We arrived in Baltimore late at night and marched
through its deserted streets silently, as though we were criminals
instead of patriots.

On our arrival in Washington the next morning, we were marched
to barracks, dignified by the name of "Soldiers' Retreat," where a
half loaf of "soft-tack," as we had already begun to call wheat bread,
was issued, together with a piece of "salt junk," about as big and
tough as the heel of my government shoe, and a quart of coffee, —
which constituted our breakfast. Our first day in Washington was
spent in shaving, washing, polishing our brasses and buttons, and
cleaning-up for inspection. A day or two later we moved to quarters
not far from the armory, looking out on the broad Potomac, within
sight of Long Bridge and the city of Alexandria. We were at the
front, or near enough to satisfy our immediate martial desires.

The weather was so mild in that February, 1862, that many of us
used the river for bathing, and found its temperature not uncomfortable. Here and there the sound of a gun broke the serenity, but
otherwise the quiet seemed inconsistent with the war preparations
going on around us. In the distance, across the wide bay, we could
see the steeples and towers of the city of Alexandria, while up stream,
on the right, was the Long Bridge. Here and there was to be seen
the moving panorama of armed men, as a regiment crossed the
bridge ; a flash of sunlight on the polished muskets revealed them

OFFICERS ON PENNSYLVANIA AVENUE. Page 9.

to the eye ; while the white-topped army baggage-wagons filed over in constant procession, looking like sections of a whitewashed fence in motion.

The overgrown country village of that period, called Washington, can be described in a few words. There were wide streets stretching out from a common centre like a spider's web. The Capitol, with its unfinished dome ; the Patent Office, the Treasury, and the other public buildings, were in marked and classic contrast with the dilapidated, tumble-down, shabby look of the average homes, stores, groceries, and groggeries, which increased in shabbiness and dirty dilapidation as they receded from the centre. Around the muddy streets wandered the long-faced, solemn-visaged hog, uttering sage grunts. The climate of Washington was genial, but the mud was fearful. I have drilled in it, marched in it, and run from the provost-guard in it, and I think I appreciate it from actual and familiar knowledge. In the lower quarter of the city there was not a piece of sidewalk. Even Pennsylvania Avenue, with its sidewalks, was extremely dirty ; the cavalcade of teams, artillery caissons, and bag-gage-wagons, with their heavy wheels, stirred the mud into a stiff batter for the pedestrian.

Officers in tinsel and gold lace were so thick on Pennsylvania Avenue that it was a severe trial for a private to walk there. The salute exacted by officers, of bringing the hand to the visor of the cap, extending the arm to its full length, then letting it drop by the side, was tiresome when followed up with the industry required by this horde. Perhaps I exaggerate, but in a half-hour's walk on the avenue I think I have saluted two hundred officers. Brigadier-generals were more numerous there than I ever knew them to be at the front. These officers, many of whom won their positions by political wire-pulling at Washington, we privates thought the great bane of the war ; they ought to have been sent to the front rank of battle, to pursue the enemy instead of Old Abe and the members of Congress from their district, until they had learned the duties of a soldier. Mingled with these gaudy, useless officers were citizens in search of fat contracts, privates, "non-com's," and officers whose uni-forms were well worn and faded, showing that they were from the encampments and active service. Occasionally a regiment passed through the streets, on the way to camp ; all surged up and down wide Pennsylvania Avenue.

This was shortly before the battle of Fort Donelson; and the first Bull Run, being the only considerable pitched battle up to that time, was still a never-failing topic of discussion and reminiscence among the men. When we fell in with soldiers who had been in the fight, we were inquisitive.

Before enlisting, and while on a visit to a neighboring town, I was one evening at the village store, when the talk turned upon the duration of the war. Jim Tinkham, the clerk of the grocery store, announced his belief in a sixty days' war. I modestly asked for more time. The older ones agreed with Jim and argued, as was common at that time, that the Government would soon blockade all the Rebel ports and starve them out. Tinkham proposed to wager a supper for those present if the Rebels did not surrender before snow came that year. I accepted. Neither of us put up any money, and in the excitement of the weeks which followed I had forgotten the wager. During my first week in Washington, whom should I meet but Jim Tinkham, the apostle of the sixty-day theory. He was brown with sunburn, and clad in a rusty uniform which showed service in the field. He was a veteran, for he had been at the battle of Bull Run. He confidentially declared that after getting the order to retreat at that battle, he should not have stopped short of Boston if he had not been halted by a soldier with a musket, after crossing Long Bridge.

"They were enlisting a regiment for three months in our town," he said, "and I thought I'd come out with the rest of the boys and settle the war. Our regiment was camped near Alexandria, and the whole of us, the recruits, grew impatient to end the war and get home to see the folks. I tell you, we were glad when we were told to get ready for a march. We left our knapsacks and heavy luggage in camp with a few old fellows and sick ones, who grieved because they couldn't go on the excursion and help the Secesh out of Virginia.

"They gave us rations of salt junk, hardtack, sugar, and coffee. Each man carried his rubber and woollen blanket, forty rounds of cartridges, a canteen, his gun and equipments, and most of us a patent drinking-tube. I threw away the salt junk and hardtack, and filled my haversack with peach-pie, cakes, and goodies. I hadn't been on the march an hour before I realized that it might not be such fun, after all. There was a thirty-two-pound gun mooring on the road, with sixteen or eighteen horses to pull it. Finally, two or three companies were detailed to help the horses. The weather was scorching hot, but the most trying thing was the jerky way they marched us. Sometimes they'd double-quick us, and again they'd keep us standing in the road waiting in the hot sun for half an hour, then start us ahead again a little way, then halt us again, and so on. The first day we marched until after sundown, and when we halted for the night we were the tiredest crowd of men I ever saw.

"The next day was the 17th of July. I had eaten up all my pies and cakes and was hungry, so I stopped at a house and asked if they would sell me something to eat. There were three negro girls, a white woman, and her daughter, in the house. The white folks were proud and unaccommodating. They said the Yankees had stolen everything — all their 'truck,' as they called it ; but when I took out a handful of silver change, they brought me a cold Johnny-cake and some chicken. As I was leaving the house, the daughter said : 'You'n Yanks are right peart just now, but you'ns'll come back soon a right smart quicker than yer'r going, I recken !' — a prophecy we fulfilled to the letter.

"We marched helter-skelter nearly all night without orders to stop, until, just before daylight, we halted near a little building they called a church (Pohick Church). I kept on the march with my company, though my feet were blistered and my bones ached badly.

"The first gun of the fight I heard," added Tinkham, "was when we were eight or ten miles from Centreville, on the afternoon of the 18th of July, the engagement at Blackburn's ford. We were hurried up at double-quick and marched in the direction of the firing until we reached Centreville, about eleven o'clock that night. It looked like war, and no mistake, in the morning. Batteries and stacked arms lined the roads ; officers on horseback were everywhere ; regiments were marching on to the field, and excitement and enthusiasm prevailed. On the 20th more Virginians came into camp, looking, as they said, for negroes, and complaining of our soldiers. We got new rations of beef and pork, and, very early on the morning of the 21st, we marched through Centreville up the turnpike road. Near Cub Run we saw carriages and barouches which contained civilians who had driven out from Washington to witness the operations. A Connecticut boy said : 'There's our Senator !' and some of our men recognized Senator Wilson and other members of Congress. Every one of us expected to have our names in the papers when we got home. We thought it wasn't a bad idea to have the great men from Washington come out to see us thrash the Rebs.

"That day was the hottest one I ever experienced. We marched and marched and double-quicked, and didn't appear to get ahead at all. Every one of whom we inquired the distance to Manassas Junction said five miles, and after a while they would say ten miles instead of five, and we know now that that was under the truth. Then we began to throw away our blankets. After a while we turned off from the main road into a cart path which led through the woods and dry, dusty, wornout fields. At last we arrived at Sudley's ford and rested, while several regiments, under General Hunter, waded Bull Run. While here we could see shells bursting in little round clouds in the air far to the left of us down the Run. The dust rising on the roads ahead was said to be the Rebel army advancing to fight us. We were going to have a fight; there was but little doubt about it now!

"We soon followed the others across Bull Run and came to a field on a hill (near the Matthews house), where we saw dead and wounded men. It made me feel faint to look at them. A battery of the enemy had just left a position in front of us. An officer here rode up, pointed toward the enemy, and said something which was not distinguishable to me, but the boys began exclaiming: 'Hurrah, they are running!' — 'The Rebels are running!' — 'It's General McDowell! He says they are running!' On the right of us was a battery, in the field, the guns of which were fired as fast as the men could load. One of the men on the battery told me afterward that they made the Rebel battery change position every fifteen minutes. We advanced to the crest, fired a volley, and saw the Rebels running toward the road below (the Warrenton turnpike). Then we were ordered to lie down and load. We aimed at the puffs of smoke we saw rising in front and on the left of us. The men were all a good deal excited. Our rear rank had singed the hair of the front rank, who were more afraid of them than of the Rebels.

"The next thing I remember was the order to advance, which we did under a scattering fire; we crossed the turnpike, and ascending a little way, were halted in a depression or cut in the road which runs from Sudley's ford. The boys were saying constantly, in great glee:

'We've whipped them.' 'We'll hang Jeff Davis to a sour apple-tree.'
'They are running.' 'The war is over.' About noon there wasn't
much firing, and we were of the opinion that the enemy had all run
away. There was a small wooden house on the hill, rising from the
left-hand side of the road as we were going, where, we afterward
heard, a Mrs. Henry, an invalid, had been killed in the engagement.

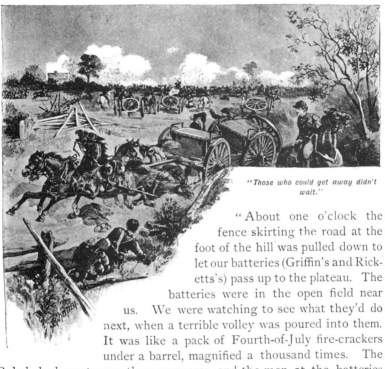

*"Those who could get away didn't
wait."*

"About one o'clock the
fence skirting the road at the
foot of the hill was pulled down to
let our batteries (Griffin's and Ricketts's) pass up to the plateau. The
batteries were in the open field near
us. We were watching to see what they'd do
next, when a terrible volley was poured into them.
It was like a pack of Fourth-of-July fire-crackers
under a barrel, magnified a thousand times. The
Rebels had crept upon them unawares, and the men at the batteries
were about all killed or wounded."

Here let me interrupt Tinkham's narrative to say that one of the
artillery-men there engaged has since told me that, though he had
been in several battles since, he had seldom seen worse destruction
in so short a time. He said they saw a regiment advancing, and the
natural inference was that they were Rebels. But an officer insisted
it was a New York regiment which was expected for support, and so

no order was given to fire on them. "Then came a tremendous explosion of musketry," said the artillery-man, "and all was confusion. Wounded men with dripping wounds were clinging to caissons, to which were attached frightened and wounded horses. Horses attached to caissons rushed through the infantry ranks. I saw three horses galloping off, dragging a fourth, which was dead.

"The dead cannoneers lay with the rammers of the guns and sponges and lanyards still in their hands. The battery was annihilated by those volleys in a moment. Those who could get away didn't wait. We had no supports near enough to protect us properly, and the enemy were within seventy yards of us when that volley was fired. Our battery being demolished in that way was the beginning of our defeat at Bull Run," said this old regular.

"Did the volunteers fight well?" I inquired.

"Yes, the men fought well and showed pluck. I've seen a good deal worse fighting and I've seen better since. I saw the Rebels advance and try to drag away those eleven guns three times, but they were driven back by steady volleys from our infantry. Then some of our men tried to drag the guns away, but were ordered to take their places in the ranks to fight. They couldn't be spared!"

But to return to Tinkham's recollections of the fight:

"It must have been four o'clock in the afternoon," he said, "at a time when our fire had become scattered and feeble, that the rumor passed from one to another that the Rebels had got reënforcements. Where are ours? we asked. There was no confusion or panic then, but discouragement. And at this juncture, from the woods ahead, on each side of the Sudley ford road, there came terrible volleys. The Confederates were in earnest. A wounded Southerner lying near me said earnestly and repeatedly: 'Thank God, I die for my country!' Our men began to feel it was no use to fight without reënforcements. They fell back steadily, cursing their generals because no reënforcements were sent to them. The men had now in most cases been marching and fighting thirteen hours. The absence of general officers convinced us more than anything else that it was no use to fight longer. The enemy were pressing us, and we fell back. We didn't run!" Complaint against the officers, like this by Tinkham, was common among the privates with whom I talked. Said another man to me:

"The fault was, we were not well disciplined or officered. I noticed in the reports that several Rebel generals and commissioned officers were killed and wounded. You'll notice, on the other hand, that but very few of ours were.[1] Companies, and in some instances regiments, were commanded by non-commissioned officers, on account of the absence of those of higher rank."

Stampede of the Baggage-Wagons.

An old regular said to me regarding the stampede :

"That was the fault of the officers who allowed the baggage-wagons to come to the front, instead of being parked at Centreville. The stampede and confusion began among them first. Why, the men were so little frightened when they began to fall back in groups scattered through the fields that I saw them stop frequently to pick blackberries. Frightened men don't act in that way. At Cub Run, between the Stone Bridge and Centreville, the irresponsible teamsters, with the baggage-wagons, were all crowded together near the bridge, and were in a desperate hurry to cross. A rebel battery began dropping shell in among them, and thus demolished some of the wagons and blocked the way. The confusion and hurry and excitement then

---

[1] The official reports show the losses of officers to be — Federal: killed, 19; wounded, 64; missing, 40; total, 123. Confederate: killed, 25 ; wounded, 63; missing, 1; total, 89. Of losses of enlisted men — Federal: killed, 462; wounded, 947; missing, 1176; total, 2585. Confederate: killed, 362; wounded, 1519; missing, 12; total, 1893.

began. The drivers on the south side, finding they couldn't cross with their wagons, now began to cut their traces and mount their horses and hurry away. Those who drove baggage-wagons on the safe side of Cub Run then began to desert them and cut the traces and shout and gallop off. The infantry, seeing this confusion and not understanding the cause of it, quickened their pace. Soon the narrow road became filled with flying troops, horses, baggage-wagons, and carriages. Then the volunteers began to throw away their muskets and equipments, so as to stand an even chance in the race. Here and there, all along the route, abandoned wagons had been overturned and were blocking the way. One white-headed citizen, an old man, looking very sorrowful, stood directing the soldiers on their way to Washington, saying : 'You'd better hurry on, or the cavalry will cut off your retreat !' The houses all along the route were filled with wounded men, while the ambulances were filled with officers hastening to Washington. Soldiers here and there marched in groups, and sorrowfully discussed the situation and its causes. The expression heard on every side among them was : 'Why were not the reserves brought up from Centreville to help us ?' 'Why didn't they bring up the troops from Fairfax Court House ?'" — questions, it seems to me, hard to answer, even if they did come from private soldiers running away from the field of Bull Run !

" ' Think ? think ? ' he cried, ' what right have you to think ? *I* do the thinking for this regiment ! ' "   Page 17.

CHAPTER II.

WHILE we were in camp at Washington in February, 1862, we were drilled to an extent which to the raw "thinking soldier" seemed unnecessary. Our colonel was a strict disciplinarian. His efforts to drill out of us the methods of action and thought common to citizens, and to substitute in place thereof blind, unquestioning obedience to military rules, were not always appreciated at their true value. In my company there was an old drill-sergeant (let us call him Sergeant Hackett) who was in sympathetic accord with the colonel. He had occasion to reprove me often, and finally to inflict a blast of profanity at which my self-respect rebelled. Knowing that swearing was a breach of discipline, I waited confidently upon the colonel, with the manner of one gentleman calling upon another. After the usual salute, I opened complaint by saying:

"Colonel, Mr. Hacket has ——"

The colonel interrupted me angrily, and with fire in his eye, exclaimed:

"'*Mister*'? There *are* no misters in the army."

"I thought, sir ——" I began apologetically.

"Think? think?" he cried, "What right have *you* to think? *I* do the thinking for this regiment! Go to your quarters!"

I did not tarry. There seemed to be no common ground on which he and I could argue questions of personal etiquette. But I should do injustice to his character as a commander if I failed to illustrate another manner of reproof which he sometimes applied.

One day, noticing a corporal in soiled gloves, he said: "Corporal, you set a bad example to the men with your soiled gloves. Why do you?"

"I've had no pay, sir, since entering the service, and can't afford to hire washing."

The colonel drew from his pocket a pair of gloves spotlessly white, and handing them to the corporal said : " Put on those ; I washed them myself ! "

This was an unforgotten lesson to the whole regiment that it was a soldier's duty to attend himself to his personal neatness.

In a camp of soldiers, rumor, with her thousand tongues, is always speaking. The rank and file and under-officers of the line are not taken into the confidence of their superiors. Hence the private soldier is usually in ignorance as to his destination. What he lacks in information is usually made up in surmise and conjecture ; every hint is caught at and worked out in possible and impossible combinations. He plans and fights imaginary battles. He manœuvres for position, with pencil and chalk, on fanciful fields, at the same time knowing no more of the part he is actually performing in some great or little plan than the knapsack he bears. He makes some shrewd guesses (the Yankee's birthright), but he knows absolutely nothing. It is this which makes the good-will and confidence of the rank and file in the commander so important a factor in the *morale* of an army.

How we received the report or whence it came I know not, but it was rumored one morning that we were about to move. The order in reality came at last, to the stress and dismay of the sutlers and the little German woman who kept the grocery round the corner. We left her disconsolate over the cakes, pies, and goodies liberally purchased, but which were yet unpaid for when we fell into two ranks, were counted off, and marched to conquer the prejudices of other sutlers.

We took the cars (early in March, I think), and were hurried through Hagerstown and other little sleepy-looking villages of Maryland. The next morning found us at Sandy Hook, about half a mile from Harper's Ferry ; thence, after about three hours' delay, we marched to a place opposite the promontory on and around which is situated the picturesque village of Harper's Ferry, at the confluence of the Potomac and Shenandoah rivers. It was cold at our camping-place, between the canal and the river. There were no rations awaiting our arrival, and we were suffering from the hunger so common to soldiers. Who ever saw one off duty who was not in pursuit of something to eat? We couldn't get anything for love or money. We had at last reached a place where the people showed some of the distress incidental to war, and a strong disinclination to feed or believe in us. We were grieved, but it couldn't be helped. Their reception was as frosty as the weather. Our genial and winning address made no impression on these Yankee-hating Marylanders, and their refusal to feed us threw a shadow over us as uncomfortable as the shadow of their hills. No wonder John Brown failed in such a place as this.

The bridge from the Maryland to the Virginia or Harper's Ferry shore had been destroyed by fire, leaving only the granite abutments (which were afterward built upon again), and we were soon set at work conveying some flat-bottomed scows from Sandy Hook to Harper's Ferry. As early as nine o'clock about one hundred men came down opposite the ferry, just above the old bridge, and broke into little groups, in military precision. Four or five with spades and other implements improvised a wooden abutment on the shore; another party rowed against the stream, moored a scow, and let it drift down until it was opposite the wooden abutment; then a party of ten advanced, each two men carrying a claw-balk, or timbers fitted with a claw, one of which held the gunwale of the boat, the other the shore abutment. Twenty men now came down on the left with planks, one inch thick, six inches wide, and fifteen feet long, narrowed at each end; these they laid across the five joists or balks, and returned on the right.

Another party meanwhile moored another boat, which dropped down-stream opposite the one already bridged; five joists, each twenty feet long, were laid upon the gunwale by five men; these were fastened by those in the boat, by means of ropes, to cleats or hooks provided for the purpose on the side of the scows, which were shoved off from the shore until the shore end of the balk rested upon the shore boat. These were covered with planks in the same manner as before; side-rails of joists were lashed down with ropes to secure the whole. So one after another of the boats was dropped into position until a bridge several hundred feet long reached from the Maryland to the Virginia shore, for the passage of artillery and every description of munitions for an army.

Owing to the force of the current, a large rope cable was stretched from shore to shore fifty feet above the bridge, and the upper end of each boat was stayed to the cable by a smaller rope. The clock-like precision with which these men worked showed them to be the drilled engineers and pontoniers of the regular army. After the bridge was built, a slight, short man, with sandy hair, in military dress, came out upon it and congratulated the engineers on their success. This unassuming man was George B. McClellan, commander of the Army of the Potomac.

It was the first boat-bridge thrown out in active service of the army of the United States, and it was on this that the army of General Banks crossed to the Virginia shore in 1862. Hour after hour this frail-looking bridge, which by force of the current swung almost in a semicircle between the two shores, was crowded with men and the material of an army. Officers were not allowed to trot their horses ; troops in crossing were given the order, " Route step," as the oscillation of the cadence step or trotting horse is dangerous to the stability of a bridge of any kind, much more of the seemingly frail structure of boats and timbers, put together with ropes, here described.

I crossed the bridge soon after it was laid ; visited Jefferson Rock, the ruins of the burned armory, and the town in general. The occasional crack of a musket among the hills on the other side of the Shenandoah told that the rebel scouts were still there. Colonel Geary's men were engaged in driving them from the hills, preparatory to the advance of General Banks. During the day fifteen or twenty were captured and marched through the town, presenting a generally shabby and unmilitary appearance. They did not impress me as they did afterward when charging on our lines, with their unmusical yell and dauntless front.

The craggy heights about Harper's Ferry are exceedingly picturesque. Here, around this promontory, the waters of the Shenandoah and Potomac meet with murmurs of congratulation, and go dancing on joyfully, hand in hand, to the ocean. The headland, around which the village of Harper's Ferry is built, is noticeable for its ruggedness, but its bold outlines are subdued into something like pastoral beauty by contrast with the huge, irregular heights which rise grandly above on either side, and look down upon it. Maryland Heights, precipitous, rock-ribbed, and angular, frown, as it were, at their rougher rival, Loudon Heights, on the opposite Virginia side below, while Harper's Ferry lies demure and modest between them.

The ruins of the burned armory of the United States were noticeable from the Maryland shore; also the masses of men moving in ceaseless tramp over the long and almost crescent-like bridge. The murmur of many voices, the mellow, abrupt call of the negro drivers to their mules, the glistening arms of the infantry reflected in the sunlight, the dull rumble of artillery-wheels and baggage-wagons, live in memory to-day, after a lapse of

The Runaway Car.

years, as one of the pictures of " war's wrinkled front," framed in the routine of more ordinary scenes of army life.

One of my early army passions was collecting mementos of historic interest. For weeks I carried in my knapsack a brick taken from the old engine-house where John Brown so coolly fought, while his sons lay dying by his side.

Near the ruins of the armory was a rough, extemporized barricade across the railroad which ran around the northern shore, upon a foundation built on solid masonry, rising from the river's edge. The barricade was made of broken and fire-bruised machinery, twisted muskets and bayonets, the débris of the armory. I had obtained a pass, and, prospecting around the village, had wandered along the shore to the barricade described. Among its material was a hand-car without driving machinery or brake — simply a platform on wheels. I succeeded, after laboring a long time, in getting the car upon the railroad, and pushed it forward up the incline of the track about a mile. Blocking the wheels, I visited a cave near there, obtaining specimens of minerals and stalagmites, and loading them upon my chariot, started on the down-grade, with a strong wind as assistant motive-power. My car soon began to obtain a rapidity of motion that astonished me. The farther I went the greater the speed. I had no idea so much momentum could be obtained on a slight down-grade. I rushed on like the wind. Blue-coated comrades shouted in derision as I passed them. I remember saluting two or three officers, who gazed at me with dazed and amused countenances, as I rushed at break-neck speed along the track toward the barricade from which I had started. I was rather confused, but could see distinctly enough that there was soon to be a smash-up. I saw discord ahead unless I could avoid the collision ; and as that seemed impracticable, I jumped and struck on the softest spot I could find in my hasty survey. The knees of my trousers were badly torn, and I was bruised in more spots than one would deem possible, but got to my feet in season to see the climax. My carriage struck the barricade with such force as to send it over, with a dull crash, into the river below! It cured me forever of any desire to ride where no provision has been made for stopping the vehicle. I tell this incident as a specimen of the scrapes an idle soldier may fall into.

The next day we were sent by rail back to Washington, and into camp upon our old grounds. A few mornings afterward an inspection was ordered. It came with the usual hurry and parade. Knapsacks and equipments were in shining order ; every musket, bayonet, and button, boot and belt, as bright as rubbing and fear of censure or police duty could make them. Inspection over, the last jingle of ramrod in resounding musket was heard, and we were dismissed, with an intimation that on the morrow we were to go on a march.

The sun rose through the mists of the morning, — one of those quiet mornings when every sound is heard with distinctness. The waters of the Potomac were like a sheet of glass as we took up our line of march across the Long Bridge, making the old structure shake with our cadence step. Our moods varied; some laughed and joked; some, in suppressed tones, talked with their comrades as to their destination. Not much was said about fighting, but I, for one, did a great deal of thinking on that tender subject.

After we passed the fort, which commanded the bridge on the Virginia side, we encountered one of the most powerful allies of the Rebel hosts, particularly during the winter and spring campaigns in Virginia, — MUD. No country can beat a Virginia road for mud. We struck it thick. It was knee-deep. It was verily "heavy marching." The foot sank very insidiously into the mud, and reluctantly came out again; it had to be coaxed, and while you were persuading your reluctant left, the willing right was sinking into unknown depths; it came out of the mud like the noise of a suction-pump when the water is exhausted.

The order was given, " Route step "; we climbed the banks of the road in search of firm earth, but it couldn't be found, so we went on pumping away, making about one foot in depth to two in advance. Our feet seemingly weighed twenty pounds each. We carried a number six into the unknown depths of mud, but it came out a number twelve, elongated, yellow, and nasty; it had lost its fair proportions, and would be mistaken for anything but a foot, if not attached to a leg. It seemed impossible that we should ever be able to find our feet in their primitive condition again. Occasionally a boot or shoe would be left in the mud, and it would take an exploring expedition to find it. Oh, that disgusting, sticking mud! Wad Rider declared that if Virginia was once in the Union, she was now in the mud. A big Irish comrade, Jim O'Brien, facetiously took up the declension of mud, — mud, mudder, murder, pulling a foot out at each variation for emphasis. Jack E. declared it would be impossible to dislodge an enemy stuck in the mud as we were.

The army resembled, more than anything else, a congregation of flies, making a pilgrimage through molasses. The boys called their feet "pontoons," "mud-hooks," "soil-excavators," and other names not quite so polite. When we halted to rest by the wayside, our feet were in the way of ourselves and everybody else. " Keep your mud-hooks out of my way," " Save your pontoons for another bridge," were heard on all sides, mingled with all the reckless, profane, and quaint jokes common to the army, and which are not for print.

The mud was in constant league with the enemy; an efficient ally in defensive warfare; equivalent to reënforcements of twenty thousand infantry. To realize the situation, spread tar a foot deep all

Pulling Mud in Virginia.

over your back-yard, and then try to walk through it ; particularly is this experiment recommended to those citizens who were constantly crying, "Why doesn't the army move?" It took the military valor all out of a man. Any one would think, from reading the Northern newspapers, that we soldiers had macadamized roads to charge over at the enemy. It would have pleased us much to have seen those "On to Richmond" fellows put over a five-mile course in the Virginia mud, loaded with a forty-pound knapsack, sixty rounds of cartridges, and haversacks filled with four days' rations.

Without exagggeration, the mud has never got full credit for the immense help it afforded the enemy, as it prevented us from advancing upon them. The ever-present foe, winter and spring, in Old Virginia was Mud. Summer and fall it was Dust, which was preferable ; though marching without water, with dust filling one's nostrils and throat, was not a pleasant accompaniment with our "salt horse" and "hard-tack."

The first night out we went into camp near a small brook, where we washed off enough of the mud to recognize our feet. We had hard-tack and coffee for supper. And didn't it "go good"! What sauce ever equalled that of hunger? Truly the feast is in the palate. How we slept! Feet wet, boots for a pillow, the mud oozing up around our rubber blankets, but making a soft bed withal, and we sleeping the dreamless sleep of tired men. I would be willing, occasionally, to make another such march, through the same mud, for such a sleep.

At early daylight we fell in for rations of hot coffee and hard-tack. Immediately after we took up our line of march, or, as Wad Rider expressed it, "began to pull mud." With intervals of rest, we "pulled mud," until about four o'clock in the afternoon, when we halted near Manassas Junction. It was strange that the enemy could not have been chivalrous enough to meet us half-way, and save us the trials and troubles of wallowing through all that mud. Then the Quaker guns! Who has not heard of the "Quaker guns" at Manassas? We met the logs, mounted on wheels, around the fortifications of Manassas, and can assure you they were not so formidable as the mud.

After thoroughly inspecting our enemies, — the logs, — we re-formed our ranks and took the back track for Washington. The rain soon began to fall, coming down literally in sheets ; it ran down our backs in rivulets, and we should have run had we met the enemy about that time — that is, if the mud had permitted; for there is nothing which will so take the courage out of a soldier as to wet the seat of his trousers. On we went, pumping and churning up and down in the mud, till about ten o'clock, when we pitched camp near the road-side, as wet and bedraggled a set of men as ever panted for military glory, or pursued the bubble reputation at the wooden cannon's mouth. We arrived at our old camp near Washington the following evening.

Virginia mud has never been fully comprehended; but I hope those who read these pages will catch a faint glimmering of the reality. To be fully understood, one must march in it, sleep in it, be encompassed round about by it. Great is mud — Virginia mud!

CHAPTER III.

THE manner in which orders are transmitted to the individual groups of an army might be compared to the motion that a boy gives to a row of bricks which he has set up on end within striking distance of each other. He pushes the first brick, and the impetus thus given is conveyed down the line in rapid succession, until each brick has responded to the movement. If the machine is well adjusted in all its parts, and the master mechanic, known as the commanding general, understands his business, he is able to run it so perfectly as to control the movements of brigades, divisions, and corps. In the early spring of 1862, when the Army of the Potomac was getting ready to move from Washington, the constant drill and discipline, the brightening of arms and polishing of buttons, and the exasperating fussiness on the part of company and regimental officers during inspections, conveyed to us a hint, as one of our comrades expressed it, that " some one higher in command was punching them to punch us." There was unusual activity upon the Potomac in front of our camp. Numerous steamtugs were pulling huge sailing vessels here and there, and large transports, loaded with soldiers, horses, bales of hay, and munitions for an army, swept majestically down the broad river. Every description of water conveyance, from a canal-boat to a huge three-decked steamboat, seemed to have been pressed into the service of the army.

The troops south of the city broke camp, and came marching, in well-disciplined regiments, through the town. I remember that the Seventh Massachusetts seemed to be finely disciplined, as it halted on the river-banks before our camp. I imagined the men looked serious over leaving their comfortable winter-quarters at Brightwood for the uncertainties of the coming campaign. At last, when drills and inspections had made us almost frantic with neatness and clean-

liness, we got marching orders.   I shall not forget that last inspection.   Our adjutant was a short old fellow, who had seen much
service in the regular army.   He gave his orders in an explosive
manner, and previous to giving them his under lip would work in
curious muscular contractions, so that the long imperial which decorated it would be worked up, under and over his nose, like the rammer
of a musket in the act of loading.   At that last inspection, previous
to the opening campaign, he gave the order with a long roll to the r's :
"Preparrrre to open rrrranks."   The ranks were open, and he was
twisting his mouth and elevating his imperial for another order, when
an unlucky citizen, who was not conversant with military rules, passed
between the ranks.   The adjutant, pale with anger, hastily followed
the citizen, who was very tall.   The distance from the toe of our
adjutant's boot, to the citizen's flank was too great for the adjutant,
who yet kept up a vigorous kicking into air, until at last, with a prodigious outlay of muscular force, his foot reached the enemy, but
with such recoil as to land him on his back in the mud.

We formed in two ranks and marched on board a little steamer
lying at the wharf near our quarters.   "Anything for a change," said
Wad Rider, really delighted to move.   All heavy baggage was left
behind.   I had clung to the contents of my knapsack with dogged
tenacity ; but, notwithstanding my most earnest protest, I was required to disgorge about one-half of them, including a pair of heavy
boots and my choice brick from the Harper's Ferry engine-house.
To my mind I was now entirely destitute of comforts.

The general opinion among us was that at last we were on our
way to made an end of the Confederacy.   We gathered in little knots
on the deck, here and there a party playing "penny ante"; others
slept or dozed, but the majority smoked and discussed the probabilities of our destination, about which we really knew as little as the
babes in the wood.   That we were sailing down the Potomac was
apparent.

The next day we arrived at Old Point Comfort, and looked with
open-eyed wonder at Fortress Monroe, huge and frowning.   Negroes
were plentier than blackberries, and went about their work with an
air of importance born of their new-found freedom.   These were the
"contrabands" for whom General Butler had recently invented that
sobriquet.   We pitched our tents amid the charred and blackened

ruins of what had been the beautiful and aristocratic village of Hampton. The first thing I noticed about the ruins, unaccustomed as I was to Southern architecture, was the absence of cellars. The only building left standing of all the village was the massive old Episcopal church. Here Washington had worshipped, and its broad aisles had echoed to the footsteps of armed men during the Revolution. In the church-yard the tombs had been broken open. Many tombstones were broken and overthrown, and at the corner of the church a big hole showed that some one with a greater desire for possessing curiosities than reverence for ancient landmarks had been digging for the corner-stone and its buried mementos.

Along the shore which looks towards Fortress Monroe were landed artillery, baggage-wagons, pontoon trains and boats, and the level land back of this was crowded with the tents of the soldiers. Here and there were groups frying hard-tack and bacon. Near at hand was the irrepressible army mule, hitched to and eating out of pontoon boats ; those who had eaten their ration of grain and hay were trying their teeth, with promise of success, in eating the boats. An army mule was hungrier than a soldier, and would eat anything, especially a pontoon boat or rubber blanket. The scene was a busy one. The red cap, white leggings, and baggy trousers of the Zouaves mingled with the blue uniforms and dark trimmings of the regular infantrymen, the short jackets and yellow trimmings of the cavalry, the red stripes of the artillery, and the dark blue with orange trimmings of the engineers ; together with the ragged, many-colored costumes of the black laborers and teamsters, all busy at something.

During our short stay here I made several excursions, extending two or three miles from the place, partly out of curiosity, and partly from the constant impression on a soldier's mind that his merits deserve something better to eat than the commissary furnishes. It seemed to me in all my army experience that nature delighted in creating wants and withholding supplies, and that rations were wanting in an inverse proportion to my capacity to consume them.

In one of my rambles I came to a small dwelling such as unpretentious people, of very modest means, would occupy at the North. I knocked at the door and a middle-aged woman responded, with, as I imagined, contemptuous glance at my uniform, and inquired my errand. I asked her if she could give me something to eat if I would pay her for it. She replied, "Come in yer and I recon I can give ye somethin ter eat."

The room into which I was invited was a neat, but poorly furnished kitchen-like place, in which, besides the matron, were two girls, one black and the other white, each about ten years of age. On the broad hearth of an open fireplace a fire was burning, and before this a johnny-cake of white corn meal was soon set to cook in a spider, elevated at an angle so as to face the fire. The little colored girl was set the task of tending it, superintended by the little white girl, who stamped, frowned, and scolded the little black imperiously at every fancied neglect of duty. The matron offered a word of suggestion at times as if she was training her little daughter as a housekeeper, and at the same time, in the art and duties of government. It was a new and suggestive scene to me. The cowed patience of the black and the exacting temper of the white were in marked contrast.

I entered into conversation with the mistress upon the all-absorbing topic — the war — and incidentally, slavery came in as a part of the topic.

"Are you'n Yanks goin to interfer with our servants?" asked she imperiously. I answered that I didn't know, but if so, there would, doubtless, be compensation given to Union people whose negroes were liberated.

I thought, from the expression of her face, that the idea of compensation was not an unfamiliar one to her.

"What is your black girl worth?" I inquired, curious to get an idea of the valuation of such property.

"Thet yer?" looking the girl over from head to foot, with the cool, calculating look which a Yankee farmer would give an ox or cow, "I recon IT is worth five hundred dollars."

It is needless for me to say, the word "IT" in this connection struck a Northern boy as having a business and property basis which he had not been accustomed to hearing applied to human souls and bodies.

One morning we broke camp and went marching up the Peninsula. The roads were very poor, and muddy with recent rains, and were crowded with the indescribable material of the vast army which was slowly creeping through the mud over the flat, wooded country.

It was a bright day in April — a perfect Virginia day ; the grass was green beneath our feet, the buds of the trees were just unrolling into leaves under the warming sun of spring, and in the woods the birds were singing. The march was at first orderly, but under the unaccustomed burden of heavy equipments and knapsacks, and the warmth of the weather, the men straggled along the roads, mingling with the baggage-wagons, ambulances, and pontoon trains, in seeming confusion.

During our second day's march it rained, and the muddy roads, cut up and kneaded, as it were, by the teams preceding us, left them in a state of semi-liquid filth hardly possible to describe or imagine. When we arrived at Big Bethel the rain was coming down in sheets. A dozen houses of very ordinary character, scattered over an area of a third of a mile, constituted what was called the village. Just outside and west of the town was an insignificant building from which the hamlet takes its name. It did not seem large enough or of sufficient consequence to give name to a place as small as Big Bethel. Before our arrival it had evidently been occupied as officers' barracks for the enemy, and it looked very little like a church.

There was a rude but very significant drawing on the plaster of the walls, which if not complimentary was amusing.

A hotel was depicted, and on its sign was inscribed " Richmond." Jeff Davis was standing in the doorway, and with an immense pair of cowhides was booting McClellan from the door, and underneath the sketch was the inscription, " Merry Mack ! "

It was significant only so far as it proved a prophecy.

I visited one of the dwelling-houses just outside of the fortifications (if the insignificant rifle-pits could be called such) for the purpose of obtaining something more palatable than hard-tack, salt beef, or pork, which, with coffee, were the marching rations. The woman of the house was communicative, and expressed her surprise at the great number of Yanks who had " come down to invade our soil." She said she had a son in the Confederate army, or, as she expressed it, " in our army," and then tearfully said she should tremble for her boy every time she heard of a battle. I expressed the opinion that we should go into Richmond without much fighting. " No ! " said she, with the emphasis of conviction, " you all's will drink hot blood before you all's get thar ! " I inquired if she knew anything about the skirmish which took place at Big Bethel. She replied by saying, "Why, Major Winthrop died right in yer!" pointing to a small sleeping-room which opened from the main room in which we were. She added, "When you all were fighting, Major Winthrop was way ahead and was shot; he was a brave man, but we have brave men too." I asked her if she knew who shot him, and she replied that a colored boy belonging to one of the officers shot him. During the engagement, the colored boy, standing by his master, saw Winthrop in advance, and said, "See that officer! Can I take your rifle and shoot him?" The master assented, and the boy shot Major Winthrop. He was then brought to this house. One or two days after the fight, she said, the boy was "playing over yon, in that yer yard," — pointing to the yard of a neighboring house, — with his mate, when the rifle they were playing with was accidentally discharged, and the colored boy who shot Winthrop was killed. "How old was the boy?" I asked. "About forty," she replied. At the right of the road was an open, marshy piece of land, and it was over this Major Winthrop was leading his men when shot. The woody intervale just beyond the marshy land was occupied by the enemy's works, which consisted of five rifle-pits, each a few rods in length, and one of them commanding the marshy opening mentioned. This is but one of several different accounts as to the manner of Winthrop's death.

While wandering about, I came to the house of a Mrs. T——, whose husband was said to be a captain in the Confederate service and a "fire-eating" secessionist. Here some of our men were put on guard for a short time, until relieved by guards from other parts of the army as they came up, whereupon we went on. A large, good-looking woman, about forty years old, who, I learned, was Mrs. T——, was crying profusely, and I could not induce her to tell me what about. One of the soldiers said her grief was caused by the fact that some of our men had helped themselves to the contents of cupboard and cellar. She was superintending the loading of an old farm wagon, into which she was putting a large family of colored people, with numerous bundles. The only white person on the load as it started away was the mistress, who sat amid her dark chattels in desolation and tears. Returning to the house after this exodus, I found letters, papers, and odds and ends of various kinds littering the floor, whether overturned in the haste of the mistress or by the visiting soldiers I could only guess. As I passed into what had evidently been the best room, or parlor, I found a fellow-soldier intently poring over the illustrations of a large book, which proved to be an elegantly bound and illustrated family Bible. Upon my approach he began tearing out the illustrations, but I arrested his hand and rebuked him. He resented my interference, saying, " Some one is going for these things before the army gets through here if I don't." It was impossible to keep out the vandal " Yanks "; they flowed through the house, a constant

Mrs. T—— leaving her Home.

stream, from cellar to garret, until there was no more any need of a guard, as there was no longer anything to guard. I felt so hopeless of protecting the family Bible, that at last it occurred to me that the only way to save it was to carry it off myself. I gave it to one of our colored teamsters to carry into camp for me. After our arrival at Yorktown I hunted him up, but he informed me that he had " drapped it." No other building at Big Bethel was so devastated, and I did not see another building so treated on our whole route. The men detailed to guard it declined to protect the property of one who was in arms fighting against us.

After leaving Big Bethel we began to feel the weight of our knapsacks. Castaway overcoats, blankets, parade-coats, and shoes were scattered along the route in reckless profusion, being dropped by the overloaded soldiers, as if after ploughing the roads with heavy teams they were sowing them for a harvest. I lightened my knapsack without much regret, for I could not see the sense of carrying a blanket or overcoat when I could pick one up almost anywhere along the march. Very likely the same philosophy actuated those who preceded me or came after. The colored people along our route occupied themselves in picking up this scattered property. They had on their faces a distrustful look, as if uncertain of the tenure of their harvest.

The march up the Peninsula seemed very slow, yet it was impossible to increase our speed, owing to the bad condition of the roads. I learned in time that marching on paper and the actual march made two very different impressions. I can easily understand and excuse our fireside heroes, who fought their or our battles at home over comfortable breakfast-tables, without impediments of any kind to circumscribe their fancied operations; it is so much easier to manoeuvre and fight large armies around the corner grocery, where the destinies of the human race have been so often discussed and settled, than to fight, march, and manoeuvre in mud and rain, in the face of a brave and vigilant enemy.

To each baggage-wagon were attached four or six mules, driven usually by a colored man, with only one rein, or line, and that line attached to the bit of the near leading mule, while the driver rode in a saddle upon the near wheel mule. Each train was accompanied by a guard, and while the guard urged the drivers the drivers urged the mules. The drivers were usually expert and understood well the wayward, sportive natures of the creatures over whose destinies they presided. On our way to Yorktown our pontoon and baggage-trains were sometimes blocked for miles, and the heaviest trains were often unloaded by the guard to facilitate their removal from the mud. Those wagons which were loaded with whiskey were most lovingly guarded, and when unloaded the barrels were often lightened before they were returned to the wagons. It did seem at times as if there were needless delays with the trains, partly due, no doubt, to fear of danger ahead. While I was guarding our pontoon trains after leav-

ing Big Bethel, the teams stopped all along the line. Hurrying to
the front, I found one of the leading teams badly mired, but not
enough to justify the stopping of the whole train. The lazy colored
driver was comfortably asleep in the saddle.

" Get that team out of the mud ! " I yelled, bringing him to his
senses.

He flourished his long whip, shouted his mule lingo at the team,
and the mules pulled frantically, but not together.

" Can't you make your mules pull together ? " I inquired.

" Dem mules pull right smart ! " said the driver.

Cocking and capping' my unloaded musket, I brought it to the
shoulder, and again commanded the driver, " Get that team out of
the mud ! "

The negro rolled his eyes wildly and woke up all over. He first
patted his saddle mule, spoke to each one, and then, flourishing his
long whip with a crack like a pistol, shouted, " Go 'long dar ! what I
feed yo' fo' ! " and the mule team left the slough in a very expeditious
manner. Thereafter I had an unfailing argument, which, if but seldom used, was all the more potent. The teamsters of our army
would have been much more efficient if they had been organized and
uniformed as soldiers. Our light artillery was seldom seen stuck in
the mud.

When procuring luxuries of eggs or milk we paid the people at
first in silver, and they gave us local scrip in change ; but we found
on attempting to pay it out again that they were rather reluctant to
receive it, even at that early stage in Confederate finance, and much
preferred Yankee silver or notes.

On the afternoon of April 5, 1862, the advance of our column
was brought to a standstill, with the right in front of Yorktown and
the left by the enemy's works at Lee's mills. We pitched our camp
on Wormly Creek, near the Moore house on the York River, in sight
of the enemy's water battery and their defensive works at Gloucester
Point. The day after our arrival I was detailed to go to Shipping
Point, some eight miles distant, on the York River, and we made the
march, with pack mules, over the very worst mud roads I had ever
seen in all my experience. A depot of supplies had been established
here, and speedily the roads leading to this place were corduroyed
and thus rendered decently passable. We found the place had been

strongly fortified by the Confederates, and contained about two hundred log huts built for their accommodation. They were, however, rendered useless to them by being flanked or cut off by our advance. In one of the huts, evidently belonging to one of their officers, I picked up a paper, which proved to contain a detail of negro servants from different plantations to work upon the fortifications, which showed that the Confederates were even then using their slaves for military purposes, thus leaving their soldiers fresh for other military duties. The camp and fortifications were almost on a level with the water of the river, very muddy and dirty, and we were not sorry to be recalled to our camp at Yorktown.

One of the impediments to an immediate attack on Yorktown was the difficulty of using light artillery in the muddy fields in our front, and at that time the topography of the country ahead was but little understood, and had to be learned by reconnoisance in force. We had settled down to the siege of Yorktown ; began bridging the streams between us and the enemy, constructing and improving the roads for the rapid transit of supplies, and for the advance. The first parallel was opened about a mile from the enemy's fortifications, extending along the entire front of their works, which reached from the York River on the left to Warwick Creek on the right, along a line about four miles in length. Fourteen batteries and three redoubts were planted, heavily armed with ordnance.

We were near Battery No. 1, not far from the York River. On it were mounted several two-hundred-pound guns, which commanded the enemy's water batteries. One day I was in a redoubt on the left, and saw General McClellan with the Prince de Joinville, examining the enemy's works through their field-glasses. They very soon drew the fire of the observant enemy, who opened with one of their heavy guns on the group, sending the first shot howling and hissing over and very close to their heads ; another, quickly following it, struck in the parapet of the redoubt. The French prince, seemingly quite startled, jumped and glanced nervously around, while McClellan quietly knocked the ashes from his cigar. When I afterwards heard McClellan accused of cowardice, I knew the accusation was false.

Several of our war-vessels made their appearance in the York River, and occasionally threw a shot at the enemy's works ; but most of them were kept busy at Hampton Roads, watching for the ironclad

General McClellan and Prince de Joinville before Yorktown.   Page 36.

Merrimac, which was still afloat. The firing from the enemy's lines was of little consequence, not amounting to over ten or twelve shots each day, a number of these being directed at the huge balloon which went up daily on a tour of inspection, from near General Fitz John Porter's headquarters. One day the balloon broke from its mooring of ropes, and sailed majestically over the enemy's works ; but fortunately for its occupants, it soon met a counter-current of air which returned it safe to our lines. The month of April was a dreary one, much of the time rainy and uncomfortable. It was a common expectation among us that we were about to end the rebellion. One of my comrades wrote home to his father that we should probably finish up the war in season for him to be at home to teach the village school the following winter ; in fact, I believe he partly engaged to teach it.

Another wrote to his mother : "We have got them hemmed in on every side, and the only reason they don't run is because they can't." We had at last corduroyed every road and bridged every creek ; our guns and mortars were in position ; Battery No. 1 had actually opened on the enemy's works, Saturday, May 3d, 1862, and it was expected that our whole line would open on them in the morning. About two o'clock of Saturday night, or rather Sunday morning, while on guard duty, I observed a bright illumination, as if a fire had broken out within the enemy's lines. Several guns were fired from their works during the early morning hours, but soon after daylight of May 4th it was reported that they had abandoned their works in our front, and we very quickly found the report to be true. As soon as I was relieved from guard duty, I went over on "French leave" to view our enemy's fortifications. They were prodigiously strong. A few tumble-down tents and houses and seventy pieces of heavy ordnance had been abandoned as the price of the enemy's safe retreat.

Upon returning to camp I found rations were being issued and preparations for pursuit being made, and that very afternoon we struck our tents and took up our lines of march, with our faces turned hopefully towards Richmond. A sergeant belonging to a neighboring regiment, whose acquaintance I had formed before Yorktown, jocosely remarked, as he passed me on the march, "I shall meet you on the road to glory!" Later, in looking over the rude head-boards which were used to mark the soldiers' graves near Williamsburg, I found his name.

There was much talk of buried torpedoes in front of the enemy's works, and it was rumored that one officer and several men had been blown to atoms by them ; also that the officer in command had a force of Confederate prisoners at work removing them. We saw a number of sticks stuck in the ground both inside and outside the earthworks, with white rags attached, which were said to indicate the location of the buried torpedoes already discovered.

Williamsburg is twelve miles from Yorktown, but the women and children, of whom we were continually inquiring the distance, gave us very indefinite but characteristic replies.

" How far is it to Williamsburg?" I inquired of an old darkey. " Right smart distance, massa," was the reply. I asked the same question of a white man, and got the same reply.

" How many miles?" I repeated, not feeling satisfied with so much indefiniteness. " Right smart of them, I recon, stranger," came the vague reply.

I concluded they either did not use miles in that country or didn't care to give us information.

A comrade in Hooker's division gave me an account of his experiences about as follows : " Marching over the muddy road late in the afternoon, we found our farther advance prevented by a force which had preceded us, and we halted in the mud by the roadside just as it began to rain. About five o'clock we resumed our march by crossing over to the Hampton road, and did not halt till eleven in the evening, when we lay down in our blankets, bedraggled, wet, and tired, chewing hard-tack and the cud of reflection, the tenor of which was, ' Why did we come for a soldier?' Before daylight we were on the march, plodding in the rain through the mire. By daybreak we came out on the edge of the dense woods in front of Fort Magruder and its cordon of redoubts stretching across the Peninsula, which is here narrowed by the head-waters of two streams which empty into the York on the one hand and the James River on the other. Here we had an opportunity of viewing the situation while waiting for orders to attack. The main fort, called Magruder, was a strong earthwork with a bastioned front and a wide ditch. In front of this muddy-looking heap of dirt was a level plain, sprinkled plentifully with smaller earthworks ; while between us and the level plain the dense forest, for a distance of a quarter of a mile, had been felled, thus forming a labyrinth of tangled abatis difficult to penetrate. A mile away lay the village of Williamsburg.

"We were soon sent out as skirmishers, with orders to advance as near the enemy's rifle-pits as possible. They immediately opened fire upon us with heavy guns from the fort, while from their rifle pits came a hum of bullets and crackle of musketry. Their heavy shot came crushing among the tangled abatis of falling timber, and ploughed up the dirt in our front, rebounding and tearing through the branches of the woods in our rear. The constant hissing of the bullets, with their sharp *ping* or *bizz* whispering around and some-

Bramhall's Battery.

times into us, gave me a sickening feeling and a cold perspiration. I felt weak around my knees — a sort of faintness and lack of strength in the joints of my legs, as if they would sink from under me. These symptoms did not decrease when several of my comrades were hit. The little rifle-pits in our front fairly blazed with musketry, and the continuous *snap, snap, crack, crack* was murderous. Seeing I was not killed at once, in spite of all the noise, my knees recovered from their unpleasant limpness, and my mind gradually regained its balance and composure. I never afterwards felt these disturbing influences to the same degree.

"We slowly retired from stump to stump and from log to log, finally regaining the edge of the wood, and took our position near Webber's and Bramhall's batteries, which had just got into position on the right of the road, not over seven hundred yards from the hostile fort. While getting into position, several of the battery men were killed, as they immediately drew the artillery fire of the enemy, which opened with a noise and violence that astonished me.

"Our two batteries were admirably handled, throwing a number of shot and shell into the enemy's works, speedily silencing them, and by nine o'clock the field in our front, including the rifle-pits, was completely 'cleaned out' of artillery and infantry. Shortly after-wards we advanced along the edge of the wood to the left of Fort Magruder, and about eleven o'clock we saw emerging from the little ravine to the left of the fort a swarm of Confederates, who opened on us with a terrible and deadly fire. Then they charged upon us with their peculiar yell. We took all the advantage possible of the stumps and trees as we were pushed back, until we reached the edge of the wood again, where we halted and fired upon the enemy from behind all the cover the situation afforded. We were none of us too proud, not even those who had the dignity of shoulder-straps to support, to dodge behind a tree or stump. I called out to a comrade, 'Why don't you get behind a tree?' 'Confound it,' said he, 'there ain't enough for the officers.'

"I don't mean to accuse officers of cowardice, but we had sud-denly found out that they showed the same general inclination not to get shot as privates did, and were anxious to avail themselves of the privilege of their rank by getting in our rear. I have always thought that pride was a good substitute for courage, if well backed by a con-scientious sense of duty ; and most of our men, officers as well as privates, were too proud to show the fear which I have no doubt they felt in common with myself. Occasionally a soldier would show symptoms which pride could not overcome. One of our men, Spin-ney, ran into the woods and was not seen until after the engagement. Some time afterwards, when he had proved a good soldier, I asked him why he ran, and he replied that every bullet which went by his head said 'Spinney,' and he thought they were calling for him. In all the pictures of battles I had seen before I ever saw a battle, the officers were at the front on prancing steeds, or with uplifted swords were leading their followers to the charge. Of course, I was surprised to find that in a real battle the officer gets in the rear of his men, as is his right and duty, — that is, if his ideas of duty do not carry him so far to the rear as to make his sword useless.

"The 'Rebs' forced us back by their charge, and our central lines were almost broken. The forces withdrawn from our right had taken the infantry support from our batteries, one of which, consisting of four guns, was captured. We were tired, wet, and exhausted when supports came up, and we were allowed to fall back from under the enemy's fire, but still in easy reach of the battle. I asked one of my comrades how he felt, and his reply was characteristic of the prevailing sentiment : 'I should feel like a hero if I wasn't so blank wet.' The bullets had cut queer antics among our men. A private who had a canteen of whiskey when he went into the engagement, on endeavoring to take a drink found the canteen quite empty, as a bullet had tapped it for him. Another had a part of his thumb-nail taken off. Another had a bullet pass into the toe of his boot, down between two toes, and out along the sole of his foot, without much injury. Another had a scalp wound from a bullet, which took off a strip of hair about three inches in length from the top of his head. Two of my regiment were killed outright and fourteen badly wounded, besides quite a number slightly injured. Thus I have chronicled my first day's fight, and I don't believe any of my regiment were ambitious to 'chase the enemy any farther' just at present. Refreshed with hot coffee and hard-tack, we rested from the fight, well satisfied that we had done our duty. When morning dawned, with it came the intelligence that the enemy had abandoned their works in our front, and were again in full retreat, leaving their wounded in our hands."

A theory generally entertained is, that Hancock's brilliant action on our right caused the retreat of the rebels. The facts, I imagine, are that the rebels only intended to fight till night, and under cover of the darkness, continue their retreat, and thus save their trains and rear-guard from capture.

On the morning following the fight Couch's men took possession of Fort Magruder and the abandoned redoubts, and a force was sent out to bury the dead.

In this first battle of the Peninsula, whose only redeeming feature was the bravery of those who fought it, our loss was shown by official report to have been : in killed, wounded, and prisoners, 2228 ; of these 1700 were of Hooker's force. The loss of the enemy was 1560 ; the protection their position afforded accounting for their small loss as compared with ours.

After the engagement I went over the field in front of the enemy's fort. Advancing through the tangled mass of logs and stumps, I saw one of our men aiming over the branch of a fallen tree, which lay among the tangled abatis. I called to him, but he did not turn or move. Advancing nearer, I put my hand on his shoulder, looked in his face, and started back. He was dead ! — shot through the brain ; and so suddenly had the end come that his rigid hand grasped his musket, and he still preserved the attitude of watchfulness — literally occupying his post after death. At another place we came upon one of our men who had evidently died from wounds. Near one of his hands was a Testament, and on his breast lay an ambrotype picture of a group of children and another of a young woman. We searched in vain for his name. It was neither in his book nor upon his clothing ; and, unknown, this private hero was buried on what was doubtless his first battle-field. The pictures were afterwards put on exhibition for identification.

The 6th of May was a beautiful morning, with birds singing among the thickets in which lay the dead. The next morning we marched through quaint, old-fashioned Williamsburg. The most substantial buildings of the town were those of William and Mary College, which were of brick. In most of the houses there were no signs of life ; blinds and shutters were closed, but a white hand was occasionally seen through the blinds, showing that a woman was gazing stealthily at us. Occasionally a family of black people stood in the doorway, the women and children greeting us with senseless giggles, and in one instance waving their red handkerchiefs. I asked one of the black women where the white people were, and she replied, " Dey's done gone and run away." We kindled fires from that almost inexhaustible source of supply, the Virginia fences, cooked our coffee, sang our songs, and smoked our pipes, thoughtless of the morrow. We quarrelled with nothing, except the pigs that wandered at will in field and wood, and which we occasionally converted into pork.

On our tramp to White House Landing, on the Pamunkey River, we began to realize some of the more substantial discomforts of a march ; the dust, rising in clouds, filled our nostrils and throats, and thoroughly impregnated our clothing, hair, and skin, producing intolerable choking and smothering sensations ; our usual thirst was intensified, and made us ready to break ranks at sight of a brook, and swarm like bees around every well on the route. No one can imagine the intolerable thirst of a dusty march who has not had a live experience of it ; canteens often replenished were speedily emptied, and, unless water was readily attainable, there was great suffering. During the frequent showers, which came down with the liberality common to the climate, it was not unusual to see men drinking from a puddle in the road ; and at one place where water was scarce I saw men crowding round a mud-puddle drinking heartily, while in one edge of it lay a dead mule. There was little to choose between the mud and the dust, and we usually had one or the other in profusion.

Near New Kent Court-House, a little settlement of two or three houses, we came upon several Confederate sick. One of them was full of fighting talk. I asked him what he was fighting for. He said he didn't know, except it be "not to get licked!" "I reckon you uns have got a powerful spite against we uns, and that's what you uns all come down to fight we uns for, and invade our soil!" I could not argue with a prisoner, and a sick man at that, on equal terms ; so I replenished his canteen, and induced one of my comrades to give him some of his rations. From the number of interviews held at different times with our Confederate prisoners, I gathered the general impression that their private soldiers knew but very little about the causes of the war, but were fighting "not to get licked," which is so strong a feeling in human nature that I may say it will account for much hard fighting on both sides. In one of the little cabins surrounding the principal residence were a mulatto woman and her children. She was quite comely, and, with her children, was pretty well dressed. She was a bitter Yankee-hater, and, we inferred, the domestic manager of the household. She declared that "the colored people didn' want to be niggers for the Yanks !"

Our corps arrived at White House Landing, May 22, 1862, and here we found a large portion of our army, which was encamped on the wide, level plain between the wood-skirted road and the Pamunkey

River, occupying tents of all descriptions. Another camp was located at Cumberland Landing, a few miles below White House. The first night after our arrival was a stormy and tempestuous one, and it was evident that an attack from the enemy was expected, as we received orders to lie upon our arms. The Pamunkey is navigable to this point, having sufficient depth, but is very narrow, — in fact, so narrow that some of the larger steamers could not turn, for their stem and stern would reach either bank, except at selected places. The broad plain was crowded with tents, baggage-wagons, pontoon trains, and artillery, — all the accompaniments of a vast army.

Our drummer boy, always getting into scrapes, was here rewarded for some of his mischief. He had gathered together large numbers of rejected cartridges, and having arranged an explosion was " hoist by his own petard." Our surgeon was a talkative man, and while dressing our drummer's wounds (which were in that portion of his anatomy covered by his coat-tail), proceeded to tell his squirming, petulant patient about a good little Kansas boy, whose wounds he dressed at one time. The little fellow, naturally ill humored and rendered doubly so by his smarts, interrupted and astounded the surgeon by exclaiming ; " What do you suppose I care for a little Kansas boy ; I guess he wasn't blowed up so he couldn't sit down ! "

Here some of the regiments who came out from home in a Zouave uniform changed their bright clothes for the regular army blue, and, as marching orders came with the sunrise, moved off the field, leaving windrows of old clothes on the plain.

CHAPTER IV.

THE roads were narrow and very muddy between the White House and the Chickahominy, and it was with great trouble that our trains were moved over them. A few miles west of the Pamunkey we found the country beautiful and undulating, with graceful round-topped hills, here and there crowned with trees and clothed in the varied tints of early summer. The picture is present with me as I write ; the beautiful, undulating country, dotted with tents, and the picturesque groups of men around their camp-fires at the hush of evening.

On our entire march up the Peninsula, we did not see a dozen white men left upon the soil. At last, on the twenty-third of May, we arrived upon the banks of the sluggish Chickahominy, — a small mill-stream, forty or fifty feet wide, with swampy lowland bordering on either side ; the tops of the trees growing in the swamp being about on a level with the crests of the bluffs just beyond, on the Richmond side. Our first camp was pitched on the hills in the vicinity of Gaines's Farm.

The engineers soon began the construction of bridges for the passage of the troops, as it was very important to gain a foothold on the west bank, preparatory to our advance. While Duane's bridge was being constructed, we were ordered on duty along the banks : and upon approaching the river we found, in the thickets near it, one of our dead cavalrymen lying in the water, evidently having been killed while watering his horse. The bridges were thrown out with marvellous quickness, and the corduroy approaches were soon constructed. A small force was ordered to cross, to reconnoitre and to observe the condition of the roads with respect to the passage of artillery. I happened to be one of that squad. With orders not to return the fire if assailed, we advanced across the bridge and through the woods, a quarter of a mile ; and, seeing the sloughy condition of the roads, were returning, when the crack of a rifle told us the enemy were upon us. At the first fire one of our men fell. He entreated

Rescuing Wounded Comrades.

us to leave him and save ourselves ; while we were carrying him, the enemy wounded two more of our men, but not seriously. On each side of the narrow defile were woods with but little screening underbrush, and it was through this we were advancing when attacked. We could not see the enemy, who were secreted in the tree tops around us, but the *zip, zip* of their bullets pursued us as we retreated.

The comrade who had been shot, apparently through the lungs, was examined by our surgeon, who at first thought the case fatal, as the bullet came out of the chest on the side opposite to which it entered; but it was found that the bullet had been deflected by a rib, and glanced round, beneath the skin, only causing a painful flesh-wound. In three weeks our comrade was on light duty about camp. Before seeing very much service we discovered that a man may be hit with bullets in a great many places without killing him. Later I saw a man who had both his eyes destroyed by a bullet without injuring the bridge of his nose, or otherwise marking his face.

In the barn at Gaines's Farm there were a number of Confederate sick and wounded, — men captured in some skirmish during our advance; and while taking a peep at them through a crack, I saw a North Carolina lieutenant whom I recognized as a former school acquaintance. I obtained permission to speak to him, but they told me he was violent and bitter in his language. On approaching him, and inquiring if he knew me, something like a smile of recognition lighted up his face; hesitating a moment, he finally extended his hand. We talked for fifteen or twenty minutes about our school-fellows and early days, but not one word about the war. In two days I visited the barn again, and upon inquiring for him was told by one of the men in charge, " That cock is done crowing." I asked where he was buried. " He isn't buried; they have carried him out! " I stepped into the barn-yard and found him thrown upon a heap of dirt. It was impossible to express all the indignation I felt; I emphatically said that none but cowards would have been guilty of such an act. I was ordered off for thus expressing my mind. Undoubtedly he had been very bitter, but that was no excuse. I mention this as the only instance I ever knew where a dead enemy, or even a prisoner, was insulted by our soldiers. No *soldier* would have committed such a foul act. It was reserved for some miserable " skulker" who, to avoid the active duties of a soldier, had taken refuge in a hospital.

Considerable foraging was done, on the sly, about the neighboring plantations, but as a rule foraging was severely condemned by our commanders. There was much tobacco raised in this section of country, and we found the barns filled with the best quality of tobacco in leaf; this we appropriated without objection on the part of our officers. As all trades were represented in our ranks, that of cigar maker was included, and the army rioted in cigars without enriching the sutlers.

By the lower bridges two of the army corps were sent across to take position near Seven Pines. Some of the bridges were of boats, with corduroy approaches. While they were in process of finishing, on the night of May 30, a terrible storm occurred; the rain-fall was immense, and the thunder the most terrific I ever heard, its sharp, crackling rattle at times sounding like the cannonading of an engagement. When morning dawned, our boat bridges were found dangling midway in a stream which covered the whole swampy and bottom land on both sides the original channel, and the water was waist-deep throughout the greater part of the swamp.

THE BATTLE OF SEVEN PINES (FAIR OAKS).

WE were ordered on duty with Sumner's corps, which was stationed at Tyler's house, and held the centre of the general line of the army. Not long after noon of the 31st, we heard the dull reverberation of cannonading in the direction of Seven Pines, and the companies and regiments fell into line, ready to march at a moment's notice. About two in the afternoon the march was begun to the approaches of Sumner's upper bridge, also called the "Grapevine" bridge, which had been built of logs over the swampy bottom, and which was sustained in place by ropes tied to stumps on the up-stream side. At first it seemed impossible to cross, so swollen was the stream by the overflow; but when the troops were well on the bridge, it was held in place by the moving weight and rendered passable, although covered with water and swaying in the rushing torrent, which every moment threatened to float it away piecemeal. The men grumbled some, after the manner of soldiers. "If this bridge goes down I can't swim a stroke," said one. "Well," said "Little" Day, always making the best of everything, "there will be, in that case, plenty of logs for you to float on." If we had gone down with all our marching equipments, there would have been but little chance even for a good swimmer. Kirby's battery of Napoleon guns preceded us; we found them mired on the west shore. They were unlimbered, and the men of different regiments tugged and lifted at them, knee-deep in the mire, until they were extricated, and finally almost carried them to dry land, or rather firm land, as by no stretch of courtesy could anything in the vicinity be called dry.

Sedgwick's division, being nearer the Grapevine bridge, took the lead at that crossing, while Richardson's division moved toward Sumner's lower bridge. There French's brigade crossed by wading to the waist, the other brigades being ordered to turn back and follow Sedgwick. It was this delay which kept Richardson out of the first day's fight.

A private of the Fifteenth Massachusetts (Gorman's brigade) afterward gave me his recollections of that forced march through water and mud. "Most of our artillery," he said, "became so badly mired that we were obliged to proceed without it, but the little battery of twelve-pound Napoleon guns, commanded by an energetic regular officer (Lieutenant Kirby), notwithstanding it was continually mired to its axles,

Bringing in a Confederate Prisoner.

was pluckily dragged along by horses and men. Despite the mire, we cracked jokes at each other, shouted and sang in high spirits, and toiled through the morass in the direction of the heavy firing."

About 3.30 P.M. we began to meet stragglers from the front.

They all told in substance the same story: " Our companies and regiments are all cut to pieces!" One straggler had a strapping Confederate prisoner in charge. He inquired for a Pennsylvania regiment, saying that during the fight in the woods he lost his company, and while trying to find his way out came across the " reb," and was trying to "take him in." " Stranger," said the prisoner, " yer wouldn't have taken me in if I'd known yer war lost."

" Meanwhile the thunder of the conflict grew louder and louder, and about five o'clock we came upon fragments of regiments of that part of Couch's command which had become isolated at Fair Oaks Station ; they had fallen back half a mile or so, and when we joined them beyond the Courtney house they were hotly engaged with the enemy, who were in overwhelming numbers.

" As we came up through a stumpy field we were greeted with the quick *crack, crack* of the infantry in our front. The smoke of battle hung in clouds over the field, and through it could be seen the flashes of the artillery. The *ping, zip, zip* of bullets, and the wounded men limping from the front or carried by comrades, were a prelude to the storm to come. We formed on the left of Abercrombie's shattered brigade, near the Adams house, and were welcomed with hearty cheers. Presently there was a terrible explosion of musketry, and the bullets pattered around us, causing many to drop ; a line of smoke ahead showed where this destructive fire came from. Kirby's five Napoleon guns came up, and in the angle of the woods opened with splendid precision upon the Confederate columns. The recoil of the pieces was often so great as to bury the wheels nearly to the hub in mud. Soon the 'rebel yell' was heard as they charged on the right of Kirby's battery, which changed front to the right, and delivered a destructive fire of canister. This caused the enemy to break in confusion, and retreat to the cover of the woods. Shortly afterward the enemy developed in greater force in our front, and the hum of shot and shell was almost incessant ; but in a few minutes the fire slackened, and the Confederate lines came dashing upon us with their shrill yells. We received them with a volley from our rifles, and the battery gave them its compliments. The gray masses of the enemy were seen dimly through the smoke, scattering to cover. Presently the order ran down the line, ' Fix bayonets !' While waiting the moment for the final order, John Milan said : ' It's light infantry we

"That night we lay under the stars, thinking of the events of the day and the expected conflict of the morrow."   Page 51.

are, boys, and they expect us to fly over them criss-cross fences.'
Then the final order came: 'Guide right — Double-quick — Charge!'
Our whole line went off at double-quick, shouting as we ran. Some
scattering shots were fired by the enemy as we struggled over the
fences, and then their line broke and dissolved from view.

"That night we lay under the stars, thinking of the events of the
day and the expected conflict of the morrow. Until dawn of Sunday
(June 1) our officers were busy gathering together the scattered and
separated forces. About five o'clock next morning we heard firing
on our left flank, which was covered by Richardson's division of Sumner's corps. It was a line of Confederate pickets deploying in an
open field on the south side of Fair Oaks Station. Shortly after six
o'clock there was a furious fire of musketry on our left, which continued for an hour.

"During the day I went over a portion of the battle-field in the
road through the woods, where the Confederates had made the unsuccessful charge upon Kirby's battery. Here the dead lay very thick,
and a number of their wounded were hidden in the thickets. They
had fallen in many instances on their faces in the headlong charge;
some with their legs torn off, some with shattered arms, and others
with ghastly wounds in the head.

"On the 2d of June the whole line moved forward, and from Fair
Oaks to the Williamsburg road occupied the positions which had been
held previous to the battle. About that time I went over the battle-
ground in front of Casey's position where the battle began. Many
of the dead remained unburied. Some of the men who first took
possession of the works informed me that they found large quantities
of Confederate arms; also a number of the enemy who had become
intoxicated on Yankee whiskey. The camp had been well plundered,
and the enemy had adopted a system of exchange in dress, throwing
aside their ragged uniforms, and clothing themselves in the more
comfortable and cleanly garments of the Federal soldiers. I saw a
Sibley tent in which I counted over two hundred bullet-holes."

A comrade who visited the scene of the charge made by Sedgwick's men said that in the woods beyond, where the Confederate
lines had been formed, a number had been killed while in the act of
getting over the fence, and were suspended in the positions in which
they had been shot. In the woods just beyond this fence were some

swampy pools, to which a number of the enemy's wounded had crept for water and died during the night. There were two or three of these pools of stagnant water, around which were clusters of wounded and dead men.

When my company reached the vicinity of Fair Oaks, about a week after the battle, I was surprised to find how many limbs of trees had been cut away by bullets and shot. At one place a cannon-ball had apparently passed entirely through the stem of a large tree, splitting it for some distance; but the springy wood had closed together again so closely that the point of a bayonet could not be inserted in its track. The forests in the rear were marked in such a manner by bullets as to indicate that the enemy must have shot at times a long way over their intended mark.

In the advance, where Naglee's brigade made its struggle until overwhelmed by the enemy, graves were plenty in every direction, and some of the enemy's dead were found standing, in the swamp near by, in the position in which they were shot. They had decomposed so rapidly that the flesh had partly dropped from the bones.

Many of Casey's men had lost their knapsacks, blankets, and clothing, as well as their tents, and were in a sad plight for soldiering.

Thereafter our lines were constantly engaged in skirmishing, and we were kept in position for battle day after day, expecting an attack. Often the bugler at brigade headquarters sounded the alarm to "fall in," on one day sounding it ten times. During one of the frequent thunder-storms the Confederates made reconnoissance, and fired volleys so timed that they might be mistaken for thunder; but our men were not deceived and stood to their arms, expecting an attack. At one time the men in our rear were practising the drill with blank cartridges, and were mistaken for the enemy. Thus the alarms of war kept our attention occupied.

CHAPTER V.

Chapin

FROM the beginning of the Peninsular campaign, it had been the expectation of McClellan, and undoubtedly the intention of the administration, to reinforce the army before Richmond, by marching McDowell's force overland to its support.

McClellan, with this in view, had made his base of supplies at White House, and early in his operations before the rebel capital, had thrown forward his right wing, at Hanover Court-House, to clear away all opposition to McDowell's advance. The Union army was pressing upon Richmond, arousing the fears of the Confederate leaders, and inspiring confidence and hope in the Union cause.

The disturbing factor, which prevented the desired junction of forces, was the fear of Stonewall Jackson working upon the apprehensions of the war-council at Washington.

Lee had entrusted this able soldier with the execution of a bold and ingenious plan to prevent any combination of our forces. After engaging and threatening Fremont's army at Franklin, Jackson turned and attacked the portion of Banks's force at Front Royal, hurling him in retreat down the valley, and following him to within two miles of Harper's Ferry.

The sudden appearance of Jackson at Winchester, shattered, as if by the crash of a cannonade, the combinations which had been formed for the defeat of the rebel army, and undoubtedly saved that army from present defeat, and the Confederate capital from capture.

McDowell's order to advance and reinforce McClellan was countermanded, and he was instead sent to head off and catch Jackson, who had thus upset the plans of McClellan, confounded the war-council at Washington, and paralyzed and rendered non-effective the force of sixty thousand men, under McDowell, Banks, and Fremont. Then, by secret movements which baffled detection, Stonewall Jackson united his force with that of Lee, in time to take part in the final and decisive attack on the Union army before Richmond.

Lee, keen-eyed and astute, had written to Jackson, under date of June 16, 1862 : " The present seems favorable for a junction of your army with this. . . . Unless McClellan can be driven out of his intrenchments he will move, by positions under cover of his heavy guns, within shelling distance of Richmond."

Thus Lee reinforced his own army with the army that had already disrupted the Union plans.

The fundamental weakness of McClellan's position before Richmond was that his communications with his base at White House was nearly a prolongation of his line of operations before the Confederate capital. This situation required that a large force should be posted on the east side of the Chickahominy, to cover and protect his communications.

To this disadvantage in position was added a moral one, which had great influence in all calculations made by the eminently cautious and able Union commander. This was the inefficiency of his secret service bureau, which persistently magnified the numbers in the rebel army. When Lee had eighty thousand, this bureau reported a force of two hundred thousand ; thus by its blunders playing an effective part for the Confederate leaders. It hampered the action of the Union commander in every battle, and exaggerated into timidity and fatal indecision his bias for hesitation. It was a common conceit among the soldiers that the spy system of our army was run in the interests of the Confederacy.

Lee, having produced as it were, by one blow, the concentration of his own army, and the division of his enemy, determined to attack, defeat, and destroy in detail, the separated wings of the army before him.

McClellan, meantime, comprehending the difficulties of his situation, and the impossibility of receiving reinforcement from McDowell, debated the advisability of changing his base to James River, which would give him a shorter line of operations against Richmond, and one free from the inherent difficulties presented by that at White House. Had he been able to change his base at once, it would have given him the prestige of doing from choice that which was afterward forced upon him.

When, on the morning of June 25th, 1862, he found Jackson within striking distance of his right wing, McClellan immediately penetrated Lee's real purpose, and decided to withdraw Porter's corps to the south side of the Chickahominy, and with his united army effect the change of base to James River.

As a necessary preliminary he engaged the threatening rebel force with Porter's corps, for, as he states in his report, an immediate withdrawal without fighting would have exposed the rear of his army, and enabled Jackson to intercept the movement to the James.

McClellan supposed the attack on his right wing was being made by Jackson's force alone, while the stubborn resistance met led the rebel commander to suppose that the entire Union army was in his front. Both assumptions were an illustration of the mistakes which are the inseparable incidents of war.

The position of Porter had almost the aspect of a forlorn hope, attacked as he was by nearly sixty thousand men.

The plan of the Confederate commander was for Jackson to so manœuvre as to uncover the passages of the stream at Meadow and Mechanicsville bridges, then crossing his whole force, sweep down the north bank of the Chickahominy and break McClellan's communications with White House. But by various devices, put in operation by the Union commander, Jackson was delayed, and did not arrive until a day after the time expected.

The principal device used to delay Jackson was the sending out, with light marching orders, of a force, consisting of the Eighteenth Massachusetts and Seventeenth Pennsylvania regiments, a battery of flying artillery, and a squad of light cavalry, under command of General Stoneman.

GAINES'S MILL.

On the afternoon of June 25th General A. P. Hill, after crossing the Chickahominy, drove away the small force of observation stationed at Mechanicsville, — thus enabling him to unite the division of Longstreet and D. H. Hill with his own. He then began a movement down the north bank of the Chickahominy, where he encountered McCall's division intrenched on the almost perpendicular bank of Beaver Dam Creek. The Confederate army was advancing by the Mechanicsville road, which runs nearly parallel at this point with the commanding intrenchments of the Union line, and thus unconsciously exposed his flank to the artillery and musketry fire.

The Union guns withheld their fire until the head of the rebel column was nearly across the creek, when they suddenly poured in a destructive artillery and infantry fire, causing the enemy to break and fly in confusion. Although constant firing continued until nine o'clock in the afternoon, no further attempt to force the passage was made. The Confederate loss, as estimated by Longstreet, was four thousand men, while that of the Union army loss was not over three hundred.

The next morning Jackson came up and turned the Union position, when Porter prudently fell back to Gaines's Mill.

The battle of Gaines's Mill was fought by Porter against overwhelming odds, June 27th. Porter's force, numbering only 20,335 men, described the arc of a circle on the hills between Cold Harbor and the Chickahominy, and covered the approaches to the bridges which connected this wing with the south banks of the river. Sykes's division on the right was in the woods and clearings extending to the rear of Cold Harbor, while Morell's on our extreme left, occupied a wooded crest rising abruptly from a deep ravine. The ground in front was open, but on that side from which the Confederates made their approach was a thick and tangled wood, through

"Suddenly there came a troop of cavalry, wildly rushing upon the artillery."   Page 57.

which ran a sluggish stream. McCall's division, which bore the brunt of the previous day's encounter, was posted in the rear, forming a second line.

The Confederate force, numbering nearly sixty thousand men, began the attack at about 2.30 in the afternoon. General A. P. Hill led the attack, and from the stubborn resistance met was soon of the opinion that the entire Army of the Potomac was in his front.

The deadly fire of our infantry and artillery hurled back and disorganized the attacking forces. For two hours the incessant roar of the conflict was heard. About four o'clock Jackson's and Longstreet's divisions came into the fight, and a general concerted attack was made on the compact lines of the Union position Our men answered the rebel yell with defiant cheers, and drove back their hosts which came swarming out of the woods and across the ravine.

The conflict was incessant up to seven o'clock, yet the Union lines were not broken, and it seemed that night only would end the contest.

Such was the situation when Whiting's troops, *en masse,* came across the ravine and up the hill, through the smoke, with wild yells. The Union lines, struggling with this overwhelming force, were broken about sundown, near the centre of Morell's division. Our forces at this point were falling back, under cover of the heavy guns, to a new position (not in confusion, but coolly and in order), when an unlooked-for event occurred. Suddenly there came a troop of cavalry, wildly rushing upon the artillery, whose gunners had, up to this time, stood firmly to their work. Thinking that they were being charged by the enemy, they were thrown into confusion and deserted their guns. It proved to be the Union cavalry, commanded by St. George Cook, who had received orders to keep below the hill, but had charged the enemy in the face of a terrible fire, and been thrown back upon the Union line and batteries, with horses frantic and uncontrollable.

Jackson, seizing this pivotal moment, with an impetuous charge, took possession of the crest, and the Union force, stubbornly fighting, fell back to the woods on the Chickahominy. Here the approaches to the bridge were crowded, in dire confusion, with skulkers, stragglers, and the wounded ; but at this critical moment French's and Meagher's brigades, opportunely sent by Sumner, arrived on the field, and under cover of their steady columns, the worn-out and shattered battalions were re-formed.

Our left wing was still unbroken, but the key to the Union position having been carried, they were forced to fall back also. Welcome night dropped her sable mantle over the terrible scenes of the conflict, and silently the heroic men, who had withstood the enemy against a superior force, retreated to the south of the Chickahominy, destroying the bridges to prevent pursuit.

The curious part of this battle was, that while 60,000 men attacked 20,000 under Porter, and supposed, as shown by their report, that they had the entire Union army in their front, the main body of the Union army, numbering over 70,000 men, was confronted by 25,000 Confederates, behind the defences of Richmond. So much it is necessary to say that the chapter which follows may be clearly understood.

CHAPTER VI.

O N the 25th of June preparations were made for a general advance from our position at Fair Oaks. Our pickets on the left were moved forward to an open field crossed by the Williamsburg road, and our lines then pushed forward beyond a swampy belt of timber, which for several days had been contested ground. Our troops, going in with a dash, met little serious resistance. The ground was so marshy in places that our men were obliged to cluster round the roots of trees or stand knee-deep in water. On the 27th (the day of the battle of Gaines's Mill) and the 28th the enemy in our front were unusually demonstrative, if not active. Our pickets were often so near the enemy's outposts as to hear them talk. One of my comrades told me of a conversation he overheard one night between two of the "Johnnies."

"Uncle Robert," said one, "is goin' to gobble up the Yankee army and bring 'em to Richmond."

"Well," said his comrade, with a touch of incredulity in his tones, "we uns'll have a right smart of 'em to feed; and what are we uns goin' to do with 'em when we uns catch 'em?"

"Oh," said the other, with a touch of contempt, "every one of we uns will have a Yank to tote our traps!"

On the 27th one of my comrades, while on picket, heard orders given as if to a large body of men — "From right of companies to rear in a column — right face. Don't get into a dozen ranks there. Why don't they move forward up the path?" These commands excited our vigilance. What puzzled us was that we could not hear the tramp of men, which is usual in moving large bodies of troops, when near enough to hear their voices. Later we knew that the Confederates in our front were keeping up a big show with a small number of troops. We heard the heavy booming of cannon, which told of Porter's battle on the north side of the Chickahominy, and on that day a balloon was seen over the Confederate capital. Every sign pointed to unusual activity in our front. Then Porter followed us to the south side of the Chickahominy, and the whole aspect of affairs was changed.

Details were made to destroy such stores

Campaigning through the
Swamp.

as could not easily be removed in wagons, and some of our officers, high in rank, set an unselfish example by destroying their personal baggage. Fires were not allowed in the work of destruction. Tents were cut and slashed with knives; canteens punched with bayonets; clothing cut into shreds; sugar and whiskey overturned on the ground, which absorbed them. Some of our men stealthily imitated mother earth as regards the whiskey. Most of our officers appreciated the gravity of the situation, and were considerate enough to keep sober, in more senses than one. Early on the morning of the 29th the work of destruction was complete, our picket-line was relieved, and with faces that reflected the gloom of our hearts, we turned our backs upon Richmond, and started upon the retreat. The gloom was rather that of surprise than of knowledge, as the movement was but slightly understood by the mass of the army, or for that matter by most of the officers.

The weather was suffocatingly hot: dust rose in clouds, completely enveloping the marching army; it filled our nostrils and throats, and covered every part of our clothing as if ashes had been sifted upon us. About nine o'clock line of battle was formed near Allen's farm. Occasionally the report of a sharp-shooter's rifle was heard in the woods. Some of the men took advantage of such shade as was afforded by scattering trees and went to sleep. All were suddenly brought to their feet by a tremendous explosion of artillery. The enemy had opened from the woods south of the railroad, with great vigor and precision. This attack was, after some sharp fighting, repelled, and, slinging knapsacks, the march was again resumed over the dusty roads. It was scorching hot when we arrived at Savage's Station, and there again we formed line of battle.

Franklin's corps, which had fallen back from Golding's farm, joined us here, and a detail was made as at other places to destroy supplies; immense piles of flour, hard bread in boxes, clothing, arms, and ammunition were burned, smashed, and scattered. Two trains of railroad cars, loaded with ammunition and other supplies, were here fired, set in motion toward each other, and under a full head of steam came thundering down the track like flaming meteors. When they met in collision there was a terrible explosion. Other trains and locomotives were precipitated from the demolished Bottom's bridge. Clouds of smoke rose at various points north of us, showing that the work of destruction was going on in other places.

Here, awaiting the approach of the enemy, we halted, while wagons of every description passed over the road on the retreat. It was now five o'clock in the afternoon (though official reports put it as early as four), when dense clouds of dust, rising in long lines from the roads beyond, warned us of the approach of our antagonists. Soon they advanced from the edge of the woods and opened fire from the whole mass of their artillery. Our guns responded. For nearly an hour not a musket was heard, but the air vibrated with the artillery explosions. Then the infantry became engaged in the woods. Even after the shadows of night covered the scene with their uncertain light, the conflict went on, until nine o'clock, when to the deep-toned Union cheers there were no answering high-pitched rebel yells.

Our regiment occupied till after sundown a position opposite the hospital camp near the station. It was then ordered to charge the enemy, which was done under cover of the heavy smoke that hung over the field. At nine o'clock they began to care for the wounded, and to carry them to the amputating-table. Our "Little Day" was wounded through the arm, but bandaged it himself. Wad Rider got another slight scalp-wound, which led him to remark, "Them cusses always aim for my head." Pendleton got what he called a ventilator through the side of his hat, the bullet grazing his head. One of the chaplains was indefatigable in his care of the wounded, and finally preferred to be taken prisoner rather than desert them.

Turning their backs upon the battle-field and the hospital camp of twenty-five hundred sick and wounded, who were abandoned to the enemy, the troops resumed their march. The long trains, of five thousand wagons and two thousand five hundred head of beef, had by this time crossed White Oak Swamp. The defile over which the army passed was narrow, but it possessed the compensating advantage that no attack could be made on the flank, because of the morass on either side. As fast as the rear-guard passed, trees were felled across the road to obstruct pursuit. Before daylight the Grand Army was across the swamp, with the bridge destroyed in the rear.

GLENDALE.

DURING the early morning hours of Monday, June 30th, our regiment was halted near a barn used as a temporary hospital. The boys lay down, weary and footsore with fighting and marching. They were aroused about eight o'clock and resumed their march. At eleven they were halted near Nelson's farm. The country here began to change from swamp and wood to cultivated fields.

McCall's division, now numbering only about six thousand men, was formed nearly parallel to the New Market road, with his batteries in rear of the infantry. Kearney was within supporting distance on his right, guarding the space between the New Market and Charles City roads, while Sumner's corps, with Hooker's division, were formed in the rear of McCall's advance line. To force the Union army from this key position and divide it, Longstreet gave battle. At 2.30 P.M., advancing with A. P. Hill by the Charles City road, he attacked with fury McCall's division. A heavy force of the enemy, passing through the woods, was hurled upon General Seymour's brigade, holding the left, who maintained a stubborn fight for two hours, finally causing him to fall back. Knieriem's and Diederichs's batteries were badly demoralized at this point. One of their officers blubbered outright. "Are you wounded? Are you killed?" asked Hooker's ironical jokers. "No; mine battery disgraces me vorse dan det," was his reply.

Six companies of a Pennsylvania regiment were stationed in two log shanties and some rude breastworks, as support to the two pieces of artillery posted on the hill in the rear, and in advance of the third brigade. The enemy opened on them with artillery, and also advanced an infantry force behind them by a ravine, upon which the Pennsylvanians broke and fled in confusion. Streaming to the rear they broke through Hooker's lines, and even fired upon his men, but took no further part in the conflict of the day. A colonel of one of these demoralized regiments came in advance of his men, dashing to the rear, and as Hooker's men were moving to the fight exclaimed, " My men are all cut to pieces; hurry up and save my poor men," all the time showing signs of fear, and a very picture of distress. Hooker's men "double quicked" by him, derisively exclaiming, "Dry up, you old fool! No wonder your men broke with such a coward in command!

You are a nice son of a gun for an officer! Pull your eagles off and don't disgrace them! Go home to your mother, you ain't worth the powder and lead it would require to shoot you!" All this may seem tame in the recital, but every sally was followed by a roar of laughter which mingled with the roar of battle at the front, to which they were hurrying, and was funny to them.

The crowning attack of the day was on Randall's battery, on McCall's right. It was of a peculiar and desperate character unusual in the history of war. McCall, in his report of the battle, describes it as "advancing in wedge shape, without order, with trailing arms, in perfect recklessness." Feeling over-confident in his ability to repel the attack with artillery, orders were given by the officer in command for the infantry to withhold their fire until the artillery were done with them.

In one dense mass, without order, a perfect mob of desperate men, with trailing arms, shouting, screaming, on they came, with an impetuosity and fury impossible to describe.

Vainly the artillery of the Federals tore great gaps and paths through this torrent of men pouring in upon them; closing up their shattered ranks, on they came with a fury which defied ordinary artillery calculations, until they were among the guns and gunners and infantry supports. Here occurred a hand-to-hand struggle over the guns seldom witnessed in battle.

The rebels cut the traces, bayoneted and shot the horses, and overturned the guns, intent upon preventing their removal.

With clubbed muskets and bayonets our men resisted. Bayonets were locked, oaths, bayonet-thrusts, and pistol-shots were given and exchanged, and in some instances men fell mutually pierced in the struggle. An acquaintance, who was in this hand-to-hand conflict, and took part as an artillerist, told me afterwards that the enemy had advanced so near when the last order was given to fire that he was obliged to discharge the rammer from his gun as well as the shot at the enemy. Said he, "Our sergeant shouted to the boys, as the rebs came yelling like mad upon us, 'Don't run from them.' I thought to myself, 'I ain't going to git from no such ragged fellows as they be.' One of them shot my hoss and I punched him with a bayonet. Another reb came up yelling, 'Surrender, you durned Yanks, to the Sixtieth Virginia!' Whereupon a big gunner knocked him over the head with his rammer."

" ' Here by the oak,' our men would say, in answer to their calls."   Page 65.

An attack which had occurred at 4 P.M. on Kearney's lines was much of the same nature as the attack described — a determined assault *en masse.* Thompson's battery swept the sloping ground over which the rebels were advancing. Notwithstanding their heavy loss the enemy pressed on with undaunted persistency, which, as General Kearney in his report said, "put artillery out of calculation." But the well-directed volleys of the Sixty-third Pennsylvania and Thirty-seventh New York accomplished what grape and canister had failed to do, and the foes were hurled back, under this withering fire, in confusion.

When McCall's division gave way the enemy, who had turned the left of the Union line, came down upon Sumner's troops, who soon received the order, "Forward, guide right"; and at double quick, while the batteries in the rear threw shot and shell over their heads into the ranks of the enemy, they pressed forward upon them. For a few moments the enemy resisted, then broke for the cover of the woods and melted away in the twilight shadows gathering over the field. Our artillery continued to shell the woods, and the din of musketry did not cease until long after dark. This Union victory insured the safety of the army, which until that hour had been in peril.

During the night many of the enemy's stragglers were captured. Hooker's men, who heard them in the strip of woods calling out the names of their regiments, stationed squads at different points to answer and direct them into the Union lines, where they were captured. "Here by the oak," our men would say in answer to their calls, and thus gathered in these lost children of the Confederacy. Our regiment captured five or six stragglers in much the same manner. Many of them were under the influence of stimulants. It was current talk at that time — to account for the desperate, reckless charges made during the day — that the Confederates were plied with whiskey. I am not of that opinion, as whiskey will not make men brave. Those captured wore a medley of garments which could hardly be called a uniform, though gray and butternut were the prevailing colors. Some of them had a strip of carpet for a blanket, but the raggedness of their outfit was no discredit to soldiers who fought as bravely as did these men.

Franklin's force, which had been disputing the passage of White Oak Swamp during the day, at dark retreated from that position, which made it prudent to retire our whole force from Glendale, as

Jackson's forces at White Oak bridge would soon be upon us. By daylight began our march to Malvern, the pioneers felling trees in the rear.

Acres and acres of waving grain, ripe for the reapers, were seen on every side. The troops marched through the wheat, cutting off the tops and gathering them into their haversacks, for, except in more than ordinarily provident cases, they were out of rations and hungry, as well as lame and stiff from marching. The bands, which had been silent so long before Richmond, here began playing patriotic airs, with a very inspiring effect. As they neared James River and caught sight of our gun-boats, a cheer went up from each regiment. About eleven o'clock in the morning they took position on the Malvern plateau.

MALVERN HILL.

THE *morale* of the army, notwithstanding its toilsome midnight marches and daily battles, with insufficient sleep and scanty food, was excellent. Its comparatively raw masses were now an army of veterans, tried in the fire of battle.

Our stragglers, their courage revived by sight of the gunboats, came up the hill, seeking their regiments. One squad encountered half a dozen of the enemy's cavalry and charged them with empty muskets. Another squad came in with a Confederate wagon, in which were several wounded comrades rescued from the battle-field. Another squad had their haversacks filled with honey, and bore marks of a battle with bees. During the morning long lines of men with dusty garments and powder-blackened faces climbed the steep Quaker road. Footsore, hungry, and wearied, but not disheartened, these tired men took their positions and prepared for another day of conflict. The private soldiers were quick to perceive the advantages which the possession of Malvern Hill gave us, and such expressions as "How is this for Johnny Reb!" were heard on every hand. Wad Rider, complacently and keenly viewing the surrounding, said, "Satan himself couldn't whip us out of this!" As soon as it was in position near the north front of the hill, our regiment was given the order, "In place — rest," and in a few minutes the men were asleep, lying beside their muskets.

Early in the forenoon skirmishing began along the new line. Some of the troops, while going up the hill to take their positions on the field, were fired upon by the enemy's batteries. Small parties advanced within musket-shot, evidently reconnoitring our position, and fired from the cover of the woods on our men. Shells from our gun-boats on the James came hoarsely spluttering over the heads of the troops. Occasionally hostile regiments appeared from the woods below the crest of the hill, and were as often driven back by our artillery.

The fighting of the day might be described as a succession of daring attacks and bloody repulses. Heavy firing began at different points soon after noon, followed by a lull. About three o'clock there was heard an explosion of artillery, with the well-known rebel yell, followed by the cheering of our men. The crash of artillery was even at this time terrible. Soon it partly died away and was followed by roaring volleys, and then the regular *snap, crack, crack* of firing at will of the musketry. It was the attack of G. B. Anderson's brigade of D. H. Hill's division upon Couch's front. In a hand-to-hand struggle at this time, the Thirty-sixth New York captured the colors of the Fourteenth North Carolina and a number of prisoners. Couch then advanced his line to a grove, which gave a stronger position and a better range for the musketry. An assault at the same time was made along the left, but was speedily repulsed by the batteries. At four o'clock there was quiet, but the storm of battle at six o'clock burst upon Malvern cliff. Brigade after brigade came up the hill with impetuous courage, breasting the storm of canister, grape, and shell which devastated their ranks. Half-way up they would break in disorder, before the destructive cannonade and the deadly volleys of musketry. Vainly they were rallied. It was more than human courage could endure.

After D. H. Hill, Magruder made his attack. Our guns, grouped around the Crew house, opened upon the Confederates, as with fierce yells they charged up the slope. In some instances our infantry, being sheltered by the inequalities of the ground in front of the guns, withheld their fire until the charging column was within a few yards of them. Sometimes the enemy attacked from the cover of the ravine on the left, but they never reached the crest. Night came, yet the fight went on, with cheers answering to yells and gun answering to gun. The lurid flashes of artillery along the hostile lines, in the gathering darkness; the crackle of musketry, with flashes seen in the distance like fire-flies; the hoarse shriek of the huge shells from the gun-boats, thrown into the woods, made it a scene of terrible grandeur. The ground in front of Porter and Couch was literally covered with the dead and wounded. At nine o'clock the sounds of the battle died away, and cheer after cheer went up from the victors on the hill.

During the battle of Malvern Hill the infantry where my regiment was posted was not brought into active opposition to the enemy. They lay on the ground in front of the guns, which threw shot, shell, and canister over their heads. Several times after three o'clock brigades were sent from this position to act as supports where the attack was heaviest on Couch's lines. Just after three o'clock the artillery fire was heavy on our brigade, but the loss was light, owing to the protection afforded to the infantry by the inequalities of the ground. Between six and seven o'clock our company was detailed to guard prisoners; and about that time, as one of my comrades said, General Hooker rode by on his white horse, which formed a very marked contrast to his very red face. He rode leisurely and complacently, as if in no alarm or excitement, but looked very warm. Behind a bluff, not far from the Crew house, was the extemporized hospital towards which stretcher-bearers were carrying the wounded; those able to walk were hobbling, and in some instances were using a reversed musket for a crutch.

All of the prisoners were "played-out" men who had evidently seen hard service with marching, fighting, and short rations. Some of them were morose and defiant. The most intelligent were generally the best natured. The Virginians would usually remark, "You all will never conquer we alls." In general they were poorly clad.

Thus ended the Union advance on Richmond. The grand Army of the Potomac forced its way to within sight of the enemy's capital, only to fall back, in a desperate struggle of seven successive days, to the James River. Yet it preserved its trains, its courage, and its undaunted front, and inflicted upon the enemy heavier losses than it sustained. Though crowded back in the final movement, our army defeated the enemy on every battle-field but one during the seven days. The moral advantage was on the side of the Confederates;

the physical on the side of the Federals. We had inflicted a loss of about 20,000 on the enemy, while sustaining a loss of but 15,849. The fighting of our private soldiers had brought no discredit to the American name. The Peninsular campaign showed their devotion, bravery, and discipline, and its lessons had an influence on all the future of the Army of the Potomac. The North was in humiliation over the result, while the Confederates rejoiced.

ON THE JAMES.

THE next morning at daybreak our regiment moved with its squad of prisoners down the road to Haxall's. Here, for some reason, they were halted for two or three hours while regiments, trains, and cattle moved over the narrow defile, jumbled in confusion together. There were loud discussions as to the right of way, and a deal of growling among the soldiers at retreating, after giving the "rebs" such a whipping; but most of them seemed to think "Little Mac" knew what he was about, and the enthusiasm for him grew in intensity rather than decreased. The halt gave leisure for talk with the prisoners. One of them was a good-looking, intelligent fellow about twenty-two years of age. He informed one of my comrades that he belonged to a North Carolina regiment. He was a college graduate, and the prospect of spending a summer at the North did not seem to displease him. He confidentially said that he had been a Union man just as long as he could, and finally went into the Confederate army to save his property and reputation and to avoid conscription. He added : "There are thousands in the South just like me. We didn't want the war, and resisted the sentiment of secession as long as we could. Now it has gone so far we've got to fight or sever all the associations with which our lives are interlinked. I know it is a desperate chance for the South. Look at your men, how they are disciplined, fed, and clothed, and then see how our men are fed and clothed. They are brave men, but they can't stand it forever. Southern men have got fight in them, and you will find them hard to conquer."

One lean "Johnny" was loud in his praise of Stonewall Jackson, saying : "He's a general, he is. If you uns had some good general like him, I reckon you uns could lick we uns. 'Old Jack' marches we uns most to death ; a Confed that's under Stonewall has got to march."

"Does your general abuse you — swear at you to make you march ?" inquired one of his listeners.

"Swear ?" answered the Confederate ; "no. Ewell he does the swearing ; Stonewall does the praying. When Stonewall wants us to march he looks at us soberly, just as if he was sorry for we uns, but

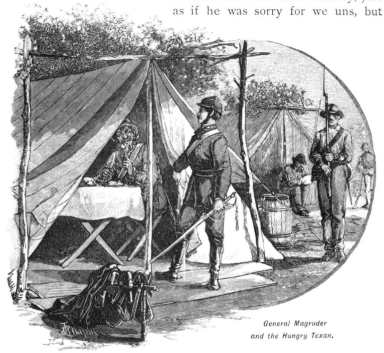

General Magruder
and the Hungry Texan.

couldn't help it, and says, 'Men, we've got to make a long march.' We always know when there is going to be a long march and some right smart fighting, for Old Jack is powerful on prayer just before a big fight."

"Did you ever see General Lee ?" I inquired of one of them.

"Yes, I was a sort of orderly for 'Uncle Robert' for a while. He's mighty calm-like when a fight is going on."

"Our General Magruder," said another, "thinks a powerful heap of what he eats and wears. He allers has a right smart of truck. There was a Texas feller one time who had straggled from his brigade, and he were a pert one, he were, stranger. He were hungry enough to eat a general, buttons and all — that Texas feller were. He saw Magruder's table all spread, with a heap of good fixins on it, and I'll be dog-goned if he didn't walk in, pert as you please, grabbed a knife and fork, and opened fire all along the line of them fixin's. Magruder heard some one in his tent, and pranced in and asked that Texas chap what brought him thar. The Texan 'lowed he were hungry. Then the general, stiff and grand-like, said, 'Do you know, sir, at whose table you'r eating?' That Texas chap, he kept drivin' in the pickets on them chick'ns, and he said to the gen'ral, said he, 'No, old hoss, and I ain't no ways partic'lar, nether, since I've come solderin'.'"

"What did Magruder do?" asked one of his Yankee listeners. "Do? why, he saw them chicken fixin's were spiled, and he jest put his arm under his coat-tail, pulled his hat over his eyes — and walked out. And that Texan hoss didn't leave anything on that thar table 'cept ther plates, not even his compliments. Who wor he? He wor one of Whitin's Texans. They ain't got no manners, they hain't. He wor powerful hungry, stranger, that chap wor."

About ten o'clock in the morning the regiment resumed its march. It reached Harrison's Landing about four in the afternoon, just as it began to rain in torrents. Here the men were relieved from guard duty and allowed the privilege of making themselves as comfortable as was possible under the circumstances. The level land which terminates in bluffs on the James River was covered with hundreds of acres of wheat ready for the harvest. The process of cutting for the army began without delay, and before night every blade of it was in use for bedding and forage ; not a vestige remained to tell of the waving grain which had covered the plain a few hours before. The fields whereon it stood were trampled under foot ; not even a stubble stood in sight. Great fields of mud were the resting-place of the army. It was almost as muddy as if the waters of the deluge had just receded from the face of the earth. Mules, horses, and men were alike smeared and spotted with mire, and the ardor of the army was somewhat dampened thereby.

At Harrison's Landing the army settled down to a period of rest, which was much needed.   The heat during the day was intolerable, and prevented much exercise.   Men lay under their shelter, smoked, told stories, discussed the scenes and battles of the previous month, and when evening came on visited each other's camps and sang the popular songs of the day.   Those vampires of the army, the sutlers, charged double prices for everything they had to sell, until the soldiers began to regard them as their natural enemies.   No change smaller than ten cents circulated in camp.   It was the smallest price charged for anything.   Sutler's pasteboard checks were in good demand as change, and were very useful in playing the game of "bluff."   Thus the army whiled away the month of July.   During August some of the prisoners captured from us on the seven days' retreat arrived in our lines for exchange.   They were a sorry-looking crowd — emaciated, hungry, sick, ragged, and dirty.   They did not have a high opinion of the entertainment they had received at Belle Isle and Libby prison.

"What kind of a place is Belle Island?" was asked, "it has a pretty name."   "It is a low point of land, sticking out into the river opposite Richmond, like a mackerel's head.   The land is so low that water came right up under us nights."

"Did they give you good food?"   "Humph! maggoty beans and such stuff.   I tell you it seems good to get hold of our hard-tack!   I was almost starved all the time I was down there."

"You have got a good appetite," said one, "they didn't steal that."

"No," said the ex-prisoner, "they were awfully afraid of over-feeding us."

During one of those quiet, still August nights, dark, and as close and muggy as only a night in "dog days" can be, some time after midnight, the whole camp was roused by the furious and rapid bursting of shells in our very midst.   Imagine, if you can, a midnight shelling of a closely packed camp of fifty thousand men, without giving them one hint or thought of warning; imagine our dazed appearance as we rolled from under our canvas coverings, and the running and dodging here and there, trying to escape from the objective point of the missiles.   Of course the camp was a perfect pandemonium during the half hour that the shelling lasted.   We soon discovered that the visitors came from a battery across the

James River, and in twenty minutes a few of our guns silenced them completely. Most of these shells burst over and amongst us who occupied the centre of the camp, near the old Harrison's Landing road. This road was lined on either side with large shade-trees, which were probably of some assistance to the enemy in training their guns.

While at Harrison's Landing there was a great deal of sickness. But, more than any other ailment, homesickness was prevalent. It made the most fearful inroads among the commissioned officers. Many sent in their resignations, which were promptly returned disapproved. One, who had not shown a disposition, proportionate to his rank, to face the enemy, hired two men to carry him on a stretcher to the hospital boat; and this valiant officer was absent from the army nearly a whole year. We believed at that time that some of the hospitals at the North, for the sake of the money made on each ration, sheltered and retained skulkers. In contrast with this was the noble action of men who insisted on joining their commands before their wounds were fairly healed, or while not yet recovered from sickness.

Bathing and swimming in the James was a luxury to us soldiers, and did much, no doubt, towards improving the health of the army. Boxes with goodies from home came by express in great numbers. One of my friends at one time received a whole cheese, and for a week was the envy of the company.

One of the most important members of the company was the cook. He was a fat "son of a gun," though he was more at home with the fire under his camp-kettles than when himself under fire from the enemy. He maintained a sort of martial law among us hungry fellows, and woe to the man who provoked his displeasure; he would surely come short in his provender some way. He used to boil his dirty clothes in the camp kettles in which he cooked our food, coffee, and soups, and although the procedure was not popular among the men, no one dared to remonstrate for fear of the consequences to his rations. I had at this time such a realization of the importance of the position of company-cook that I was of the opinion that nothing short of a brigadier-general should hold it; and as we had so many more of those than seemed useful in a fight, I thought it would be a valuable innovation to install them as cooks.

Hooker's brigade moved towards Malvern Hill on the 2d of August, and on the 4th attacked the enemy near Glendale. On the 15th all was bustle and confusion, getting ready for some movement — perhaps another advance on Richmond. But instead we took up our line of march down the Peninsula. The people on the way openly expressed hatred of us and sympathy with the rebellion. No guards were posted over the houses as heretofore, and we used the fences to boil our coffee, without reproach from our officers. At one house, near the landing, a notice was posted forbidding the burial of a Yankee on the estate. That house was very quickly and deliberately burned to the ground. Steamboats and wagons were crowded with our sick. After rapid marches we arrived at Hampton, and embarked again for Alexandria.

CHAPTER VII.

THE removal of the Army of the Potomac from its new base on the James, and the setting aside of McClellan from its command, has been a prolific source of discussion and recrimination. There is much that can be said both in favor of and against its removal, which a dispassionate man might assent to as pertinent and just.

On one hand it is claimed that the unhealthy situation in which the army would be placed while inactive amid the low and marshy land on the north of the James during August and September, made its removal expedient. While on the other hand it is certain that the months following would be no more fatal than those which had preceded, and that the sanitary condition of the army would compare favorably with that of any other in the field. It is again urged that it was advisable to concentrate the military forces then in Virginia into one army.

It is generally admitted by military critics that if the Army of the Potomac was not to be reinforced while on the James, it would be better to remove it and consolidate with the other forces in Virginia. McClellan urged that it was cheaper and easier to reinforce him on the James, and less demoralizing, than to remove the army to Acquia Creek; that the army on the James was practically within ten miles of Richmond, with water transportation within twelve miles during its whole contemplated advance; while at Acquia Creek the army would be seventy miles from Richmond with difficult land transportation all the way.

Halleck's memorandum of his visit to the headquarters of the Army of the Potomac, July 25th, discloses the intention of McClellan "To cross the James at that point, attack Petersburg and cut off the enemy's communications by that route south."

To this plan Halleck objected, and in his memorandum says:

"I stated to him very frankly my views in regard to the danger
and impracticability of the plan." Two years afterwards Grant found
the true defence of Washington to be on the James (a position
gained by immense and disproportionate loss to that of the enemy),
and then adopting the plan McClellan proposed, took Richmond, and
destroyed Lee's army.

The situation was not materially different so far as Washington
was concerned, except that in 1862 there would have been a much
larger number left for its defences than in 1864.

All questions of this nature should be determined by military
rules rather than by prejudice. It is an accepted maxim in war never
to do that which your enemy wishes you to do. From this well-
grounded maxim let us consider the withdrawal of the army from
the James.

Lee's report of the operations of the Army of Northern Virginia
shows what he desired by his saying: "In order to keep McClellan
stationary, or, if possible, to cause him to withdraw, General D. H.
Hill, commanding on the south side of James River, was directed to
threaten his communications by seizing favorable positions below
Westover, from which to attack the transports on the river."

We have in this report the authority of Lee himself as to what
he considered desirable, and it is a curious fact that Halleck's wishes
were in perfect accord with the Confederate commander's in a desire
to remove the Army of the James, and that he finally achieved, by
reason of his high official position, that which Lee failed to attain
by strategy. No more sarcastic presentation of his want of wisdom
could be offered than this fact. Again, upon the advisability of reinforcing Jackson on reaching Gordonsville, Lee in his report says,
"Jackson ascertained that the force under General Pope was superior
to his own, but the uncertainty that then surrounded the designs of
General McClellan rendered it inexpedient to reinforce him from the
army at Richmond."

It was not until the movement from Harrison's Landing was fully
disclosed that Lee ventured to reinforce Jackson.

Halleck, while holding his exalted position, thus showed his
greatest ability in anticipating and acting in unison with the designs
of the enemy, and was a stumbling-block in the path to success of
every general who succeeded McClellan in command of that army,

until Grant's high position and strong will finally excluded him from its management.

One of the most potent causes of the removal of the army from the James, no doubt, was want of accord in political sentiment between its commander and the administration.

If McClellan had preserved that modest reticence in regard to political affairs which afterwards characterized Grant, it would have been wiser for him and better for the country. No doubt his letter to President Lincoln, written July 7th, from Harrison's Landing, offering advice on the slavery question, stirred up a deep sentiment against him among the friends of the administration, who thenceforth brought great pressure upon Mr. Lincoln for his removal. The subjects discussed by that letter, however correct its views may have been, were not military, and might justly have been considered by Mr. Lincoln as impertinent.

General John Pope, whose successes in the West had commended him to the administration, was appointed to command the scattered forces under Banks, Fremont, and McDowell, and had wisely consolidated them into one army.

Some of Pope's characteristics are revealed by his answers to questions, while before the committee on the conduct of the war, just after his appointment, June 26, to the command of the army before Washington. In expounding to the committee his military views, he said: "By lying off on their flank, if they should have forty or fifty thousand men, I could whip them. If they should have seventy or eighty thousand I would attack their flank and force them, in order to get rid of me, to follow me out into the mountains, which would be what you would want, I should suppose."

Committee: "Suppose you had the army that was here on the first day of March last, do you suppose you would find any obstacle to prevent your marching to New Orleans?" "I should suppose not."

Having astonished and delighted the committee he proceeded to electrify the army by an address in which military rules were revolutionized or set aside.

In that address he says: "I have come to you from the West where we have always seen the backs of our enemies — where the policy has been attack and not defence. I presume I've been called here

Stuart's Cavalry raiding Catlett's Station.

to pursue the same system. I desire you to dismiss from your minds certain phrases which I am sorry to find much in vogue among you. I hear constantly of 'taking strong positions and holding them,' of 'lines of retreat, and bases of supplies.' Let us discard such ideas. The strongest position a soldier should desire to occupy is one from which he can most easily advance against the enemy. Success and glory are in the advance, disaster and shame lurk in the rear."

Fate, in interpreting Pope's military principles, was decidedly ironical. His forces, numbering nearly fifty thousand men, were concentrated into one body, lying along the line of the Orange and Alexandria Railroad, in front of Washington and in the direction of Gordonsville.

This disposition threatened Lee's communications with southwestern Virginia, which the Confederate commander was quick to perceive. To prevent it Lee sent forward Jackson's force of twenty-five thousand men towards Gordonsville where they arrived July 19. But because this force was too weak to risk aggressive movements, he was reinforced by A. P. Hill's division, and August 8, crossed the Rapidan, moving towards Culpeper.

Pope had promptly hurried forward Bank's corps, which met the enemy near Cedar Mountain, August 9. The force under General Banks numbered only about eight thousand men. They acted under written instructions from a member of Pope's staff, which were, "to deploy his skirmishers, if the enemy advances, and attack him immediately as he approaches." Although his force was but little more than one-third that of his antagonist, Banks attacked him with great impetuosity, and defeated him.

After the action of Cedar Mountain the army, under Jackson, fell back to Gordonsville; being there reinforced by Longstreet's division, it advanced to the Rapidan, and on the 20th of August crossed that river.

Pope, much more judicious in his movements than his exposition of military principles would suggest, forgot to "lie off" on Lee's flank, and, also heedless of his great maxim that "strong positions and lines of retreat were to be disregarded," prudently retired beyond the Rappahannock. He evidently found Jackson unaware that he had a flank for him to lay off on, or was singularly obtuse to the fact that his antagonist was likely to bring out this horrible strategic spectre.

Lee now began to make it lively for the western general. Leaving Longstreet as a blind at the ford, covered by Pope, who was absent-mindedly guarding it and thus neglecting his vast opportunities of "lying off on Lee's flank" and of putting in force his western usage "of seeking the enemy and beating him when found," Lee sent Jackson up the south bank of the Rappahannock, which he crossed, August 22d, at Warrenton Springs. At the same time Stuart's cavalry made an expedition to cut the railroad communications in rear of Pope's army and thus give a new reading to that general's famous maxim that "disaster and shame lurk in the rear." They thus succeeded in giving a new and vigorous interpretation to Pope's address. The army supplies which they captured at Catlett's Station were immense.

Jackson, meanwhile, turned Pope's right and by forced marches of thirty-five miles a day continued the flank march. Turning east towards Salem, he crossed the Bull Run Mountains through Thoroughfare Gap, and at sunset on the 26th had reached Bristow Station on the railroad. This he destroyed and at the same time hurried Stuart's cavalry to Manassas Junction, seven miles nearer still to Washington. Here several hundred prisoners and immense stores of army supplies were captured.

While Jackson, without reference to his flank or communications, was illustrating Pope's address to his army, that general determined to bag him, and he was not modest in proclaiming the fact. Jackson might be called the great Confederate Flea, for when Pope put down his military hand where he was, he wasn't there!

Lee must have had a settled contempt for his adversary or he

Hooker's Men raiding the Box of Chickens.

never would have attempted this daring raid in our rear. He evidently did not appreciate Pope's "lying off on his flank!"

It is greatly to be regretted that during the entire campaign Pope did not find time to spring upon the Confederate leader this terrible "Jack in the box." It would certainly have marked a new era in military strategy.

Why didn't he do it? Would the results have been too dark and terrible even to inflict upon an enemy?

On the 27th Hooker with his division was sent out from Warrenton

Junction, and after marching nine miles he encountered, at Bristow's Station, Ewell's division *en masse,* and attacked them with his characteristic skill and bravery. His attack was sudden and the enemy fled. They must have been making themselves comfortable, since good things in process of cooking were left behind them ; bread was found baking in Dutch ovens, dough in pans, while in the houses their sympathizers had been making ready to entertain Confederate guests. One of our men came out of a house with two bags of peanuts, a Confederate substitute for coffee, and said to a comrade, " Hey ! Jim, here's peanuts enough to set up a circus ! " The civilians, who were not anxious to entertain the Yanks, had, as one of the boys afterwards explained to me, been laying themselves out for the Confederates and had "killed the fatted calf." At one house there were found two or three barrels of cakes which the mistress protested were for family use, but which, notwithstanding, were speedily converted to the use of Uncle Sam's wayward children in blue.

One squad of Hooker's men introducing themselves into a house, found three females sitting on a box. They were politely assisted to their feet by our gallant and hungry patriots, and the box examined. It was found to contain chickens all cooked.

The skies were now darkened by the smoke of burning trains which Jackson had left in his track. At the close of the skirmish, which had been short and sharp, General Pope arrived and learned, for the first time, that Jackson was in front of him with his whole corps.

Banks was ordered to take Porter's place at Warrenton Junction, while Porter was sent to bring up his forces, and Kearny, five miles distant at Greenwich, was ordered up. This would have been a brilliant move and sufficient to oppose Jackson and separate him from Lee's army, thereby preventing a junction of his forces. But in addition Pope ordered Reno's division and also Sigel's and McDowell's from Greenwich to Manassas. Ewell, when he modestly retired from Bristow's Station, burned the bridge across Bull Run, thus intimating that he did not care for Hooker's company.

Jackson did not care to stay at Manassas waiting for Pope, his command being separated from the rest of Lee's army ; he therefore retired, without asking leave of Pope, on the night of the 27th, to the old battle ground of Bull Run, where he first showed his ability as a commander, and where he gained the *sobriquet* of " Stonewall." At daylight, August 28, his whole corps was reunited at Manassas.

On the 28th Pope did not know, practically, where his own forces were, or those of the enemy who had so manœuvred as to mislead, elude, and confuse him. His divisions, scattered by contradictory and confusing orders, were held so loosely in hand, and were so isolated from each other, that so far as exercising control over them was concerned, it would almost have been as well for him to have been in the West, where he came from, as in Virginia. By the morning of the 29th he began to get clearer views of the situation.

Jackson is said to have claimed that one of the elements of his military success was the mystery with which he shrouded his movements.

CHAPTER VIII.

TWO DAYS OF THE SECOND BATTLE OF BULL RUN.

POPE'S first orders on the 29th of August were given partly with a view to the possibility of falling back beyond Bull Run. At three o'clock of that morning Pope had written to Porter that McDowell had intercepted the retreat of Jackson; that Kearney and Hooker were to attack the enemy's rear; and that Porter was to move upon Centreville at dawn of day. Porter was obeying the order when he learned its revocation through a staff-officer riding with orders to another part of the field, and at once countermarched from Manassas Junction. Meanwhile Pope had learned that Ricketts's and King's divisions had retreated, leaving open the road for Lee's advance or Jackson's retreat. He ordered Sigel to attack in order to bring Jackson to a stand if possible. Jackson was in fact leisurely awaiting attack behind his chosen stronghold of the unfinished railroad, with his skirmishers in front and for the most part veiled with thick woods. General Sigel soon developed the position of the enemy. There were gaps in Sigel's lines, the closing of which weakened the main line, itself already too thin for such an attempt. The enemy were quick to avail themselves of this weakness, and broke our lines by a furious attack, causing Sigel to fall back.

Longstreet had availed himself of the roads left open by King and Ricketts, and about noon his advance had formed on Jackson's right. After 12 o'clock McDowell brought to Porter information from General Buford, showing that Longstreet was holding the roads in force in Porter's front, and hence it was impossible, by marching on converging lines, to establish communications with the right wing of the army without giving battle. After consultation with Porter, McDowell started with King's division to go round by the Sudley Springs road. Porter waited to open up communications with McDowell, sending scouting parties through the broken country and tangled woods to the right for this purpose.

Towards noon a part of Sigel's force, under Schurz, gained a foothold on the railroad, and held on stubbornly for two hours. They were exhausted with marching, fighting, and manœuvring in the extreme heat since five in the morning.

The veterans of Heintzelman, under Kearney and Hooker, aroused from their bivouacs at two in the morning, were an hour after sunrise on the heights of Centreville, in sight of the blue hills about Thoroughfare Gap through which Longstreet was hastening to Jackson's aid. Fording Bull Run, they came upon the rusty remains of guns, bayonets, weather-beaten fragments of gun-carriages and equipments, and the bleaching skulls and bones of their comrades who had perished on the field the year before — the first sacrifices to the blunders of the war. Many fields were black from the effect of fires ignited by our shells. This fragment of the army, under Hooker and Kearney, was in a destitute condition. The horses of the field-officers in most instances had been left behind at Yorktown. The rank and file were poorly supplied with clothing, and to a large extent destitute of proper rations. Many were without blanket or blouse, some even without trousers ; others with shoeless, blistered feet were marching over rough, hot, and dusty roads. Still they were full of enthusiasm for the fight ; and as Pope, with a numerous staff, passed them on the road, he was loudly cheered. After that battle there was less cheering for the commander. At eleven o'clock they had reached the battle-field. At three Pope ordered Hooker to attack the strong position in his front. General Hooker, foreseeing that the attack promised but little chance of success, remonstrated.

Finally the order came to General Grover. "What does the General want me to do?" Grover inquired of the officer bringing the order.

"Go into the woods and charge."

"Where are my supports?"

"They are coming," was the reply.

Drawing his men up in line, he awaited the arrival of his supports, which did not come. But receiving imperative orders to "Charge at once," the men loaded their rifles and fixed bayonets. With cheers the men dashed through the tangled wood in their front. One of the regiments had its flag torn from its staff, and the eagle shot away from its top, but the men answered to the cry, "Rally round the pole." The bullets penetrated even the barrels of the muskets of the men; the stocks were shivered in their grasp. Small twigs of trees came down in showers upon their heads. So far as nature was concerned the air was a dead calm, yet the leaves of the forest were moved as by a breeze, by the bullets zipping among them. As they stormed the railroad they saw wounded Confederates clutch the embankment, hold on for a moment, and then losing their grasp, roll down the steep bank. The first line of the enemy was overthrown. On they rushed upon a second line. Bayonets and swords were used at close quarters, so stubborn was the fight.

Had this attack been properly supported, it must have broken Jackson's centre. There were many deeds performed in this action which were heroic. A father and son charged side by side. The son fell, pierced by the enemy's bullets. A quiver of grief swept over the father's face, and then he said, "I'd rather have him shot like that than see him run." Two privates, advancing through the woods, were separated from the main line, and were confronted by a squad of the enemy. They were called upon to surrender, but, standing shoulder to shoulder, they stood their ground until their assailants drew back. Then one of the two fainted from a wound; his comrade took him in his arms, and brought him safely back into our lines. So the combat went on, till a new line of the enemy advanced upon our men, and compelled them to fall back. As they were falling back, stubbornly contesting the ground, some one shouted, "Pring up the shackasses." Sure enough, up there came, at a shambling gait, a battery of howitzers mounted on the backs of those animals. Hooker's men hurried up, laughing and shouting at the operation of this quaint battery.

"What battery is that?" "The shackass pattery, py Gott;" savagely came the answer. "Get out mit der way, or we plows your hets off." That battery, with the other artillery, opened with canister at short range on the advancing line of rebels, from the fringe of woods, and checked their advance again.

Kearney was, at the same time, to have made an attack upon A. P. Hill's division, on Jackson's left, but for some unexplained reason he did not advance until Grover's brigade had been repulsed. General Kearney, the one-armed veteran, led his men in person. His soldiers wore the red square on their caps which was the insignia of "Kearney's men," or, as they were sometimes dubbed, "Phil Kearney's thieves." They went enthusiastically to the charge, supported by the troops of Reno. He doubled back the left of the enemy, and for a short time seemed to have achieved a decisive result. The enemy hurried up two brigades of Ewell's division, acting as reserve, who came down upon Kearney's thin and exhausted line, which was driven from its hard-won position. McDowell arrived at the scene of action between five and six in the af-

"Pring up the Shackasses."

ternoon, bringing up King's division, then commanded by Hatch. The enemy were making movements which were interpreted to mean a retreat, and Hatch being ordered to press them, a fierce and bloody contest for three-quarters of an hour followed. Thus ended the day of the second Bull Run, or Groveton. The enemy were readjusting their lines for another day's fighting, and Pope, misinterpreting these movements, conceived that the enemy were running away. It may be said in praise of Pope that he was never discouraged, was always sanguine of success, always ready for a fight.

As usual, so soon as the fighting ceased, many sought without orders to rescue comrades lying wounded between the opposing lines. There seemed to be a mutual understanding between the men of both armies that such parties were not to be disturbed in their mission of mercy. After the attempt of Grover and Kearney to carry the railroad embankment, the enemy followed them back and formed a line of battle in the edge of the woods. Our artillery sent their main line to the rear. It was replaced by a line of skirmishers formed in the fringe of this wood. These opened fire upon the wounded Union men who were attempting to creep to the protection of their friends. After this fire had died away along the darkling woods, little groups of men from the Union lines went stealthily about, bringing in the wounded from the exposed positions. Blankets attached to poles or muskets often served as stretchers to bear the wounded to the ambulances and surgeons. There was a great lack of organized effort to care for our wounded. Vehicles of various kinds were pressed into service. The removal of the wounded went on during the entire night, and tired soldiers were roused from their slumbers by the plaintive cries of wounded comrades passing in torturing vehicles. In one instance, a Confederate and a Union soldier were found comforting each other on the field. They were put into the same Virginia farm-cart and sent to the rear, talking and groaning in fraternal sympathy.

THE FIGHTING OF SATURDAY, AUGUST 30.

THE condition of Pope's army on Saturday, August 30, was such that a more cautious general would have hesitated before giving battle. His men were exhausted by incessant marching and fighting; thousands had straggled from their commands; the men had had but little to eat for two days previous; the horses of the artillery and cavalry were broken down from being continually in harness for over a week and from want of forage. But Pope believed he had gained a great victory on the day previous, and that the enemy were demoralized, while in fact their lines held the railroad embankment as a fortress, and for thirty-six hours there had been nothing to prevent the union of Longstreet with Jackson.

At an early hour Pope ordered a reconnoisance made in his front. At this time the enemy, in readjusting their lines, had withdrawn their troops from some of the contested ground of the day previous. Pope interpreted this movement to mean that the enemy were in full retreat, and at noon assigned McDowell to the pursuit. Porter was ordered to push forward on the Warrenton turnpike, followed by the divisions of King and Reynolds. Upon his arrival Porter brought to General Pope the intelligence that Longstreet had joined Jackson, and was the day previous in full force on the Union left.

To this information the general in command gave no heed, evidently regarding it as an invention of Porter's to excuse himself in not obeying his order to attack the flank of the enemy, rather than as an important fact most needful for him to know.

It seems strange that Pope, before determining his plans for the day, did not summon the brigade commanders of Porter's corps, to determine the truth or falsity of that general's statements, so vital were its bearings upon the impending battle.

At four o'clock in the afternoon the battle was opened by Porter. With cheers the Union force dashed up the hill, through the intervening woods, and charged the railroad cut and embankment. Hatch, on the right, with King's division, moved to the attack. The fight was most obstinate and determined, and as one line was repulsed another took its place, the Confederates resisting with bayonets and stones after their ammunition gave out, and sticking to the deep cut and embankment as to a fortress. Longstreet opened on the force, assaulting Jackson with a murderous enfilading fire of shells. It was under this cannonade that the lines of Porter were broken and partly put to flight.

On the extreme right, Hooker's, Kearney's and Ricketts's divisions, which were to have attacked by the Sudley Springs road, made no serious demonstration in that quarter. Reynolds had meantime discovered the enemy in force concealed in the woods south of the turnpike. It was here that Lee had massed for the attack planned upon our left flank. Reynolds, who during the fighting described above occupied a key position protecting Porter's left flank, was ordered by Pope (or by McDowell) to support Porter, thus uncovering the left flank of the force attacking Jackson.   Colonel G. K. Warren, in command of one of Porter's brigades, seeing the importance of this vacated position, without orders seized and held it obstinately with only a thousand men, of whom over four hundred were killed, wounded, or captured.

When Lee saw that Pope contemplated an attack north of the turnpike, he allowed the Union army to expend its strength in that direction, relying upon Jackson's well-known skill and stubbornness to repel it, while he prepared for an attack on our flank.   When half of our troops were either in actual conflict or already discomfited, then it was that Longstreet rolled like an irresistible wave upon our left.

It fell to McDowell to defend the line of retreat by the Warrenton turnpike.   A strong prejudice existed among the men against this able but unfortunate commander.   Nothing was more common during the day than to hear him denounced.   " We've got a Pope who makes more Bulls than the Pope of Rome," said one ; and "now we are gored by one of them," responded an irrepressible joker. " Sergeant," said a gray-haired officer, wounded and on a stretcher, " how does the battle go ? "   " We are holding our own," replied the non-commissioned officer, " but McDowell has charge of the left." "Then God save the left !" growled the officer, in despair.   " I'd rather shoot McDowell than Jackson," said a comrade.   "It's an outrage to put men under that traitor to be murdered," said another. He wore a peculiar head-gear which looked like a basket.   It was a common remark that Pope had his " headquarters in the saddle, and McDowell his head in a basket."   Such was the moral disadvantage under which McDowell labored with his men, and such elements have more to do with success or defeat than is generally imagined.   Since understanding McDowell's character and record better, we soldiers are glad to acknowledge his true worth as a brave, able, and long-headed commander, and to apologize for abuse which was undeserved.

Pope took prompt measures to ward off impending disaster.   The officers and privates, as a whole, by their devotion, coolness, and courage, gave steadiness to the wavering lines.   Wearied and even wounded men dragged themselves forward to the conflict for the common safety.   It was past five o'clock when Longstreet's five fresh divisions, hitherto concealed in the woods, came on, giving the rebel yell, and followed by artillery which took positions from point to point in conformity to the main line of advance. When, however, the Confederates reached the position where they had hoped to intercept our line of retreat, they unexpectedly found it defended. McLean's brigade of Schenck's division, Milroy's independent brigade, and Tower with two brigades of Ricketts's, held the line of Bald Hill. Being severely pressed, Schenck in person brought up reinforcements to McLean's support, including two brigades of Schurz's division, and fell, severely wounded, while at the head of his men.

Here it was that Colonel Fletcher Webster, son of Daniel Webster, fell while leading his regiment. Here also the brave Colonel Koltes, commanding Schurz's third brigade, was killed. Then came the struggle for the Henry house hill, the plateau which was the scene of the hardest fighting in the first Bull Run. It was bristling with the guns of Reynolds's and Reno's men, and of Sykes's regulars. The enemy made a vigorous attack. At last darkness, the succor of armies hard pressed, came. The army crossed Bull Run by the stone bridge, and by midnight were all posted on the heights of Centreville.

Notwithstanding the surprise of Longstreet's flank attack, our men were at no time completely demoralized, and certainly under the circumstances were excusable for such demoralization as did exist. While the fight was still going on, many in other parts of the field made fires and began cooking their rations of fresh beef, just issued, while some stood on fences and gun-carriages to see how the fight was progressing. The sky was clear and blue, where it was not obscured by the battle-clouds. In the distance could be seen the bold outlines of the Bull Run and Blue Ridge mountains. At one time the Eleventh Massachusetts Regiment was in the same position it had held during the first battle of Bull Run about the same time the previous year.

Our prisoners were disposed to rally us on our defeat. "What was Stonewall doing in our rear when we came so near gobbling him?" was asked of a prisoner. "Gobbling!" exclaimed the indignant rebel; "we uns are foot cavalry, we uns are. We uns can march right around you uns while you uns are getting ready. Old

Stonewall ? He was up there to get our rations ; we uns couldn't live if you Yanks didn't keep we uns in fixin's." And this was very near the sober truth. After the retreat Pope grew in disfavor with all the soldiers. One of the men, while on the march, seeing him pass called out : " Go West, young man, go West."

Irishmen, as a class, are good fighters and great growlers. "Oime sorry, begorra, that iver oie came to this divilish war," said an Irish comrade, trudging along through the mud, to Fairfax Court-House. " Ye'r mad because ye'r not a gineral and on a hoss," was the tantalizing reply of another.

" No," said our Irish growler ; "it's because it's meself that is obleged to associate with such fools as yesilf and Pope."

The general estimate of that general was well expressed, when his comrade got extremely angry at being classified with Pope.

One of my comrades had a rubber pillow, which when not inflated occupied a very small space. One who had only seen it when inflated could not be made to believe it was the same article on seeing it rolled up, but Wad Rider explained that it was like Pope, mostly wind.

The hardships of the army in this campaign were unparalleled in its experience. The field hospitals contained nearly eight thousand wounded men, and a ghastly army of dead lay on the field. The ambulances, too few for the occasion, were supplemented by hacks and carriages of every description, brought from Washington. The tender hand of woman was there to alleviate distress, and the picture of misery was qualified by the heroic grit of those who suffered.

The greatest losses in a battle are in the wounded, their ratio being as ten to one of the killed ; and it seemed as if accident exhausted its combinations in the variety of places in which a man could be wounded and yet live. I have seen men die from a trivial scratch, and others live with a fractured skull ; others were killed by a shell or shot passing very near them, without leaving a bruise or scratch upon the body, and men shot through the lungs and bowels lived and got well. During the fighting of Saturday an officer put out his foot to stop a cannon-ball, which seemed to be rolling very slowly along the ground. It took off his leg and killed him. Another picked up a shell from the ground, not thinking it was lighted, and it exploded in his hands without doing him serious injury. Jar and concussion often broke down the nervous system and produced death, while men with frightful wounds often recovered.

After that hard experience the *morale* of the army was much better than might have been expected, though some, for the first time, began to regard our cause as a losing one. Most of the soldiers believed the Confederate armies were more ably commanded than our own. Said one : " If the rebels have a small force, they manage to get into some strong place like that old railroad cut that Jackson held." Another said : " They always have the most men where the nip comes." This expressed in a nutshell two facts. When weak, the Confederates took strong defensive positions, and at the supreme moment they were superior at the point of contact. Along with stubbornness and confidence, the natural inclination of the soldiers in our ranks was towards cautiousness and economy. Sometimes they ceased the fight before receiving orders because they recognized its uselessness in advance of their commander. The common soldiers represented the average intelligence of the North, and many of them — enough to give tone to the whole — looked upon the cause as peculiarly their own. It was felt that we must keep up the fight because it was a cause that belonged to ourselves and children. Around the camp-fire, after the battle, says a comrade, we were discussing the situation. Some took gloomy views, others were more cheerful. In the midst of the profanity and loud talk, one of our men said : " Boys, let us pray," and kneeling down, in simple, touching words, which sunk deep into all our hearts, prayed for our country and for the success of our cause.

The clamor of voices stopped, and these rough men were still ; and when he rose from his knees, one who had been most profane, stepped forward, and grasping his hand, said : " Ed, I thank you ; you make me ashamed of myself."

This simple incident is related because I believe such men exerted a greater influence over the *morale* of a regiment than any of its officers. There were some men of this kind in nearly every regiment, who commanded respect by their firmness and earnest patriotism. They were the leaven in the measure which leavened the whole mass of the Union army, and whose earnestness supplied a sentiment of cohesion, when all ordinary ones failed.

It shows how rich our army was in material, when they could

afford to have such men in the ranks. This view was deeply impressed upon the great bulk of our army. It supplied a bond of union when discipline failed; and although we had fought and retreated, retreated and fought, we were neither dismayed nor badly disorganized. We were learning the trade of war thoroughly and systematically, and only needed a commander.

CHANTILLY.

THE next day after the army occupied Centreville, Sumner's and Franklin's corps were united with Pope's army.

The day was rainy, and the fords of Bull Run almost impassable. The Confederate commander, wishing to reap all possible benefit from the defeat inflicted upon the Union army, and judging them more demoralized than they really were, determined upon another flank movement, to break up our communications and compel another retreat. Jackson was assigned to this flanking movement, while Longstreet moved more slowly upon his track. Amid the rain on September 1st, Jackson

Death of General Kearney at Chantilly.

reached a cross road which connects the little river with the Warrenton turnpike (near where they intersect in the vicinity of Fairfax Court-House) and formed his lines with Ox Hill in his rear. The attack fell upon Reno's, Hooker's and Kearney's, and a part of Mc-Dowell's troops. Stevens's division of Reno's corps, being out of ammunition, was forced back in disorder. While Kearney was riding forward in the darkness and rain to view the situation in person, he rode into the enemy's lines and was killed.

In him the army lost an ideal soldier, brave, generous, of knightly bearing and undaunted courage. He was full of the poetry of action ; heroic to do and dare ; ready, alert and vigilant. He was one of the most marked figures of the times in which he lived. In his life he illustrated the highest qualities of a soldier; in his death, its heroism.

The action was severe but short, and the enemy were repulsed, but not decisively. Longstreet had come up during the night, and every preparation was made by the Confederates to renew the conflict, but the authorities at Washington feared the consequences of risking another battle so near the Capitol. The army was, therefore, withdrawn behind the defences of Washington, and Pope henceforth dropped out of participation in its battles, defeats, and destinies.

To the credit of Pope, be it said, he advised a more aggressive policy ; proposing to Halleck to attack the enemy with the fresh corps of Sumner and Franklin (which had joined him) before the enemy could be reinforced, and while yet they were weakened by the battles they had fought. In this he disclosed the spirit, courage, and insight that mark a good commander.

As the Union army fell back by squads, companies, and broken parts of regiments and brigades, for the defences of Washington, McClellan came out to meet them. To every brigade, regiment, or only a squad, he met, his only words were : " Boys, go back to your old camps." The regard the private soldiers felt for McClellan arose from a deep conviction that he would not needlessly throw away our lives ; that, with all his faults, he understood his trade.

CHAPTER IX.

MCCLELLAN AT THE HEAD OF THE GRAND ARMY.

TWO days after our second defeat at Bull Run, while yet the roads were crowded with stragglers, and despondency overshadowed all, McClellan reassumed command of the army. It was the morning of September 2d, 1862, and reorganization began at once. The demoralizing influences of a battle, whether it is a defeat or a victory, are always very great; but there is no disorganization of the machine known as a brigade, regiment, or company, except in case of utter rout, when the army becomes a mob. As soon as a vacancy occurs in battle the officer next in rank, without assignment or orders, fills the place. An officer, perhaps, finds fighting does not agree with his peculiar temperament, and resigns, or is taken sick and puts himself under the care of some sympathetic surgeon; or the demoralized private, during the fight, throws away his knapsack and fighting equipments in order to increase his speed for the rear. The sick and foot-sore straggle, the cowards skulk, and a more vicious class wilfully desert. Those who have by casualty of battle been deprived of gun, or knapsack, or haversack, or canteen, or tin cup, have to be re-supplied. A private, perchance, sees where a bullet has entered his neatly rolled blanket, which when opened out is found better adapted for ventilation than bedding. The whole military machine must be lubricated with general, special, necessary and unnecessary, ornamental and practical orders, and bound together, more or less, with red tape. Incapable officers who have been promoted by the accident of battle are restored to their former positions, and competent ones advanced. Companies are filled up with recruits. Sometimes two or more companies, thinned by the casualties of battle, are merged into one.

In no direction was the ability of McClellan so conspicuous as in organizing. Even before the soldiers knew he was again in command, they began to detect a new influence around them. In order to bring the troops upon ground with which they were already familiar, they were as far as practicable ordered to the camping-grounds occupied by each corps before the movement to the Peninsula. In a few days the *morale* of the army underwent an astonishing change for the better.

A Straggler

On the 5th of September, with shoes worn out, clothing in rags, and destitute of the necessaries for effective duty, the Army of the Potomac again left the defences of Washington, while the work of reorganization went on as it marched into Maryland to meet the enemy.

Lee had transferred the theatre of operations from the front of Richmond to the front of Washington. The harvest of the fertile valley of the Shenandoah had fallen into his hands, together with stores and munitions of war of great value to the impoverished Confederacy. To secure, as he thought, the full benefit of his victory, he crossed the Potomac into Maryland. By this movement he hoped to arouse a deep sentiment against the war at the North by bringing it nearer to our own hearthstones ; to enable the secession element in Maryland to raise the standard of revolt, and recruit his army ; and so to manœuvre as to seize Baltimore or Washington. It was a bold undertaking, and his army was poorly equipped for the task. At no time had it been so destitute and ragged, and so little calculated to impress the imagination of "My Maryland" with the fact that the despot's foot was on her soil. The western counties of Maryland were loyal or lukewarm in their Rebel sympathies, and the result showed they hardly aspired to become as miserable as the hungry, tattered horde let loose among them. Yet at no time in its previous history was the Confederate army so worthy of admiration, and of the name of Chivalry. They were heroes in rags !

McClellan, in taking command, had to confront both the enemy and Halleck. The latter was constantly telegraphing his doubts, and fears, and advice. September 9th, he telegraphed that he feared the enemy's object was to draw off the mass of our forces and then attack from the Virginia side. As late as the 13th, he telegraphed : "Until you know more certainly the enemy's force south of the Potomac, you are wrong in thus uncovering the capital." On the 14th, "I fear you are exposing your left and rear." As late as the 16th, he wrote : "I think you will find that the whole force of the enemy in your front has crossed the river."

On September 10th, McClellan wrote to Halleck asking that the ten thousand men garrisoning Harper's Ferry be ordered to join him by the most practicable route. Before he left Washington he had advised that the garrison be withdrawn by way of Hagerstown to aid in covering the Cumberland valley ; or cross the river to Maryland Heights, the military key to the position. Halleck chose to consider the possession of the town as of the first importance, and the whole campaign pivots around this fact, which resulted, as might have been expected, in the capture of the garrison. But it also had another far-reaching result not intended, for Harper's Ferry was the point whereon Lee miscalculated and miscarried in his plans. He did not propose to make any direct movement against Washington or Baltimore, but first establishing his communications with Richmond by way of the Shenandoah Valley, and by menacing Pennsylvania, he expected that McClellan would uncover Washington, and be led from his base of supplies. Then if he could defeat McClellan he might seize Baltimore or Washington, or both. Imagine his surprise after he had crossed the Potomac above Harper's Ferry, and rendered the place useless, to find it still occupied. The Federal advance had been up to this time so timid that Lee believed he could capture the garrison and again concentrate his columns before being called upon to give battle. He forthwith ordered Jackson to move by way of Williamsport across the Potomac, advance upon Martinsburg and then descend to Harper's Ferry and attack from the rear, while McLaws should capture Maryland Heights, and a force, under Walker, crossing below, should seize the heights of Loudon. Before the plan succeeded McClellan had arrived at Frederick, and on the 13th there fell into his hands a copy of Lee's official order, fully disclosing this movement in all its details. Here was an opportunity seldom presented to a general, of throwing his forces between the now divided army of his antagonist, and destroying him in detail. McClellan ordered a movement towards Maryland Heights, but not rapid enough to effect his purpose. On the 15th, Jackson, having surrounded Harper's Ferry, opened with artillery. In an hour Colonel Dixon S. Miles, who was in command, was killed, the Union guns were silenced, and the post, with its twelve thousand men (including two thousand under General Julius White, who had retreated from Martinsburg) and seventy-three pieces of artillery, surrendered at eight o'clock in the morning. Leaving General A. P. Hill to receive the surrender, and losing not a moment, Stonewall Jackson, on the night of the 15th, marched his men seventeen miles, and on the morning of the 16th had united his force with Lee at Sharpsburg.

Behold the contrast between the swift energy of the Confederates, and the leisurely march of the Union force in this great emergency! McClellan, to whom the plans of the Confederates had been revealed by Lee's captured order, was by this knowledge master of the situation. Resolved to avail himself of its advantage, he decided to move his left through Crampton's Gap and debouch into Pleasant Valley in rear and within five miles of Maryland Heights; also with a large force to seize Turner's Gap, six miles further north, before the enemy could concentrate for its defence.

At 6.20 in the afternoon of the 13th, he directed Franklin to march at daybreak upon Crampton's Gap, and closed by saying: "I ask of you, at this important moment, all your intellect and the utmost activity that a general can exercise." With such an immense stake upon the boards, we wonder he did not command Franklin to move that night, immediately on receiving the order. The distance from Franklin's position near Jefferson to the top of Crampton's Gap was but twelve miles. The roads were in good condition, the weather was fine, and we now know that had he marched to the foot of the mountains during the night, he could have debouched into Pleasant Valley, in rear of the Confederates, with little or no opposition, on the morning of the 14th. McLaws, while directing the guns from Maryland Heights upon the defenders of Harper's Ferry, learned of Franklin's advance, and at once sent back Howell Cobb, with instructions to hold the pass to the last man.

Upon Franklin's arrival at the foot of the mountain at Burkittsville, at noon of the 14th, he found the enemy posted behind a stone wall, while the artillery were on the road, well up on the heights. About 3 P.M., Bartlett's brigade, supported by the brigades of Newton and Torbert, all of Slocum's division, advanced upon the enemy, and a severe contest ensued. The enemy, overpowered, fell back up the hill, firing upon our men from behind rocks and the natural defensive positions presented by the ground, until they reached their artillery, where they made a more decided stand. Their riflemen took advantage of every possible cover of ledge and rock and tree. When Slocum's division had become actively engaged Brooks's and Irwin's brigades, of Smith's division, were sent forward and bore a part in the final struggle. Hancock's brigade was held in reserve. After a sharp action of three hours the crest was carried, — four hundred prisoners, seven hundred stand of arms, one piece of artillery, and three colors were the prizes of the Union army. Our loss was 113 killed, 418 wounded, and 2 missing.

A Vermont soldier told me that during this up-hill fight, while climbing over a ledge, he slipped and fell eighteen or twenty feet between two rocks. Rapid as had been his tumble, upon his arrival he found himself preceded by a Confederate soldier. For an instant they glared angrily at each other, when the "reb" burst out laughing, saying: "We're both in a fix. You can't gobble me, and I can't gobble you, till we know which is going to lick. Let's wait till the shooting is over, and if your side wins I'm your prisoner, and if we win you're my prisoner!" The bargain was made. "But," said my informant, "didn't that reb feel cheap when he found I'd won him!"

That night the advance of Franklin's corps rested on their arms within three and a half miles of McLaws on Maryland Heights. During the night Couch joined him, and had he attacked McLaws early in the morning (September 15th), it is possible that the garrison at Harper's Ferry would

"For an instant they glared angrily at each other."

have been saved. An hour after midnight of that morning McClellan had sent orders for Franklin to occupy the road from Rohrersville to Harper's Ferry, and hold it against an attack from Boonsboro', or in other words from Longstreet and Hill, and to destroy such force as he found in Pleasant Valley. " You will then proceed," ordered McClellan, "to Boonsboro', . . . and join the main body of the army at that place. Should you find, however, that the enemy have retreated from Boonsboro' towards Sharpsburg you will endeavor to fall upon him and cut off his retreat." But from one cause and another the plans for an overwhelming defeat miscarried.

Our corps (Sumner's) was following Reno's and Hooker's in the advance upon Turner's Gap, five miles north of the fight described above, but I personally did not get up in time to see the last blows struck. Until our arrival at Frederick, and even later, I was a straggler. The circumstance which caused me to become a demoralized unit of the army may be creditable or otherwise, but I will tell it. Just before the battle of Chantilly (September 1), I, with Wad Rider, and " Joe," the recruit, had retired to the seclusion of a neighboring wood to engage in a war of extermination against an invader of the Union blue. I had partly resumed my clothing but not my shoes. Joe had entirely re-dressed, but Wad Rider was still on undress parade. Suddenly Joe, whose quickness of sight and hearing were remarkable, shouted, " Rebs! Rebs!" Down a cross-road on our left came a squad of the enemy's cavalry. I ran barefoot, with my cartridge-box and belt over one shoulder, my musket in one hand, and my other hand holding my garments together. As I ran I heard a musket-shot, and turned to view the situation. Wad Rider, dressed in nothing but his cuticle and equipments, had killed the leading cavalryman in the pursuit, and shouting like mad for reinforcements, was retreating in light marching order upon the camp. I dashed through a stump lot, with Joe on my flank and Wad in the rear, still pursued by the enemy, who were calling upon us to surrender. The noise brought the boys swarming from the camp, and when I regained my feet, after a collision with the root of a stump, the rebels were making for the woods. Under a strong escort of comrades we returned to reclaim Wad's uniform and my shoes, but the enemy had gobbled them. Wad stripped the dead cavalryman, and assumed his clothing without saying so much as " poor fellow," and looked grotesque enough in his gray suit. "First thing you'll hear of," said Wad, " some blank fool will be shooting me for a reb ! "

As the result of my fall I had the sorest foot in camp. I was ordered to report to the hospital — a place I never had a liking for —

but I preferred to limp along in rear of the army like a true straggler. I messed with darky teamsters, or with anybody who had eatables and would receive me into good-fellowship. In some of the Maryland houses they were nursing the sick soldiers of the Union army, and many farmers gave to the hungry soldiers most of the food upon their farms. Near Middletown a woman gave me a pair of shoes, which I was not then able to wear ; while at another place an old lady, after caring for my unheroic wound, presented me with a pair of stockings which she had knit for her own son, who was in the Union army. Maryland was the first place since I had come to the front, where we were greeted with smiles from children and women. At a pleasant farm-house, near Damascus, where flowers grew in the garden, and vines climbed around the capacious veranda, a little girl peeped over the gate and said good-morning. I asked her if she was not afraid of so many passing soldiers, and she replied : "No, my father is a soldier in the army, too," and then timidly, as if afraid to dazzle me with his exalted rank, said, "He's a corporal! Do you know him?" Of course we met with some decided contrasts smacking of disloyalty.

I picked up temporary acquaintances of all kinds, but during my third day's ramble I chummed with an artilleryman, who had lost his voice. Near Damascus, we called at a pleasantly situated house, belonging to an old man about sixty or seventy years of age. He was very non-committal in his sentiments. His wife was a lady-like old woman, and her two daughters had evidently seen good society. We propounded the usual conundrum about something to eat, and exhibited money to show that we intended to pay.

The young women, when speaking of the Confederates, spoke of them as "our army," and it leaked out that they had one brother therein, and another in the paymaster's department at Washington. After supper, we were invited into the reception-room, where there was a piano. I asked for a song. One of the young women seated herself at the piano and played "My Maryland" and "Dixie," and then wheeled as if to say : "How do you like that?" My chum hoarsely whispered a request for the "Star-Spangled Banner," and she obligingly complied, and then said in a semi-saucy manner : "Is there anything else?" My friend mentioned a piece from Beethoven. "I never heard of it before," said she ; "perhaps if you should whistle it I would recognize it." But my friend's whistle was in as bad tune as his voice. "Perhaps you will play it yourself!" said the black-eyed miss, for an extinguisher! To my astonishment, no less, seemingly, than theirs, the rusty-looking artilleryman seated himself at the piano and under his hands the instrument was transformed. He played piece after piece and finally improvised a midnight march in which a band of music was heard, receding farther and farther until the whole died away in the distance. Our parting was more cordial than our reception.

Two or three miles south of Frederick, my chum was peppered with pigeon-shot while gathering our supper in a farmer's sweet-potato patch, and in the morning refused to march, so I pushed on without him. I joined a party who were driving a herd of cattle for the army. The guard hung their haversacks on the horns, and packed their knapsacks and muskets on the backs of the oxen and cows. It was in this company that I arrived at Frederick and wandered into the hospital, a church, where there were about two hundred sick inmates. Feeling lonely, I pushed on after my regiment. A battle was imminent, and many stragglers were hurrying forward to be in the fight. A friend who had been wandering at his own sweet will, barefoot and without a shirt to his back, in the track of the army, hired and persuaded with his bayonet, an unwilling darky whom he met (driving a mule attached to a two-wheeled cart) to carry him a "right smart distance" to the Antietam fight. He urged on the mule and darky at the point of the bayonet until near the battlefield, when the bursting shell caused both the darky and his mule to balk. When the darky was released from the persuasive influence of Tom, he and his mule made commendable speed for the rear. It was about noon of the 14th when I caught up with my company, and fell in line, hobbling along towards Turner's Gap, where heavy firing could be heard. At ten in the evening we relieved the force holding the main road of the Gap. During the night we could distinctly hear the rumble of the enemy's artillery, and at early dawn found they had fled, leaving their dead and wounded to our care.

CHAPTER X

A Zouave.

THE situation was such after our victory at South Mountain, that Lee, seeing the impracticability of longer holding Turner's Pass, withdrew the force there engaged into the valley of the Antietam.

On the 15th, the Union army was pushed forward in pursuit until it reached the river, where it was brought to a halt by the enemy, in force on the opposite banks.

The valley through which the Antietam takes its winding course is very beautiful. As we advanced over the ridges we looked down upon its green fields where herds of cattle were grazing, and richly laden orchards and yellow harvests lay ripening in the September sun. At our feet were undulating hills and fertile meadows, and comfortable farmhouses, some standing out boldly on eminences, others half hidden by vines or fruit trees.

The range of low hills rising on either side of the stream, relieved by deep gulleys and verdant vales; the winding turnpike on the hillsides and through green valleys; the Antietam, mostly obscured from view by trees which fringed its tortuous course, running smoothly here, or grumbling there with discontent at its rocky bed, or dashing in sparkling foam over shallow declivities ; winding far up to the foot of one range of hills, or turning back to caress the base of another, presented to the eye a beautiful picture of peace.

The enemy's position was admirably selected. Here the Antietam runs nearly south and obliquely towards the Potomac. Their lines were drawn across the angle formed by the junction of the Antietam with the Potomac, and as the Potomac at this point makes a series of

The Zouaves holding the Stone Wall in Front of Sharpsburg.

curves, forming a sort of horse-shoe bend in their rear, the Confederate army was enabled to rest both flanks on that stream, while the Antietam protected their front. Here also they were in the flank and rear of any force moving against McLaws, and in a position where all their forces could easily unite.

East of the town of Sharpsburg was a line of abrupt hills, forming a half circle with the convexity in front, rising from the river. From these their artillery could sweep the level land before them, from

right to left.   In case of defeat, their line of retreat was assured by
two fine roads running to the Potomac.

McClellan's plan of battle was comprehensive and simple.   It was
to throw his right across the river, by an unguarded ford and bridge,
below Pry's Mill; attack the Confederate left, with Hooker's and
Mansfield's corps, supported by Sumner; and when the movement
had engaged the enemy's attention, the centre and left were to force
the bridges and attack his front and right.   Had the plan been
carried out as boldly as conceived, the result would have been
decisive.

The Union commander occupied most of the day (the 16th) in
examining the ground, posting troops, and massing artillery.   During
the day an artillery engagement occurred.   In this duel the Confederates were badly worsted.   The Confederate general, D. H. Hill,
in his report, alludes to this exchange of artillery compliments, and
says : "They could not cope with the Yankee guns," and terms it,
on their part, "the most melancholy farce of the war!"

McClellan had been criticised, perhaps justly, for not making the
attack at an earlier hour, while yet Lee's force consisted only of
Longstreet's and D. H. Hill's corps.   A general, to be judged fairly
should be criticised by the facts known, or obtainable by him, before
and during the battle, rather than those gained by investigation from
the safe distance of after years.   Those who fight battles long after
their issues are decided have more time to deliberate than the actors
on the actual field.

It seems, however, that Hooker's advance was ill-timed ; it should
either have been made earlier, or delayed until the next morning.
As it was, McClellan's preparations and Hooker's movement both
warned the enemy that the attack was to be made on their left, and
gave them time to make a disposition of troops to resist it.

Hooker began his movement at four o'clock in the afternoon.   In
the twilight which follows sundown, he struck the Confederate force,
under General Hood, and after smart skirmishing they rested on their
arms during the night.

The Confederate and Union forces, at this point, occupied the
woods which are on the margin and near the cleared land on both
sides of the Hagerstown road.   Hooker was in the edge of the wood
on the east side, and the enemy in the low timbered land on the

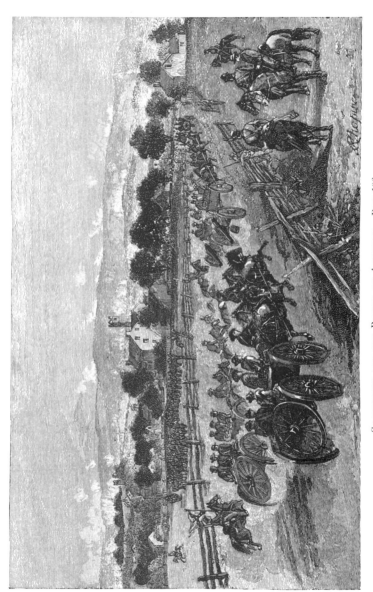

SHARPSBURG AND THE BATTLE OF ANTIETAM.   Page 106.

west side. Their pickets were so near together during the night, that their conversation could be heard from one line to the other.

At early dawn on the 17th, Hooker opened the battle by an attack on the left of the line now held by the indomitable Jackson, who made use of the numerous ledges as fortresses. The object of Hooker was to obtain possession of the Hagerstown road, and the woods on the west of it.

The chief criticism made on this part of the battle, by military critics, is that Hooker and Sumner both failed to take possession of a hill a little to the right of the place where they formed their lines, which, if occupied by our artillery, would have made it impossible for the Confederates to hold their ground, as the field is seen in reverse from its crest. It was the key to the battle-field.

Though numbering 14,000 in the reports, the force of Hooker on the field was about 9000 men. The command of Jackson was made up of two divisions, Ewell's and the "Stonewall." The Confederates claim their whole force as not over 4000 men, but Hood's report shows that Woodford's brigade of 2000 men had marched at sunrise to reinforce that part of the line, which makes the force 6000.

The Union lines advanced with enthusiasm, and after an hour of "bloody bush-whacking," the left and centre drove the Confederates into the west woods, and Ricketts gained its borders. The fight, furious and sanguinary from the first, here became terrible. The hostile lines literally tore each other to pieces, as the quick volleys and rattling fire at will, with explosions of artillery, mingled with rebel yells and Union cheers. The lines of battle surged back and forth over the ground, now strewn with the dead and dying. Ricketts, in killed and wounded, lost 951 men ; Phelps, forty-four per cent ; Gibbons's brigade, 380 men.

The Confederate loss, when reckoned by the numbers they claimed to have had at this part of their lines, was phenomenal. They lost 554 men killed and wounded, out of one brigade, and five out of six regimental commanders. Hayes's brigade lost 323 out of 550 men, including his entire staff and all his regimental commanders. Such was the furious nature of the contest waged on that field of blood.

The enemy's lines, overthrown, were falling back, and Hooker was advancing his centre under Meade, to seize the Hagerstown road and the woods beyond, when Jackson's reserve division, reinforced by the two brigades of Hood, issued from the woods and hurled Meade's lines back, bleeding and broken. Ricketts was engaged with a part of Hill's division, closed for support upon Jackson's right, while Stuart's horse artillery held Doubleday in check. Hooker had lost by death, wounds, and straggling, two-thirds of the force he carried into action. Thus stout Hooker stood at bay, wrestling for victory, when Mansfield's corps, which had bivouacked but a mile in his rear, during the previous night, came to his assistance.

While examining the ground in his front, its veteran commander fell mortally wounded, and Williams took command. They brought on the field about seven thousand men. As they came up they found Hooker's men slowly and doggedly falling back, through the cornfield between the road and the east woods.

Gordon, of Mansfield's corps, cleared the cornfield. Green's brigade went in on the left, drove the enemy before them, and delivered while pressing forward, an enfilading fire along the front of the force engaging Gordon. By nine o'clock the Union force held a line extending from Miller's house southwest to the Dunkers' Church, having driven the enemy over a mile from their first position. Their line was irregular and they had reached the climax of their powers; they were fought out.

Such was the situation when General Sumner marched his corps to the scene of action, and found Hooker wounded and leaving the field, his force broken and scattered to such a degree that Sumner declared he saw nothing of them.

Sumner's corps had three divisions : the first under Richardson, second under Sedgwick, and third under French. Up to this time the corps had never encountered a reverse. As they marched through the east woods (a grand park of fine trees, and but little underbrush) they encountered the stragglers and wounded of the broken forces in their front — men who declared themselves the only living men of their regiments. " Sometimes," says a comrade, "three or four men were helping along one wounded one, the usual accompaniment of a heavy fight. In reply to some sarcastic remark from our company, one of the stragglers said ; ' Bark now ; but you'll soon come back yelping like a dog whose tail has been stepped on.'

" Over the fences and ditches, and through the cornfield, our line swept steadily forward, Gorman's brigade leading the way, with Dana's next and Burns's bringing up the rear. Shells from unseen batteries struck our lines, but we passed beyond their fire as we reached the west woods, which we found strewn with wounded, dying, groaning rebels, and our own dead. Our flanks had literally no protection, as we marched steadily forward, and moved through the east woods without encountering the enemy. We climbed a fence, followed by Dana's brigade, were halted and aligned. The column then pressed forward, the left just reaching the little school-house-like building known now as the Dunkers' Church.

" At about this time of our advance the enemy opened with canister, which tore through our lines, and three of our company were killed and five wounded at this point ; but the men steadily closed their ranks and moved forward. It seems, from the Confederate reports, the two of their brigades holding that part of the line, had just been reinforced by eight additional brigades, hurried across from the Confederate right. These reinforcements filled a road in the woods on our left. We had marched into an ambush !"

Ten Confederate brigades, working around under cover of the woods, were on our flank, front, and rear. Then burst such a storm of battle as those who were of Sedgwick's command will never forget. Two thousand dead and wounded covered the ground in a moment. Some companies and regiments faced to the rear, fired, and met this awful volley of death with a calm front. It was one crash of musketry ; and then the terrible crackle and uproar mingled with groans and screams, curses and shrieks ! Some wildly ran, while little squads kept their discipline, and coolly marched to the right, where the broken ranks were re-formed in a new line, under cover of our batteries, and here again met the enemy and drove him back. Here the brigades of Gordon and Green came up to reinforce the shattered lines, but too late. The successes of the preceding part of the day were lost.

It was now ten o'clock in the morning, and we were occupying the east side of the Hagerstown road, near where the battle first opened under Hooker. Sedgwick had lost in this encounter 2255 men. The Third Wisconsin lost sixty per cent of its numbers.

The pressure now became terrible on Sumner's centre and left. General French, whose command had drifted off to the left, for some reason never explained, was ordered to make an attack to relieve the pressure. He attacked with the two brigades of Kimball and Weber. The enemy, forced back, took possession of the sunken road, which runs a zigzag course, at right angles with the Hagerstown pike. Here they piled rails in their front for breast-works and stubbornly contested its possession.

Meagher, with his heroic Irish brigade, fought his way to the crest of a hill overlooking this sunken road, in which the rebel force, under General Hill, was posted. These were relieved, after a stubborn fight had exhausted their ammunition, by Caldwell's brigade. The enemy, receiving reinforcements, endeavored to possess themselves of the high ground on the left; in this they were frustrated by the Fifth New Hampshire, whose heroic colonel, Cross, here began an exciting race for its possession. The two hostile forces, marching by parallel lines, delivered their fire as they marched; Cross, with his red handkerchief for a turban, his voice ringing out with excitement, urged on his men, and they won the crest.

In an effort to flank us the enemy was checked. General Barlow, in this movement, by a change of front executed with great promptness and audacity, was enabled to enfilade the enemy's lines, and captured three hundred prisoners. This success, followed up, gave us the sunken road, and the position on which stood the Piper House. This was the strongest part of the enemy's lines, and had matters been then pushed the victory would have been decisive. Into this terrible maelstrom of battle and death, three out of the six corps composing the Union army had been drawn.

Franklin's corps, which had been hurried up from the right, now came into the fight. The enemy had reinforced their endangered left heavily, and the arrival was well timed. They were massing to strike a blow directed between Sumner's right and centre, which were loosely shackled together. Franklin filled up the gap with a part of Smith's division, while another part of the division, under Colonel Irwin, drove back the Confederates abreast the Dunkers' Church.

Stretching over hills and through woods, the contending lines stood face to face. The roar of musketry rolled along the whole extent of the battle-field. Franklin now massed his men for a crushing blow, but Sumner, demoralized by the heavy fighting, ordered him to desist. It was one o'clock and the battle was practically over on the right, although firing still continued along the line until night.

It was McClellan's plan, as I have stated, to attack the enemy's left, supported by an attack on their right and centre. If successful in carrying the crest in front of Sharpsburg, it would force Lee from his line of retreat by way of Shepardstown. It would also prevent the reinforcement of the Confederate left from their right.

General McClellan had ordered Burnside, early on the 16th, to make a reconnoisance of the ground in his front. Crook, later in the day, missed his way to the bridge to take part in the assault, which shows how little the ground was understood.

McClellan says, in his report, that he ordered Burnside to hold himself in readiness to assault, and await further orders. At eight o'clock in the morning he ordered Burnside to carry the bridge and heights, and advance along their crest, upon Sharpsburg. General Jones, who commanded the entire Confederate right, says, "My whole command of six brigades, comprised only 2430 men." Making due allowance for Confederate exaggeration, the force could not have been a large one.

Notwithstanding the order to attack, General Burnside occupied the forenoon with frivolous action, and the battle on the right was over before he began the attack. This had enabled Lee heavily to reinforce his left wing, by the withdrawal of two-thirds of the right wing, under Longstreet. They had arrived in season to bring disaster to Sedgwick, and check the onslaught of Sumner. It is believed this could not, and would not, have been attempted, had Burnside acted with vigor, as at one time not over four hundred men disputed the passage of the bridge.

Our forces, under Burnside, had pierced the enemy's lines and were in the full tide of success when two thousand men, under General A. P. Hill, who had marched from Harper's Ferry (seventeen miles in seven hours), reinforced the broken Confederate lines, which resumed the offensive, recaptured a battery which had been taken from them, and hurled Burnside's force back to the protection of the bluff, with a loss of 2202 men, only 123 of whom were missing.

Burnside sent for reinforcements, weakly intimating that he could not hold his position, and afterwards withdrew the Ninth

Corps to the opposite side of the Antietam, leaving Morell's division to hold the position alone.   Thus ended the battle of Antietam.

The question of Burnside's dilatoriness in action is a mooted one. Some have supposed that he had already formed the design of supplanting McClellan, and hence purposely delayed in order to prevent his success.   Others, that he was rendered antagonistic to McClellan by the removal of Hooker's corps from his command.   Those who knew Burnside cannot for a moment accept either of these explanations.   His unselfish and generous character is so well known as at once to contradict it.   Is it not rather to be accounted for by a fact, afterwards shown on a wider field, that the man was not equal to his position?   No one who ever saw his noble, lion-like face, or grasped his manly hand, can, for a moment, believe that he willingly failed either his commander or his country.

One of McClellan's characteristics was that he seldom blamed his subordinate officers, hence though Franklin and Burnside both failed him in the critical periods of the campaign, his words of blame were confined to a simple statement of facts, in his report of operations.

The morning of the 18th dawned, and with it the question for McClellan to decide whether he should renew the conflict.   The reasons he gave for not renewing it were : "At this moment, with Virginia lost, Washington menaced, Maryland invaded, the national cause could afford no risk of defeat.   One battle lost, Lee's army could have captured our large cities, levying tribute from a fertile and undevastated country."   It is the opinion of military critics, founded on facts afterwards developed, that McClellan's decisions were wrong.   As a general commanding an army makes decisions grounded upon facts known to him at the time, and not those afterwards developed, let us see what McClellan knew at that time.   He knew that his forces which had met the enemy upon the field that day had scarcely held their own, and that the battle was substantially a draw ; that Sumner had advised against further movement on the 17th ; that his troops were exhausted, his supply trains far in the rear, while his men, in many instances, were suffering from hunger ; that Burnside had met with a repulse, and when the fight closed was calling for reinforcements, which he could not send. While these facts had weight with McClellan's cautious mind, a bolder general would have risked the hazard of battle.

The reasons given by military critics why McClellan should have resumed the offensive in the morning, are these : McClellan stood on his own base with everything at hand to aid him, while Lee was at a great distance from his base, with a difficult river in his rear. Again, our troops fought on loyal soil with a *verve* they had never shown in Virginia, and could be depended upon for greater exertions and sacrifices. The battle-field was better understood on the 17th than when the fight began, and the key position on our right was now properly appreciated. Burnside had gained a foothold on the opposite banks of the Antietam.

All facts now point to the probabilities that had we resumed the offensive on the morning of the 18th the rebel army would have been overwhelmed. Yet, as McClellan said, there was a doubt then.

Lee was, by far, the ablest general on the Confederate side, and perhaps the ablest produced by the war. Pushed to extremities we know not what new strategical resources he may have developed. One thing is certain, McClellan weighed these questions to the best of his ability at the time, and decided against resuming the offensive on the 18th, and in this he violated no received maxims or principles of war.

Our successes had been such as to compel Lee's retreat. He had crossed the river with high hopes. He had returned to the south side of the Potomac to gather together the shattered fragments of his army. The army of invasion had signally failed, and had been almost destroyed. Its venture had been fruitless and unprofitable.

Lee had begun the invasion with the *prestige* of success on his side. McClellan had begun the campaign with an army disorganized by defeat.

The Confederate chieftain had been obliged to abandon the invasion; had left his dead unburied, and many of his wounded uncared for on the field of battle, and crossed the river. He had asked for a truce to bury his dead, and had used the truce so gained to make preparations for retreat.

The Confederates claim that they fought this battle with less than 40,000 men. Yet on the 20th of October their reports show 67,808 men. September 23d, the Richmond *Enquirer* credits Lee with 60,000 men on the field of Antietam. Lee laments that his army was ruined by straggling. What was true in this respect of Lee's army was true also of the Union army.

The official report is no gauge of the number present for duty. It is doubtful if the Union army, present for duty, was much over sixty thousand men, and considering that they attacked defensive positions, selected by Lee himself, does not show so great an inequality in forces as at first would appear. The Fifth and Sixth Corps, and cavalry division, which according to McClellan's report were hardly used at all, numbered 29,550 men.

One point of criticism may be made here, and that is, that McClellan, knowing the immense enthusiasm the army had for his person, did not use this by showing himself on the field of battle. Had he done so it may be safely said it would have had a beneficial effect. Such elements should not be despised by one whose position demanded that every circumstance be used to open a road to victory; an element which has been used with such potent effect on so many doubtful battle-fields should have been conserved by its commander.

Napoleon used this enthusiasm upon the field of Austerlitz, and overwhelmed his enemies. Sheridan used it and wrung victory from disaster, and hurled a victorious force back in defeat and dismay. McClellan should have used it at Antietam. And yet, it might be said, that McClellan had already animated the army under him, as was seen after he took command of the troops. His personal presence on the field, no doubt, would have been great ; but a general during a battle should not have his headquarters movable, but be where he can be reached by every order — a centre of *intelligence*, directing and deciding. McClellan was not the kind of a general who has his " headquarters in the saddle ! "

CHAPTER XI.

A S the sun went down on the 17th of September the last sounds of battle died away along Antietam Creek. Wounded men at last could be succored, the wearied rest, the hungry find food; but thousands were sleeping the untroubled sleep of death, while the wounded wailed in anguish through the long night.

Our own losses are seen in the foreground, and their sum and detail forcibly strike the mind. Those of the enemy, equalling or surpassing ours, are seen in the distant perspective, and it required a man of less sensitive mould than McClellan not to be influenced by them. Men of the iron mould of Wellington or Grant, insensible to detail so long as a final result can be obtained, are better fitted to press home advantages gained with such terrible loss.

The private soldier, concentrating his energies and attention to the small focus of individual action, while the excitement of battle lasts, does not feel that terrible reality of suffering and death incident to the battle, which is afterwards presented to his mind, when he passes over the ground where the victims are writhing in the agony of wounds or lying prostrate in death.

"I saw," says a comrade, "something of the effects of the battle after it was over, while assisting in carrying off the wounded who remained on the field. The scene on the field over which the roaring wave of battle, with its bristling crest of bayonets and foam of smoke had surged and advanced, or recoiled and receded, baffles description. The mangled forms of comrade and foe lay stretched side by side. For over a hundred acres the dead and wounded were lying, the uniform of gray and blue intermingled."

Where Hooker had attacked and recoiled, advanced and receded, the dead and dying lay thick, reddening with their blood the broken cornstalks. In the timbered land where Jackson's men made a stand, in one place the dead lay in a long row as if they had fallen while on dress-parade. To the left of this there was a narrow road, with a high board fence on either side. Here while crowded with a Confederate force, it had been enfiladed by a Union battery, and the dead lay in every conceivable position, a few only seeming to have escaped.

Some who were killed while in the act of climbing the fence hung balanced across its boards, or were suspended by their clothing. A more terrible picture one cannot well conceive. All over the fields were strewn articles of clothing, broken muskets, canteens, and haversacks, mingled with the bloated re-

After the Battle.

mains of horses with their feet turned upward; while broken caissons, dismantled guns, and crushed wheels, strewed this memorable field.

Around the army and in its rear, for miles, every barn and house, every haystack and shelter, formed the nucleus of a hospital. Wounded men, shot through the body, head, or limbs, presenting every conceivable variety of wounds, lay groaning in anguish. The surgeons at the amputating table, in shirt sleeves, with blood-reddened hands, labored incessantly; and here the ghastly surroundings of death and suffering were as terrible as the battle-field itself.

The wounded of friend and foe were treated alike; yet the labors of the surgical department, though immense, could afford but little relief for their sufferings. The enemy always showed their sense of the humanity of our army by leaving their badly wounded in our hands to be cared for, even when they could have removed them as well as not. It was also their habit, during the entire war, to leave the burial of their dead to us. Even in this instance, where they had asked a truce for the avowed purpose, they left over twenty-seven hundred of their dead unburied. When burying their dead, in most instances, they merely heaped soil over them without digging trenches, while on our part trenches and regular burial were customary.

I noticed a marked difference between Southern and Northern men in bearing pain. A slight wound often caused the Southerner to wail and groan, and call out for help and care, while our Northern men were more self-controlled; the wounded would seldom groan, or give any noisy expression to suffering, but clench their teeth and bear it uncomplainingly. The difference was that between a warm Southern race, and the cool, phlegmatic, enduring race of the North — one, formed to endure and bear; the other, for sharp and brave encounter.

After the rebel army had evacuated Sharpsburg, I passed over the ground where hundreds of their dead lay unburied, along the roads, in the fields, and under the fences. Where their hospitals had been located there were clusters of dead and the remains of the amputating table.

The people welcomed the arrival of the Union army with every evidence of gladness, and hailed them as their deliverers.

"Bless God!" said one old lady, "you've driven them away. I've been down in my cellar three whole days!" The people, unsolicited, brought out food from concealed places to feed the hungry. The houses were crushed into shapeless masses, and riddled with shot. The churches were filled with the rebel wounded. Riderless horses were running around, and wounded ones limping about the streets. The people had had a hard time, and the contrast between our treatment of them, and that of the Confederate army (who made levies of food upon them, and their marauders who had plundered them unmercifully) was so great that I think it must have cured them forever of any desire to make common cause with those in rebellion.

The Confederate soldiers, throughout the war, were keen for plunder. They stripped and robbed the dead habitually; took their watches, greenbacks, and valuables for their own use, without any deed of transfer but their own. A battle-field won meant a harvest of gain to them, and hence every incentive to win was theirs. There were some plunderers in the Union army, more particularly among its camp followers; but the bodies of the rebels slain did not present great inducements to those actuated by avarice.

After this battle we rested on our arms, amid the picturesque hills and vales of southwestern Maryland, and here entered upon a season of recuperation. We swapped our hardtack, pork, and coffee, with the people of the region, for fresh meat and home-made bread, and indulged in all the luxuries of this delightful country. The corn which we gathered in the fields (oft-times without permission) gave us hasty-pudding and johnny-cake. With a nail, or the point of a bayonet we punched holes through a tin plate or the half of a canteen, thus converting them into graters, on which we rubbed the corn, on the ear, and obtained meal seemingly nicer and sweeter than that ground at a mill. It seemed to me that I never had eaten such johnny-cakes as were made from this meal.

While food was plenty, our army was destitute of clothing sufficient to render us comfortable in the cool nights and evenings of the fall months. A considerable number were without blankets or shirts; many without shoes or stockings. It must be remembered that in November snow sometimes fell to the depth of several inches in Virginia. Frosts in the morning were common, covering the blankets of those who slept without tents.

There was somewhere in the War Department a great delinquency in forwarding supplies of clothing, which, without entering into the controversy over the matter, seems to have been needless. It would seem that this would have been impossible if the Department had been friendly to McClellan; and this disloyalty to the commanding general cannot be too strongly condemned, as it was disloyalty to the cause of the republic, as well as injustice to the brave and patriotic masses of soldiers then suffering from neglect.

With the exception of the kindly and seasonable words of President Lincoln, thanking the general and the army, no word or order of commendation of our victories, gained fifteen days after being beaten under Pope, and driven to the defences of Washington, came to cheer us. Such was the jealousy shown by the culpable Halleck, and our able, though not over mild, Secretary of War.

General McClellan taking Leave of the Army of the Potomac.   Page 119.

After seasons of needless delay in forwarding supplies, McClellan, the last of October, put the Army of the Potomac in motion. He determined to select the line east of the Blue Ridge, and to guard the upper Potomac with the Twelfth Corps. The crossing was completed on the 2d of November, though heavy rains delayed us. McClellan contemplated (after seizing the debouches of the Shenandoah Valley) pushing directly up that valley; but fearing that his antagonist, finding the doors open, would again cross in to Maryland, formed a new plan of action. The season of high water in the Potomac had removed that danger, and he determined to operate by the east side of the Blue Ridge. Crossing by Berlin, below Harper's Ferry, masking his purpose by guarding the passes of the Blue Ridge, and by threatening to advance through them, he compelled Jackson's retention in the valley. With such success was this achieved, that, upon reaching Warrenton, on the 9th of November, Lee had sent half his army forward to Culpeper to resist this movement, while the other half was west of the Blue Ridge scattered along the valley. McClellan's next intended move was to interpose his own army between these severed divisions of Lee, by marching westward, when, — he was removed from the command. At the time of his removal it might be said of him, as Napoleon said of Turenne, " He grew bolder as he grew older."

Thus ended his career as a soldier, and his connection with that army he had fashioned into a mighty host, — an army baptized in blood, and a participant in great actions for the preservation of the Union. Had he remained at the head of the army it is safe to say the nation would not have mourned over Fredericksburg or Chancellorsville. He had provoked political antagonism, unwise as it was needless, and it was inevitable that " He must go !"

CHAPTER XII.

THE general selected to succeed McClellan was Ambrose E. Burnside — a man in the prime of life ; a graduate of West Point, and although without special fitness for his position, he had commanded a successful expedition ; a man of fine presence, patriotic, energetic, manly, generous, and respected by the army generally. He disarmed criticism to begin with by declaring himself unfit for the position.

Upon taking command he abandoned the line of operations adopted by McClellan, where a fair opportunity was presented of meeting the enemy upon equal if not advantageous grounds, and putting his army in motion from Warrenton, with Sumner leading the advance, he moved by the north bank of the Rappahannock to Falmouth, which place he reached on the afternoon of the 17th of November. Fredericksburg was then occupied by but one regiment of Confederate artillery, one of cavalry, and four of infantry.

Sumner wished to possess himself of the position at once but was restrained by Burnside, who desired first to establish his communications by way of Acquia Creek. On the 19th and 20th the grand divisions of Hooker and Franklin also reached Falmouth.

The Union army was now concentrated. The movement to seize the position, to be successful, should have been made at once ; but the pontoons for bridges, which Burnside had ordered to precede the army to this point, had not arrived. Burnside says, that in his personal interview with Halleck, that officer had assured him that everything required should receive his attention, and that he would at once order the pontoon trains spoken of in his plans.

Without entering into the controversy as to who was to blame for their non-arrival, Halleck had displayed in his "circumlocution office" at various times, so much of the science of "how not to do it " that the disposition to attribute the blame to him is almost irresistible.

Meanwhile the precious moments wasted in delay enabled the Confederates to concentrate, so that when Burnside, who had voluntarily moved away from his enemy to try a new route to Richmond, was ready to move, it was only to find his antagonist posted in an impregnable position squarely across his path.

"On the 18th, our corps and brigade," says a comrade, "arrived and went into camp opposite the little city of Fredericksburg. Here, fronting the city, on the north side of the stream was a steep bluff called 'Stafford Heights.' It is near the river opposite the town, and gradually recedes from it below. In our front, back of Fredericksburg, the hills rise one above another in natural terraces. This ridge extends from above to a point five miles below the town. It is a position of great natural defensive strength. Between this high ground and the river is the valley of the Rappahannock — a broken plain six miles in length, about a mile wide near Fredericksburg, but gradually broadening out until, where our lower bridges were finally constructed, it is at least three miles in width.

"The narrow river brought the outposts of the armies within speaking distance, and conversations, jokes, newspapers, and tobacco were exchanged by the pickets of the two armies, until prohibited. The Confederate pickets are said to have repeatedly remarked: 'Before you 'un Yanks can get to Richmond you 'uns will have to get up Early, go up a Longstreet, get under the Lee of a "Stonewall," and climb two Hills.' I never heard them say anything so allegorical as that, but while on picket one said to me: 'Why don't you 'un come over and fite we 'uns? We want yer to!' It was quite cold and many of the rebel pickets wore Federal overcoats, and when not on duty occupied holes excavated in the banks opposite us. The pickets informed us that Jackson had command of the forces then back of the city. The day after our arrival the city presented a 'first of May' aspect. Everybody was moving out; carriages of various devices were loaded with the goods of its inhabitants, who, to avoid the dangers of the battle, were leaving their homes."

Lee quickly concentrated his forces, began the construction of defensive works, and crowned them with cannon, which were destined soon to sweep the plain with an *Inferno* of fire.

Burnside's first essay was to make a crossing above the city at Schenk's Neck, as that point gave an opportunity for a direct attack on Lee's left, which, if successful, must have caused him to fall back towards the coast. This attempt so engaged the attention of Lee that it determined Burnside to surprise him by crossing at Fredericksburg, as he would be unprepared for an attack in front. But it takes time to throw out several bridges, and under the most favorable circumstances a force of
a hundred thousand
men cannot be
crossed on them
(even when there is
no resistance) un-
der several hours.

Union and Rebel Soldiers on opposite ends of the burned R.R. Bridge.

With this sur-
prise in view, how-
ever, the comman-
der concentrated
his troops near the
proposed bridges.
Hooker was in rear
of Sumner, while
the crest of the
hills on the north side were crowned with 147 pieces of artillery to command the plain and silence the ene-
my's guns. As early as three o'clock on the morning of the 11th of December, the engineer troops, assisted by the infantry, silently unloaded the pontoons.

The construction of the bridge was no sooner begun than the rebel infantry, in the town opposite, under protection of the houses and the walls of the river street, opened at short range upon the construction party. Simultaneous with this the report of two guns on the heights in our front broke the stillness of the morning air. They were the signal guns of Lee for the concentration of his troops.

FREDERICKSBURG.   Page 123.

The fire of the keen-eyed Mississippi riflemen, in the town, was so well directed that the two regiments supporting the engineers lost one hundred and fifty men, and the construction party was driven from its task. It was now ten o'clock, and as it became apparent that nothing could be done until this annoying outpost was dislodged, Burnside gave the order to open with artillery on the town and batter it down. The bombardment was terrific and seemed ridiculously disproportioned to the enemy therein, — like an elephant attacking a mosquito. It soon checked the fire of the concealed riflemen, and a volume of dense black smoke rolling up from the gray drapery-like fog showed that fire had added to the work of destruction.

Acting under the suggestion of General Hunt, chief of artillery, advantage was taken of the temporary lull which then occurred in the sharp-shooting, to send, under cover of our riflemen, who commanded the opposite bank from behind the batteaux, four regiments across the river in boats; and these captured or drove the few annoying riflemen from the town. Under their protection the bridges were completed; but all hopes of a surprise, if originally entertained, were now abandoned.

A force was pushed across the first of the upper bridges, when completed, and Captain Marcy, commanding the Twentieth Massachusetts, led the advance to clear the street leading from the bridge. He says : " Platoon after platoon was swept away ; ninety-seven officers and men being killed in a space of fifty yards."

A brigade of Sumner's men was crossed above, while below a brigade of Franklin's division was crossed, and during the night and morning of the 12th the town and plain were occupied by our forces. Thus opened the bloody and fruitless battle of Fredericksburg.

While this was taking place the enemy was concentrating and strengthening their already impregnable positions on our front and left. The crossing had been effected, but the formidable heights, thronging with men and frowning with artillery, still ominously and darkly confronted us.

" I wonder if old Burney expects us to bunt our heads into those rocks ?" said a private of my company pointing to the heights opposite. " If Johnny Reb had selected a spot to his own liking and invited us to come and be shot he would have chosen this !" said another. There was not a soldier in the ranks but saw the folly of making an attack on these impregnable rocks, and yet when ordered to attack all went forward willingly, so strong was the spirit of discipline and patriotic devotion in the face of even impossibilities.

The morning of the 12th dawned upon the army formed on the plains of Falmouth ; but forty-eight hours of precious time had already been spent since the signal gun of Lee was fired, and whatever other hopes were left to the Union army, there were no hopes of capturing the position in our front by a surprise.

The morning was foggy like the day before. Franklin's grand division held the plain on our left, communicating with the left bank by the bridges which the regular engineers had constructed. Hooker's centre grand division was still on the north bank, while the entire right grand division, under Sumner, was on the south side in the vicinity of the town.

The night of December 12th was very cold, and new troops could be detected by their incessant coughing. Burnside's reports show that there were 113,000 men in his command when the morning of the 13th dawned. He had crossed the river with two-thirds of this force and had yet formed no very definite plan of action. To let him speak for himself, however, he says, " Positive information had reached me that the enemy had built a new road in rear of the ridge or crest. . . . I decided to seize, if possible, a point on this road near Hamilton's Crossing, which would not divide the enemy's force by breaking their lines, but would place our force in position to move in rear of the crest and either force its evacuation or the capitulation of the forces occupying it. It was my intention in case this point had been gained to push Generals Sumner and Hooker against the left of the crest and prevent, at least, the removal of the artillery of the enemy if they attempted to retreat."

Whether it would have been possible for him to gain the first point or not, it is at least doubtful, if, in presence of a powerful enemy admirably posted and ably commanded, concentrated to resist his movement, it would have been wise for him to invite annihilation by dividing his forces as stated.

His chances of success were small in the first place, and his chances were ninety-nine in a hundred of being beaten or destroyed if successful. If Lee had planned the operations of his antagonist he could not have devised anything more fatal to him.

In referring to the plan of attack, that master of the anatomy of battle, Swinton, says : "Such partial attacks seldom succeed, and directed against such a citadel of strength as the Confederate position at Fredericksburg, their feeble sallies were simply ludicrous. Not a man in the ranks but felt the hopelessness of the undertaking."

The instructions received by General Franklin, who now had, in addition to his own corps, one of Hooker's, was to send forward one division at least, to seize, if possible, the heights near Hamilton's Crossing, to keep it well supported, with its line of retreat open ; while the rest of his command was to be in readiness to move at once, as soon as the fog lifted. Possibly Franklin may have been lukewarm and tardy in executing Burnside's plans, but his written orders from Burnside do not disclose that fact ; on the contrary, they show that he exceeded his instructions, or at least liberally interpreted them. Burnside may have thought the verbal understanding of the evening previous sufficient, and therefore neglected to state more definitely in his order what he expected Franklin to do ; but of one thing there is a certainty, and that is that a commander cannot "hold his men in readiness," and "keep his whole command in position," and "move the whole force against the enemy," at the same time. Franklin may have believed, as he states, and as his instructions gave him good reasons for believing (and his corps commanders seem to have arrived at the same conclusion), that Burnside had, during the night, changed his plan of making his main attack on the left. It does not, however, appear that Burnside had any well-settled plan. He seems to have been from the first simply trying experiments.

When he announced his unfitness for the position thrust upon him, he so completely gauged his own abilities, that no one has been able since to improve upon his statement.

Franklin, in obedience to his instructions to send forward one division at least, threw forward Meade's division to seize the point desired. Meade was supported on the right by Gibbon's division, with that of Doubleday held in reserve for emergencies. The point of attack indicated was on the ridge of the Federal left, near the Massaponax Valley. The Confederates occupied the wood-covered heights, the railroad in front of them, and the woods in front of that. Between nine and ten o'clock in the morning, as the sun began to dispel the heavy fog which overhung the lowlands, it revealed the long lines of Franklin's corps spread out in the valley, and lit up the gleaming bayonets of Meade's division advancing to the attack. Meade had not advanced far before he was compelled to silence a rebel battery shelling his left. This accomplished, he pressed on (led by his heavy line of skirmishers) without opposition, until, within short and destructive range, the batteries of the enemy opened on him with a converging fire of grape and canister. His lines were swept with the fiery missiles of death. Great gaps, as if by an eruption of fire beneath, were broken in his lines. Shot and shell sped through them like the ploughshares of death. The gallant attack did not falter. The First brigade penetrated the woods, drove the enemy from the railroad, crossed the crest of the wooded hill, reached the open ground beyond, drove back the force in their front, swept back their lines from right to left, captured two hundred prisoners and several colors, and wedged the attacking division between the two brigades of Archer and Lane, of A. P. Hill's division.

There comes a time with every attacking column when its strength is spent by its very impetus — when the force is disorganized by its own energy. At this climax it fails unless supported by fresh troops, if opposed by an enemy with a firm front. The climax of his exertions was reached by Meade at the point described. The enemy, broken by this impetuous charge, were rallying. On Meade's front, on the coveted road built by Lee (the better to communicate with his right wing) were Greggs's South Carolinians. In their rear, as reserve behind this road, was Jackson's second line. The disposition was such that if the road had been seized by Meade it would have resulted in nothing, and could not have been held. Meade paused not a moment but charged up the crest.

In this moment of intoxication and peril he met the new rebel line. Greggs was mortally wounded while beating down the muskets of his men, mistaking the line of Meade for Confederates. This mistake only postponed the storm of fire, for which the attacking force was not prepared. When the true character of the attack was revealed, the rebels poured a terrible fire into the faces of our men, while a fresh line under Early, from Jackson's reserve, swept forward at double quick. Exposed to a fire in front and on both flanks, disorganized by their own advance, overpowered by numbers, the gallant force under Meade drew back in disorder, pursued by the yelling and exultant Confederates.

The disaster would have been greater had not a brigade from Birney's division on the left, and one of Gibbon's on the right, aided in covering the withdrawal. Meade had attempted with five thousand men the work of fifty thousand. In the attack, Gibbon's force on Meade's right, owing to the density of the woods, had been unable to keep up the connection between the lines, and his leading division was broken by the fire of the enemy who were at that point behind the railroad embankment. Doubleday's attack was turned off to the left to meet a menace in that direction. The whole of Reynolds's corps had been put into the action where Burnside had called for "a division at least."

Meade lost forty per cent of the men engaged, and the aggregate loss in Reynolds's corps was four thousand men. Meade's forces had penetrated the lines of the enemy further than did Pickett, in his famous charge on our lines at Gettysburg, and with a smaller proportional loss because more ably commanded. It was two o'clock in the afternoon when Meade and Gibbon were driven back.

While this was taking place on our left, Sumner was ordered to assail the heights back of Fredericksburg. His orders were to push a column of a division along the plank and telegraph roads with a view to seizing the heights in rear of the town, to be supported so as to keep its line of retreat well open. The attack fell to the lot of French's division of the Second Corps (Couch's).

The plain in the rear of Fredericksburg afforded cramped space for the deployment of troops, because it was cut by fences, ditches, and the canal. While moving by the flank from the town these forces were exposed to a severe fire from the enemy's batteries on the heights above them. A citizen truthfully said to Howard's men while moving through the town : "The soldiers on those hills are looking down and laughing to see you coming up to meet them. It is just what they want." And well they might laugh, for of all the follies of the war this was doubtless the greatest and most bloody. No commander has a right to expose his men, by desperate attacks, without a reasonable chance of success, and every attack made upon those impregnable heights partook of the nature of a forlorn hope.

The force moved by the flank, and under cover of a rise in the land, formed for the attack. French's division here deployed in column with brigade front, and Hancock followed in the same order.

Longstreet held the position in rear of Fredericksburg, while his advanced line, forming the Confederate left, was posted behind the stone wall and trenches at the foot of Marye's Heights. Above these the sharp-shooters were posted, while from the semi-circular heights above their frowning batteries commanded the plain with a direct and converging fire. Back of this was the heavy Confederate reserve. Every art of field engineering had been employed to strengthen this naturally impregnable position against which the Union forces were now led. At one o'clock Couch ordered the position carried by storm; advancing to the attack from the cover of the rising land, his ranks were ploughed by a cross fire of canister, shot, and shell. Great gaps were torn through his lines, which Longstreet, in his report, says could be seen at the distance of a mile. The din was awful, the destruction terrible; but closing up their thinned ranks the men dashed on towards the formidable works, the first line of which they had not even reached, when, at short range, they were met by a storm of lead from the enemy behind the stone wall. Nothing human could withstand this terrible and destructive fire, and with a loss of half their number they were hurled back amid shouts and yells of derision from the enemy.

Close behind French came Hancock, "the superb" directing on his men to the attack. Such of French's men as retained their formations joined them. Kimball's brigade headed the line and proved worthy to lead. They gallantly advanced under the converging fire of artillery, amid the hiss of bullets, the shriek of shells, the cries of the wounded, the uproar and din of the conflict, and the cheers and yells of the attacked and attacking. The advance line reached within twenty-five feet of the stone wall, and threw up their hands and fell, wounded or dead, before it. All in vain, human valor, superhuman courage, and patriotic enthusiasm against so formidable a position! After fifteen awful minutes, with a loss of five thousand men, they were forced back.

Howard's division now came to support Hancock's hard-pressed heroes, who could not advance and would not retire, but they could do nothing more than hold the advanced line on the plain, exposed to a terrible artillery fire from the heights. Yet these disastrous attempts had taught Burnside nothing. On the opposite side of the river he was nervously walking up and down the banks, excitedly exclaiming, "That crest must be carried to-night!" He had lost the calmness so necessary to a general, and in its place was a spirit of desperation, very proper in one who heads a forlorn hope, but unsuitable to one who commands or directs an army. On Couch's left, two divisions of the Ninth Corps made several well-directed, but ineffectual, attacks to support the Second Corps.

The loss up to this time was: French, 1200; Hancock, 2000; Howard, 877. The attack had spent its force at half-past two in the afternoon. Sturgis, of the Ninth Corps, lost 1028 men in his ineffectual attack. At four o'clock Getty was sent in lower down the general line, and lost 284 men. Hooker was now ordered across the river. After reconnoitring the ground and counselling with others who had preceded him, he saw the hopelessness of such an attack, and went back to remonstrate with Burnside against ordering it. Hooker was a brave man and not always judicious, but one of the bravest acts of his life was his remonstrance with Burnside against this needless slaughter.

Behind a slight rise in the land, 150 yards from the stone wall, in front of Marye's Heights, now lay a line of infantry on their faces, while two batteries of Couch were trying to effect a breach in the stone wall through which to lead a forlorn hope. Humphrey's division, the Third, composed in part of new men, was formed in column of attack to carry out Hooker's orders. At three o'clock Humphrey directed his men, of the Second brigade (under Allenbach), forward. When they reached the rise in the land, judiciously imitating Couch's men, who preceded them, they lay down behind the ridges and opened fire against the enemy who were behind the stone wall. This determined Humphrey to assault the position with the bayonet. His first attempt was broken before it advanced fifty yards. He stopped the firing of his men, re-formed his brigade in the rear, partly in a ravine from which it had at first advanced, and in the dusk of evening instructed his men to pass right over the men lying down in their front. With cheers the men advanced, those lying down making motions and calling upon the charging column to desist, but, heedless of remonstrance, over they passed.

Says General Humphrey, in his report : " The line was somewhat disordered and in part forced to form in column, but still advanced rapidly. . . . The stone wall was a sheet of flame that enveloped the head and flank of the column." On they passed until close up to the stone wall when, met by the terrible infantry fire, the column staggered back before the destructive fire, and all efforts to rally them were in vain. The two brigades lost one thousand men in this attack.

Thus ended these murderous assaults "into the jaws of death." The losses there sustained show that better fighting never was done.

Meanwhile, at half-past two, Burnside had ordered Franklin to make another attack, with his whole force, on the left, "upon the heights immediately in his front."

As there were heights along his whole line the order was simply (when construed literally) very indefinite. General Franklin claims the order came in the form of a request, and therefore he did not feel compelled to make the attack, against his better judgment. To have obeyed the order would have exposed his men to useless slaughter. It is not easy to blame him. Had he made the attack it would simply have been more slaughter.

The Confederate position was so strong that their reserve had not been called into action, and it was just as well, and perhaps fortunate for the Union army, that Franklin failed to obey the "request" to attack all along the line when at one single point, as already narrated, a corps had previously been concentrated and hurled back in defeat with terrible loss. So decisive had been the Union repulse, that it is, at this time, difficult to see how there could arise any question as to the propriety of retiring the Union army across the Rappahannock. Urged by his corps and grand division commanders to the contrary, Burnside determined on the morrow to resume the attack, leading the Ninth Corps in person, in one more desperate assault upon the impregnable heights before him. We can but admire his obstinate courage and resolution, but must condemn the loss of that equipoise so essential to a commander. Finally entreated by General Sumner, Burnside desisted from his purpose.

The troops lay on their arms, on the plain, during Sunday and Monday, the 14th and 15th, and in the night, during a cold and driving rain-storm, the army was withdrawn to the north side of the river. The Union loss was 12,321 killed, wounded, and missing. The Confederate loss, as reported by Lee, was 5309 killed, wounded, and missing.

There is no need of any comments, only such as suggest themselves to any soldier. Burnside is dead, and we all admired his frank and manly character. His assumption of all blame for the defeat was worthy of him, but will not atone for the needless slaughter of brave men. After this battle there remained in the army no illusions respecting his capacity for this command. He has since been reported as saying : "No one would ever know how near I came to achieving a great success." And to this we will add — no one ever will.

CHAPTER XIII.

" DURING the battle of Fredericksburg," says a comrade, "my regiment, though taking no particular or very active part in the scenes described, was constantly under fire from the rebel artillery, and a portion of the time during the Sunday and Monday following the battle, while the army were hourly expecting the renewal of the conflict, were on picket duty in front of the city. While the battle was going on, the wounded were constantly passing our position *en route* for the bridges. Some among those passing to the rear were merely shirks, shamming sickness or wounds, or, in the expressive phraseology used by the boys, 'playing it,' and certainly in many instances, their acting would have done no injustice to the theatrical boards."

While the severe fighting was going on at "Marye's Heights" an officer, assisted by two able-bodied men, with the solemnity of a funeral, was being conducted to the rear. The officer was groaning in apparent anguish; his sleeve torn away and a bloody bandage pathetically spoke of a desperate wound. A colonel on provost duty halted the party. The two men were directed to the front with the assurance that their officer should receive every attention. Then turning to the captain the colonel kindly inquired: "What is the matter with you?" "I'm wounded," faintly responded the officer, with a grimace of pain on his face. A surgeon was summoned. "Dress this man's wounds!" "I didn't say I was wounded," said the officer; "I am sick and want to go over the river to be treated by my own doctor." "You can go when this surgeon has examined you and pronounced you unfit for duty," said the colonel. The officer sprang to his feet with an oath, and in tones very different from his invalid voice exclaimed: "I'll go any way!" The colonel's manner changed from respect to severity, and grasping the cowardly

officer by the collar, he directed his men to take him in charge.
The shamming officer broke away and ran to the front with so much
vigor as to show his complete recovery.

The wounded who could travel were treated with kindness, and
real sickness considerately, but those who were feigning were made
to believe "there was retribution in Israel," as Wad Rider expressed
it. I give this in-
cident as a sample
of many similar
ones constantly
being enacted in
the rear of a fight.
Surprising cures
were performed
by the provost
marshal. If men
did not take their
beds and walk,
they at least, in
some instances,
ran to the front,
whereas a few
moments previous
they were creep-
ing on all fours to
the rear.

On Sunday fol-
lowing the battle,
a flag of truce was
sent into our lines,
and parties were
permitted to bring

The Provost Marshal and Wounded Officer.

in the wounded. The rebels brought some of our wounded to the
neutral ground, where the curious spectacle might be seen of the
men of both armies engaged in friendly conversation. The best of
feeling was exhibited. Tobacco was exchanged for coffee, corndodger
for hard-tack, and there was a general inquiry for "picture papers"
on the part of the rebels, and when one was given them they were

seemingly delighted, as if that was a part of the paper that they could understand better than type.

"We 'uns will drive you'ns into the river to-morrow," said one of them. "Good-bye, blue bellies!" said another; "look out for another big licking to-morrow," said a third; all of which was said in a good-natured, joking manner, rather than that of bitter earnestness.

One of the citizens I met after the battle complained bitterly of the treatment he received from both armies. He informed me that in the town paintings, mirrors, pianos, furniture, and other valuables, had been wantonly destroyed, and then set forth his personal grievances by saying, "The rebel army tuck everything I had, and the Yankees have got the rest!"

On the 15th our company went on picket duty. By a tacit understanding there was no firing, and while conversations were not allowed, there was evidently a good feeling existing between the rank and file of the armies. During the afternoon the skies were overcast, and as darkness came on the wind moaned dismally, as if in requiem for our dead, still scattered on the plain.

About two o'clock at night, in the sleet and rain, by whose orders I know not, we stealthily crept back towards the river, which our forces had mostly crossed, though up to this time we had had no information of the army's crossing to the opposite bank. If our artillery and heavy teams had not been moved before the rain came on, it is doubtful if they could have easily reached the northern bank, so adhesive is Southern mud. When morning dawned we were boiling our coffee on the other side of the river, and the driving rain, coming down steadily, added not a little to our gloomy feelings. In the morning the enemy advanced on the plain and began to plunder and strip the dead and gather up the fragments left in our retreat. The Union artillery opened on them and drove them back.

It would be false to state that we were very cheerful. There was universal despondency. On the other hand, one of the men, detailed to cross the river and bury the dead, informed me that the rebels were very jubilant, and believed the Southern Confederacy would be acknowledged and the fighting over in another month.

The moral condition of the army after the battle may be more easily imagined than described. Gloom pervaded every rank. The feeling was deep and universal that it was of but little use to fight, unless the government could find some one to command who would not throw away our lives in useless experiments. It was evident to the most ordinary soldier in the ranks that we were superior in discipline and intelligence to the rebel rank and file, and fully as brave ; and that we were constantly out-generalled rather than whipped.

Intelligent soldiers, such as fought in our ranks, are merciless critics when they discover they are being led to useless slaughter, and there begin, under such conditions, those malign influences which in time destroy an army more surely than the enemy. There are no soldiers in the world who so soon grow dissatisfied under continued blunders of their commanders as Americans. So, while their hearts were in the war, they lacked confidence in Burnside, and had a feeling of anger against the constant interference of the "Cabinet General" at Washington. They were not tired of fighting, but of useless fighting, which brought them reproaches rather than victories. They clamored for no particular officer, but considered it due to them to have in command some one who was competent to lead them properly. They considered it madness and murder to continue in command one who had demonstrated his lack of ability so plainly as had General Burnside.

That indefinable something which can neither be weighed nor measured, called the *morale* of an army, was seriously impaired. After the battle the soldiers had leisure to look over the situation and discuss it from the standpoint of individual experience, and all the newspapers or manifestoes of the world could not convince them that they had not been needlessly whipped by attacking the enemy in his chosen position, when that position could have been flanked.

"Burnside seems a good man," said one of our boys during a discussion of the situation. "Oh, yes," said Wad Rider scornfully, "good enough for a parson, but not sensible enough for a soldier."

"He don't blame any one but himself," squeaked out a little fellow, and then with a touch of sarcasm — "and we don't either ! "

"Fellers," said Joe, who had a rough lot of common sense, "what we want is a gineral that can gineralize so as to lick them durned bragging rebs. This fight makes me so down in the mouth that I feel like a big funeral."

"One of them blasted fellers on picket said to me the other day, 'any time your'ns want a licking over thar, come over and we'll 'comerdate yer !'" said Joe explosively.

"What we want is McClellan back again!" said another with a long-drawn sigh. "Oh, go to thunder!" said Joe; "we want a fitin' man who ain't afeared to hurt them rebs!"

This croaking was universal and seemingly chronic and incurable. Made up of fancies, prejudices, sense and nonsense, the *morale* of an army is its better part, and Napoleon aptly expressed his appreciation of its prepondering value by affirming that in military affairs the *morale* is to the physical as two to one.

In the midst of this general gloom and discontent we received boxes from home, and read newspapers, and made merry over anything we could find to laugh at, with the usual careless gayety of soldiers.

"STUCK IN THE MUD."

A FORTNIGHT after the battle General Burnside essayed another move, but the moral condition of the army being well understood at Washington, the President, while not really forbidding a movement, commanded that no important one be made without informing him. The position of the Union commander was humiliating and false. The despondency and discontent increased rather than diminished; desertions were frequent, and a successful move was needful to him that he might re-establish himself in the confidence of the army — confidence was needed as a first condition of success. The people and press were clamoring for action. The President refused his resignation, while Halleck would sanction no proposition looking to a movement. Determined to extricate himself from the coil which enveloped him, he resolved to try once more the fortunes of battle, the result of which should relieve him from command of the army, or reinstate him in its good opinions.

Up to the 19th of January the roads and weather were in excellent condition. At this date the movement determined on began. The grand divisions of Hooker and Franklin moved up the river by the roads running parallel, and at night encamped at convenient distances from the fords. During the 20th preparations were made for crossing, positions selected, and passage determined upon at dawn of the morrow. During the night one of the wildest storms experienced by the army while on the march, came on, and yet all through its long, dreary hours the men worked and toiled in the cold, pelting rain to get artillery in position and to pull the pontoon boats to the river banks, in preparation for crossing. Five bridges were required, and when morning dawned not enough boats had been conveyed to the river for one. Who shall describe that toilsome night?

With the dawn came the announcement that the vigilant foe had discovered the movement, and was concentrating his forces to oppose the crossing. Meanwhile the country, which at any time afforded unequalled elements for bad roads, was now outdoing itself. The army was accustomed to mud in its varied forms, knee-deep, hub-deep; but to have it so despairingly deep as to check the discordant, unmusical braying of the mules, as if they feared their mouths would fill, to have it so deep that their ears, wafted above the waste of mud, was the only symbol of animal life, were depths to which the army had now descended for the first time, and was rather more than the mud-embargoed Army of the Potomac imagined possible.

The problem of the soldiers engaged in extricating mules and artillery and scows was no longer how to keep their shoes from filling with mud, but how to prevent their own disappearance beneath this waste of wallow. Imagine a mud engulfed train of wagons, boats, and artillery; the men laughing, shouting, and occasionally a mule so undaunted as to join his hickupping, and *errzzupping* with the chorus.

The men, staggering under the weight of rations, blankets, and equipments, formed a funeral-like procession over which a winding-sheet of mud was spread in thick and sticky perversity. The rain poured down capriciously in dreary drizzle, or in sheets like water-falls. Over all the sounds might be heard the dauntless laughter of brave men, who summon humor as a reinforcement to their aid, and as a brace to their energies, and not the unmeaning laugh of sense-less men who do not understand the situation. Hour after hour the rain continued and the difficulties and mud grew thicker and deeper. Twelve horses attached to a light cannon extricated it with difficulty from the mud, only for it to sink deeper at every halt, until nothing but the muzzle pointed in a defiant angle from the mud. Finally logs and rails were put under the wheels at every rest, to prevent their being engulfed. Ropes were attached to cannon, wagon, and pontoon, and in the rain hundreds of men worked to extricate and pull them through the mud, which clutched and held, and drew to its depths everything which came in contact with it, like the suction power attributed by Victor Hugo to the devil fish.

Four mules would be exhausted drawing a lightly loaded wagon. The disposition to laugh at the long-drawn out, ludicrous wallow of men, mules, and mud, was general. Grim humor was common. "This looks like a funeral procession stuck in the mud!" said one of the boys. "I'm afraid," said another, "we shall never get this *corps* along in season for the resurrection morning!" "Oh," said another grimly, "Burnside is going to bury the whole durned crowd in the mud, not knowing what else to do with it, and let it sprout for the resurrection!"

"Pshaw," said Wad Rider, who liked to have the last word, "we are like the caterpillar, and when we are well encrusted in the mud like a chrysalis we privates will all be hatched out into home-guards and brigadier generals!"

The rebels on the opposite banks caught the humor of the situation and shouted out offers to come over and lay the bridges if we would get up the boats, laughing, and performing various extravagant antics to express their satisfaction.

In vain long files of men pulling at ropes supplemented the labors of mud-begotten-looking mules and mud-magnified pontoon boats, caissons, and artillery. The rain descended in torrents, but could not wash the mud away from the mud-enshrouded troops, and the boats could not be brought to the banks of the river that was darkly running between the armies. Night came on and it was still raining, and though the boats were not in position, the enemy was. Morning dawned upon another day of deluge-like rain; the mud was still more persistent in its clutching, drawing in, and adhesive powers. It was no longer a question of how to go forward, but how to get back. The rations were exhausted, and the next morning the army wretchedly began its return to camp. Some ironically offered to get into the boats and row them to camp through the mud as the most expeditious manner of arriving there. An indescribable chaos of all vehicles known to the army straggled and floundered in the oozy, liquid muck; guns were stalled, pontoon boats engulfed, wagons upset by the roadside. Finally the army began to corduroy the road for the trains to return, and with laughter and jest, and oath and execration, it floundered back to its camps,

The Burnside Mud March. Page 138.

but not until the enemy had facetiously put up a big placard on the opposite shore which read "BURNSIDE STUCK IN THE MUD."

Thus ended the "Mud March" which so pertinently illustrated an answer to the public query at the North : "Why don't the army move?" and showed the difficulties and impediments to winter campaigning in Virginia.

After the armies returned to camp the mud seemed to have settled into their dispositions. Desertions were common and constant ; grumbling and dissatisfaction chronic; and enlistments at home, in spite of high bounties, slow. Eighty thousand men were absent from causes unknown or on "French furloughs," — "Walked off on their cheek" as the boys styled it, and they dared not face consequences by voluntary return. The career of General Burnside in command of the army was from this time brief.

CHAPTER XIV.

CHANCELLORSVILLE.

THE condition of disheartened distrust into which the army had now fallen was due less to defeat in battle than to a thorough want of confidence in the ability of its commander.

Amidst this general gloom the appointment of General Joseph Hooker to its command came to gladden us like the sudden appearance of the sun in cloud-darkened skies. Confidence was restored as if by magic, and as one of our boys declared, "The army seemed to have got a new back-bone." The habits of discipline which had become relaxed were resumed with the promptness characteristic of intelligent soldiers.

Hooker had been identified with the battles and history of this army from the beginning, and by his dashing bravery had won the *sobriquet* of "Fighting Joe." It was the general feeling among the rank and file that he was more likely to err from over-rashness and daring than to fail by over-caution.

The President had not promoted him to these high duties without misgivings. He had been an outspoken, unsparing critic of his superiors, and it remained to be seen if this spirit of insubordination would not react against him, and whether or not he would bear the ordeal of a command from which no commander had as yet escaped unscathed.

In a private letter addressed to him, dated January 26th, 1863, with his usual sense, quaint humor, and fatherly kindness, Mr. Lincoln said: "I have heard, in such a way as to believe it, of your recently saying that both the army and the government needed a dictator. Of course it is not for this but in spite of it that I have given you the command. Only those generals who gain successes can set up dictators. What I now ask of you is military success, and I will risk the dictatorship. . . . I much fear that the spirit you have aided to infuse into the army, of criticising their commander and withholding confidence from him, will now return upon you. Neither you, nor Napoleon if he were alive again, could get any good out of an army while such a spirit prevails. . . . Beware of rashness, but with energy and sleepless vigilance go forward and give us victories."

Hooker soon showed himself in a new phase, — that of an able administrative officer, and under his energetic administration many long-needed reforms took place. He stopped desertions, before which the Army of the Potomac was melting away like an iceberg in the tropics, by instituting a system of furloughs to the most deserving. "These," as Joe said, "allowed some of the boys to go home and brag how they fit." They proved beneficial in inspiring good conduct and cheerfulness, and also aided in checking desertions by removing the real cause.

General Kearney, at Fair Oaks, had ordered his soldiers to sew a piece of red flannel on their caps so that he might recognize them in battle. This idea General Hooker expanded into a system of corps badges of immense utility to the service.

The cavalry, which had hitherto been so non-efficient in its character as to call out the stinging criticism from Hooker, "Who ever saw a dead cavalry-man?" was now consolidated under efficient leaders, so that henceforth it was able to assert its superiority over that of the enemy. Franklin, who had been a stumbling-block, declaring that "Two thousand cavalry was enough for the whole army," was sent to the army of the Southwest, and the cumbersome "Grand Divisions" organized by Burnside done away with.

The new commander wisely deferred grand military movements during the wet months of winter. From January to April the army was occupied with drill, while its ranks were filled by the return of absentees and recruits. By the first of May the Army of the Potomac was in superb condition, numbering in infantry and artillery one hundred and twenty thousand men ; its artillery, a powerful force of four hundred guns ; its formerly despised cavalry had become a finely equipped and well-drilled body of twelve thousand. The boast of Hooker, that "It was the finest army on the planet," was not without truth. It was about to be demonstrated whether the hand which wielded this superb instrument was competent to use it.

The strength of the enemy's position in our front debarred Hooker from a direct attack, while the right flank was so disposed as to secure Lee against an assault in this direction.

In this emergency Hooker matured the exceedingly bold and able plan of operating against the enemy by passing around Lee's flank to Chancellorsville.

On the morning of April 27th, the divisions of the army, followed by pack-mules, and the men laden like mules, with rations for eight days, — salt pork, hard bread, salt, sugar, and coffee, — broke camp and went marching up the northern banks of the Rappahannock, often making wide detours behind the hills, to conceal the movement, as far as practicable, from the vigilant foe. The force consisted of the Fifth, Eleventh, and Twelfth Corps, under Meade, Howard, and Slocum.

The next morning the turning column crossed the Rappahannock by a pontoon bridge constructed on light canvas boats, twenty-seven miles above, at Kelly's Ford.

Only one small brigade of cavalry was left to clear the movements of this force; the remainder had been sent under Stoneman to break up Lee's communications with Richmond. This absence of our cavalry force, so essential for obtaining information to an army about entering the befogging, impenetrable region of the "Wilderness," was doubtless one of the powerful causes of Hooker's final defeat.

To reach Chancellorsville they crossed the Rapidan, and moved on parallel roads. The columns soon reached that river, at Germania and Ely's Fords. The water was rapid, and at first glance it seemed impracticable (in view of the heavy baggage of sixty pounds carried by each man) to cross by fording ; but the men stripped and, bearing their baggage aloft on their heads, or on bayonets, waded shoulder deep the swift-running river. One who had been carried away by the current, and was picked up by the cavalry stationed below, said to the author, "Old Joe Hooker thought of most everything, but forgot to give us swimming lessons!"

Bonfires were kindled on the banks, and the crossing was continued all night. To say that the men were in good spirits would but faintly express their good humor and hilarity. Every hardship, impediment, or accident, was surmounted with laughter and joke, for the rank and file, acute judges of military movements, recognized in the march they were making one of those battles with legs, which are often equivalent to a victory. They humorously congratulated each other that they had a commander at last who knew how to use their legs as well as their arms. They recognized that they were doing a big thing, or as one of them said, "Going to give the rebs an awful thump on the flank."

At the fords they captured some prisoners, who joked them on their heavy luggage. "When you 'uns capture we 'uns, you 'uns don't get much but a reb; but if we 'uns capture you 'uns we' uns get a heap of truck."

"We've got eight days' rations to last us to Richmond," said one of our men in response. "You 'uns will need to carry a year's rations before you get thar!" was the retort.

The point of concentration was reached on the afternoon of April 30th, and so far the movement was a grand success.

Fifty thousand men, heavily weighted, had marched nearly forty miles in two days, crossed two difficult rivers, with the loss of only six men and two mules. It was truly, as Swinton characterized it, "the stride of a giant." In the evening the Second Corps, under Couch, came up, and amid enthusiastic cheers Hooker arrived and took up his quarters at Chancellor House, an old-fashioned brick building, with massive pillars extending from the ground to the roof, surrounded by its rude negro cabins. Hooker issued a glowing proclamation to his army, saying, "The enemy must either ingloriously fly or come out from behind his defences and give us battle upon our own ground, where certain destruction awaits him."

There was much in the situation to justify this boast, for he had seized one of the two lines of retreat left open to Lee; was threatening the other, and had taken, by this daring move, Lee's whole fortified line in reverse. The Confederate general, however, as the sequel proved, was not one of those commanders to be easily compelled into the *rôle* assigned him by an opponent, but with a daring genius which compels our admiration, sought to retrieve the situation of extreme peril in which Hooker, with a master grasp of the elements of war, had placed him. From the time of his arrival at Chancellorsville, however, an inexplicable stupor seemed to have taken possession of Hooker's faculties, and he who had seized the situation with the grasp of a Titan was soon to let it fall from his hand with the nervelessness of a paralytic.

During the movement detailed, and as a cover and mask to it, General Sedgwick crossed the Rappahannock below Fredericksburg, thus engaging Lee's attention by a menace in his front. Demonstrations of this nature were made until the 30th, which assisted in the successful lodgement gained at Chancellorsville.

Seeing his peril, and that these movements in his front were but a mask to the real movement, Lee, leaving Early with a small force to hold the heights, put his columns in motion to meet Hooker, before he should have advanced from Chancellorsville and seized his communications with Richmond.

The plateau at Chancellorsville is hemmed in by a region covered with a dense growth of dwarfed pines and scrub oaks, intertwined and interlaced by a profusion of vines, creepers, and briars. The distance by direct lines, to Fredericksburg, was about ten miles, with two excellent roads, and on both sides of these roads, a few miles from the plateau, were open spaces on which to deploy troops, and where the Union army could avail itself of its superiority in artillery.

Leaving Sickles's corps, which had just arrived, in rear of Chancellor House as a reserve, Hooker gave orders to advance and form line of battle with the left covering Banks's Ford, and the right resting on Tabernacle Church. The passage through the tangled thickets broke up companies and regiments into crowds; men were separated from their commands and absolutely lost in the woods. They were in inextricable confusion, but almost out of the thickets, and about three miles from Chancellorsville, when they struck the enemy's advance. It was not a heavy force and there was no reason why we could not have continued the march, as the army was almost out of the hindering thickets; the general line was a good one, and Slocum's right had taken possession of high commanding ground, which dominated the surrounding country and commanded Chancellorsville. The left column had moved out on the river road five miles, under Humphrey and Griffin, and was in sight of Banks's Ford, which was practically uncovered by the movement. This fact alone should have prevented a retrograde movement, as it shortened communications with the portion of the army under Sedgwick by twelve miles, and practically united the two wings of our army. Here also our surplus artillery was parked. From here we could debouch in rear of Fredericksburg. There was absolutely every reason for desiring to get out of the Wilderness, and none for remaining in it. It was then, however, that Hooker issued that inexplicable order for the army to fall back to Chancellorsville, an order not understood at the time, and the cause of astonishment to every student of the movement since.

Officers and men received the order with mingled incredulity and astonishment, and the phlegmatic Couch was so overwhelmed with a sense of its folly, that he hurried Warren to Chancellorsville to remonstrate. But Hooker adhered doggedly to his resolution, and, followed step by step by the enemy, our army fell back to fight a defensive battle upon the plateau at Chancellorsville. Here Hooker closed up his front lines to render the defence easier; felled the trees in his front to render approach perilous and difficult, and blocked the approaches to the plateau.

His right wing under Howard, at Dowdall's Tavern was, how-ever, weak and unprotected. There were only two regiments faced on that flank, and a weak picket of only two companies of the Seventeenth Connecticut, constituted the entire outpost.

Notwithstanding the incomprehensible mistakes of Hooker, hith-erto detailed, Lee's position was one of great peril. His enemy's position was practically unassailable in front, and he had sent out Stuart's cavalry to see if there was not some assailable point in the Union lines. While anxiously discussing his plans with Jackson, it is said that Stuart brought him intelligence of the exposed con-dition of our right wing.

Lee clearly understood the advantage and disadvantage of Hooker's position, that the impenetrable thickets by which he was shut in condemned him to inactivity; that his cavalry force was small, and that therefore he could not venture upon movements which in a more open country, or with a large cavalry force as eyes for his army, would have been possible. So when Jackson proposed the bold plan of making a great march to strike the Union army on the exposed flank, he saw it was about the only movement which gave promise of success against Hooker's position. For to attack that general in front would be inviting defeat, and practically taking the bull by the horns.

At daybreak May 2d, Jackson began his march, with a force of twenty-six thousand men which, with other dispositions, left with Lee on the Union front only seven brigades. Lee masked his own weakness and Jackson's movement by artillery demonstrations along Hooker's entire front, as if about to attack.

Moving south by a wide detour of by-paths and roads but little used or known, Jackson, late in the afternoon, reached the Orange plank road. From the top of a wooded hill in the vicinity he saw the Eleventh Corps spread out on the plateau near Dowdall's Tavern, and that the plank road would lead him to our front instead of our flank. Leaving his old brigade, therefore, on this road, he continued his march until at about five o'clock he reached the turnpike which led him to the desired point. Here in the thickets he silently made his preparations for the attack.

Secretly as the march had been conducted, it had not been unperceived. As early as nine o'clock Birney had reported to Hooker that his outposts had seen a large column accompanied by trains about a mile and a half from his front. While at first Hooker thought this indicated the retreat of the enemy on Orange Court-House, he at once sent an order to Howard to be prepared for the enemy from whatever direction he might advance, and to determine on the position he would take if attacked on the flank, adding : " No artificial defences worth mentioning have been thrown up, and there seems to be a scarcity of troops at that point. Please advance your pickets for purposes of observation." [1] The timely issue of this order

[1] Copy of Hooker's order to Major-General Slocum and Major-General Howard :

Headquarters Army of the Potomac.
CHANCELLORSVILLE, VA., May 2d, 1863, 9.30 A.M.

I am directed by the Major-General Commanding, to say that the dispositions you have made of your corps has been with a view to a front attack by the enemy. If he should throw himself upon your flank, he wishes you to examine the ground and determine upon the position you will take in that event, in order that you may be prepared for him in whatever direction he advances. He suggests that you have heavy reserves well in hand to meet this contingency. The right of your line does not appear to be strong enough. No artificial defences worth naming have been thrown up, and there appears to be a scarcity of troops at that point, and not, in the General's opinion, as favorably posted as might be. I have good reasons to suppose the enemy is moving on our right. Please advance your pickets for purposes of observation, as far as may be safe, in order to obtain timely information of their approach.

(Signed)   JAMES H. ALLEN,
Brigadier and Aide-de-Camp.

by Hooker, it seems to us, shifts a large part of the responsibility for the disaster which followed, from his own to Howard's
shoulders.[1]

Sickles, with two divisions, started out in pursuit of the moving
column at one in the afternoon, and the Third Georgia was surrounded and captured by Berdan's sharp-shooters. From them
Sickles obtained information which showed that instead of a retreat
it was a menace against some point in our lines. Pleasanton's and
Sickles's scouts and spies came in with information, which duly
reached Howard, that Jackson was coming. General Schimmel-
pfennig, in command of a brigade, says the movement of the enemy
on our flank was reported full two hours before the charge. It is
even reported that Howard censured the scouts for lying, and treated
them with cool disdain. Be that true or false, although he had had
plenty of time since Hooker's order was issued, he had neither
strengthened his flank nor taken the ordinary precautions demanded
by his situation.

About sundown the soldiers of the Eleventh Corps, with stacked
arms, were boiling their coffee, smoking their pipes, lounging in
groups, and playing cards among the baggage-wagons, pack-mules
and teamsters, when rabbits, deer, and other game, driven by Jackson's advance, came into our lines. Some of the men were chasing
the rabbits with shouts and laughter, and all were unprepared, when
a few shots were heard along the road, and Jackson's men, who had
preserved their organization even in the dense thickets which tore
their clothes to tatters, burst upon them like a clap of thunder from
a cloudless sky. Before the men could seize their arms the rebels
rushed upon all parts of Gilsa's brigade, formed at this part of the
line. The slight intrenchments were attacked in the rear, and the
men driven in upon each other in huddles, with no chance to rally.
Our men fought as well as their situation allowed.

Everything was in confusion. No change of front was possible,
and the officers, isolated from the rank and file, could not rally them.
The impetuosity of Jackson's attack was terrible. A soldier of the

---

[1] Regarding this order, H. M. Kellog, a clerk at the Adjutant-General's office, of the
Eleventh Corps, says: "This order *was not on record or on file*, and was not placed there
until June 30th, two days after General Hooker had been relieved. The corps was then at
Emettsburgh, Md."

Eleventh Corps said afterwards to me, " It was a perfect whirlwind of men. The enemy seemed to come from every direction."

The flying fugitives disordered such lines as in vain tried to form. In ten minutes sixteen hundred men of Deven's division, on this flank, were killed, wounded, captured, or put to flight, and a confused mass of flying men, pack-mules, baggage-wagons, and riderless horses, broke through and disordered every line which endeavored to make a stand. In this way they overran Schurz's division, occupying intrenchments across the road on which the Eleventh Corps was posted.

Bushbeck, with his brigade, held the extreme left of the corps, preserved his line formation, and made a gallant fight. Howard rallied the fugitives and heroically endeavored to stem the tide of disaster; but the enemy enveloped his flanks, took his lines in reverse, and broke them into a mob. Bushbeck's brigade alone retained its formation and retired in good order through the crowd of fugitives now streaming to the Chancellorsville plateau. The right wing was being swept away and disaster threatened the entire army. Jackson, in the midst of his force, which now consisted of only his centre formation of four brigades, with the simple order of " Forward! Forward!" constantly reiterated, urged them on, and took our defences in reverse. Jackson had now reached the Mineral Springs road which leads to United States Ford by passing north of Chancellorsville, and conceived, it is said, the bold plan of out-flanking our army by this route.

" HAZEL GROVE."

At the first attack of Jackson, Howard sent to General Pleasanton for a regiment of cavalry. The aide-de-camp bearing this message found Pleasanton with General Sickles at Hazel Grove, a large open clearing about a mile west from Chancellorsville, and half a mile to the left from the plank road. Near the northwest corner of this field in open battery, were the Tenth and Eleventh New York Independent Batteries, and Battery H, First Ohio.

There was so little thought of an attack among these artillerymen, that they had unbridled their horses and were feeding them. Martin's horse battery occupied another part of the field, while the Eighth Pennsylvania Cavalry here stood to horse waiting for orders.

To that regiment the order to report to General Howard came. When Major Huey gave this order he found several of his officers playing a social game of cards, and as Major Keenan mounted he jokingly said, " Major, you've spoiled a good game of cards! "[1]

The regiment went forward on a wood road towards the plank road, with no thoughts of a present encounter. Major Keenan and other officers were riding at the head of the column. They had almost reached the plank road when they discovered that they were surrounded by the enemy's skirmishers, who were in the dense thickets which skirted the road.

Major Huey, without hesitation, determining to cut his way through, gave the order, " Draw sabres and charge! " Then ensued a scene that baffles description.[2]

Led by those officers who were riding at the front, the column dashed forward. Both horses and men seemed frenzied with excitement. The enemy was trampled under the horses' feet, and struck down with the sabre.

Reaching the plank road, a few yards distant, our men found it literally crowded with the enemy. Here they turned to the left and charged ; shooting, sabring, and trampling under their horses' feet those who could not escape.[3]

In turn the Confederates, from the wood-skirted sides of the road, threw at them their unloaded muskets, and bayoneted the men on the flank of the charging column. Resolved to sell their lives as dearly as possible, amid shouts and imprecations, the clanking of

---

[1] Andrew B. Wells, Captain of Company F, Eighth Pennsylvania Cavalry, says: "This was twenty minutes past six ; I looked at my watch to see how long we had been playing cards."

[2] Penncook Huey, in his book, " The Charge of the Eighth Pennsylvania Cavalry at Chancellorsville," says, " The regiment did not make its charge at Hazel Grove on the 2d of May, 1863 (as the enemy did not appear there until after the regiment had left), the charge having been made before that time on the plank road. The woods in front of Hazel Grove, where the charge is represented to have been made, was so thick that a bird could scarcely fly through it, much less could a cavalry charge have been made, as some writer has stated."

[3] The regiment had been forced to move in column, on account of the dense thickets skirting the road, and the whole regiment therefore did not get through. The rear squadron cut its way through in another direction. The men who were not killed or dismounted, came out on the other side of this road, and were re-formed in rear of the artillery that was then going into line on the left of the plank road, and though it was purely accidental, they materially assisted in checking the enemy's advance.

equipments, and neighing of steeds, and the shrieks and yells of the enemy, the column cut its way through this mass of men for a distance of a hundred yards, when the enemy poured in a volley of musketry, killing many private soldiers, and with them Major Keenan, Captain Arrowsmith, and Adjutant Haddock.

The position at Hazel Grove controlled the communication between our advance force at the Furnace and the main army.

A few moments after the departure of the Eighth Cavalry from Hazel Grove, a sharp fire of musketry was heard in the direction of the Eleventh Corps. The chief of artillery being absent, Captain J. P. Huntington, First Ohio Artillery, next in rank, assumed command.

The batteries which were in close column, resting on the wood through

Major Keenan's Charge on the Plank Road.

which the enemy were advancing, were in an awkward and perilous position. Every moment the firing of the advancing enemy grew louder.

While endeavoring to get his guns in position, a mob of fugitives from the Eleventh Corps, and a lot of Third Corps' forges, battery-wagons, and ambulances, broke through the incomplete formation, while a regiment of cavalry occupied for a time the ground on which the battery was forming.[1]

[1] Captain Huntington, in a note to the writer, says, "The assertion of General Pleasanton, that the retreating and abandoned guns belonging to the Eleventh Corps were put in position here, is not true."

Soon Archer's brigade, forming the extreme right of the rebel line, issued from the wood. Says Captain Huntington, "They probably did not anticipate resistance at this point, having reason to believe that everything in that quarter had been well started to the rear. A storm of canister from our eighteen pieces, and from Martin's horse battery of four pieces, in battery on the south side of the field, at an angle to our line, enlightened them on the subject." This was the critical moment, and Captain Huntington justly

Martin's Horse Battery at Hazel Grove.

says had Archer's men reached this position, the results would have been serious. They regained cover of the woods and opened a heavy fire with musketry. Meanwhile Archer's troops took possession of our rifle-pits in the direction of the plank road, and opened an enfilading fire on our batteries. Captain Huntington changed front with the rifle battery, and swept the woods, while Martin's horse battery kept up a cross fire on the enemy.

This timely and gallant conduct of the officers and men of Whipple's Artillery, which was unsupported by either infantry or cavalry, checked the enemy's advance in this direction.

The enemy's fire gradually slackened, and by the time Sickles's troops reached Hazel Grove the fighting at that point was practically over.

The plateau at Chancellorsville, where the various roads intersect, contains not over sixty acres, and was at this time encumbered with parked artillery and wagons of every description. It would be fatal to the army to have confusion and stampede occur here, for it was not only the single means of communication between the different parts of the army, but was the one point where the disorganized fragments coming in on all the roads could be rallied and re-formed.

Realizing this, Hooker flamed out with his old fighting spirit. He endeavored to stay the torrent of flying men. His old division, then under Berry, advanced in good order, while the fugitives swayed around it. These tough old veterans formed on the first crest west of the Chancellor House plateau, while Hayes's Brigade of the Second Corps came up to support his right, and the Twelfth Artillery formed in the rear of Fairview. By seven o'clock thirty-seven guns were thundering over the heads of Berry's men into the woods beyond.

In the meantime Birney's division had formed on the south of the position so magnificently contested by Captain Huntington, and thus was stayed the advance of Jackson, which, like the simoon of the desert, had been sweeping our right wing into destruction, and threatening disaster to the whole army.

Darkness came on and comparative silence succeeded this terrible eruption of battle. The enemy, after Huntington's cannonade, abandoned the earthwork running southeasterly across the woods, and it remained unoccupied. Jackson rode out to reconnoitre this position, which would give him the key to Hooker's interior defences, and was returning with his staff, when he rode accidentally upon some of Birney's skirmishers, who fired upon the group. He wheeled, and to avoid the shower of bullets, rode into the thickets, where the Eighteenth North Carolina formed his line. Mistaking them in the darkness for Union cavalry, they poured into the group a close volley, and Jackson was mortally wounded. Thus fell the bravest and most skilful of all Lee's lieutenants. In his death the Confederacy lost its greatest soldier, and one who had by his dashing flank attacks hitherto proved so terrible to the Federal army.

Death of Lieutenant-Colonel McVicar at Spottsylvania. Page 153.

It has been fashionable since, as it was at the time, to attribute this disaster to the cowardly elements which were supposed to exist in the Germans of the Eleventh Corps, and to their dissatisfaction over the displacement of Sigel by Howard. This is a great injustice to many brave men. Only a few cavalry, less than a company, cleared the front of the Eleventh Corps. There should have been at least a brigade. This was Hooker's mistake. The great weight of blame, however, falls upon Howard, who did not take those precautions so essential to the situation, and allowed himself to be surprised. General Doubleday, in his book on the Civil War, justly observes : " I assert that when a force is not deployed, but is struck suddenly and violently on its flank, resistance is impracticable." Couch takes similar views, and such are the views of many military men. Howard received notification and definite instruction from his commander, and yet failed to be prepared for the menaced attack.[1] No general is excusable who allows himself to be surprised.

[1] Regarding the order issued by Hooker to Generals Slocum and Howard, it is but justice to Howard to say he denies ever receiving it.

NOTE. — On the 30th of April, the Sixth New York Cavalry was sent forward by General Pleasanton to reconnoitre in the direction of Spottsylvania. They were returning by moonlight the same night, when they encountered the Fifth Virginia Cavalry, barring their passage to Chancellorsville. Lieutenant-Colonel McVickers, commanding the regiment, ordered a charge with sabres, and routed them. The brave McVickers was mortally wounded in this encounter. It was said that Stuart and his staff were with the defeated party.

CHAPTER XV.

SATURDAY night Sickles had massed Birney s division near Hazel Grove. Berry's division and Hayes's brigade of Couch's corps ranged themselves north of Fairview,. while Williams, leaving his artillery planted on Fairview as a barrier, advanced and supported Sickles. The latter, enthusiastic and untiring, had requested of Hooker permission to make a night attack.[1] The coveted order was given, and at eleven o'clock, while darkness enshrouded the thickets, his men cautiously advanced. The mournful notes of the whippoorwill, the crackling of the underbrush beneath the feet of stealthily advancing men, the low-toned command alone broke the silence.

Peering into the darkness, halting here and there to catch the faintest sound, the advancing line suddenly encountered the enemy, who were approaching cautiously through the thickets bent upon the same errand. A blinding flash illumined the darkness and the terrible discharge of musketry resounded through the woods. The foes charged each other with mutual yells, cheers, and shouts, and the Union artillery, which had hurried down the road at the first alarm, advanced into the thickets and opened within a hundred yards of the enemy's lines. The dark wood was now lit up with lurid flashes of artillery and the fire-fly sparkle of rifles. From the forest depths there burst forth the terrible uproar of battle. The deep tones of the cannon marked time to the incessant roll

---

[1] Captain Huntington, whose artillery had defended Hazel Grove, says: "About midnight I was awakened by the passage of a column of troops near our bivouac. I asked an officer what was up. He replied that they were going to drive the enemy out of the woods at the point of the bayonet. In reply to my wish that they would have a good time doing it, he said, 'They belong to Kearney's old division, that never yet went back!' The cold-steel part of the programme was not long adhered to, for the roar of musketry soon became deafening."

of musketry, which, like the explosion of long strings of fire-crackers, ran along the whole line where the contestants retreated or advanced to the attack.

The impossibility of giving orders in the darkness, among the tangled thickets, soon produced its effects. Brigades were broken into regiments, regiments into companies, and these into smaller groups, while friend and foe seemed con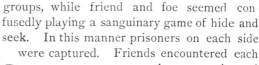fusedly playing a sanguinary game of hide and seek. In this manner prisoners on each side were captured. Friends encountered each other as enemies and each mistook foes for friends.

A comrade who participated in this attack afterwards related the following incident : "About a dozen of us got broken off as short as a pipe-stem from our regiment, and we weren't fools enough to 'halloo' before we got out of the woods. There were six of us, and Matt Jenkins, a little corporal with a big voice, was the ranking man of the squad. We had lost the p'ints of the compass as completely as if there were none, though there was no mistaking where the fight was. We were cautiously groping through the brushwood, where the occasional flash of musketry only made us all the blinder, when a blaze and the roar of a volley on our front showed us that we had encountered an enemy. Their shot, however, had pattered

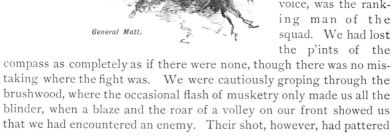

General Matt.

all around without injuring any of us. Our little corporal, with his big voice, which sounded for all the world like a major-general's, shouted out : 'Reserve your fire, men!' and then gave orders to captain this and major that and colonel some one else, as if he was in command of a brigade. 'Thunder!' said some one in the party we had encountered, 'you needn't make all that fuss ; we'll surrender!' and then," said my informant, with a chuckle, "about twenty of our own company, including the captain, came in and surrendered to Matt Jenkins!" Ever afterwards we called him "General Matt."

The contestants were in confusion, running into each other at haphazard. The Federals had captured the intrenchments lying across the wood and several cannon previously abandoned by the Eleventh Corps. The battle gradually died away, only blazing out here and there fitfully as little squads encountered each other in the tangled wilderness.

It was past midnight ; the moon now shone brightly, and the woods were strewn with dead and wounded, and the wearied contestants needed rest. Silence succeeded the dismal uproar and lurid lights of midnight battle. The result of this contest was that the approach to the ridge, so grandly defended by Captain Huntington, was cleared, and the enemy driven from the hills opposite Fairview by Birney ; but Berry had not been able to drive away the Confederates holding the left slopes.

Sunday morning, May 3d, the situation was by no means discouraging, but for the incomprehensible mental torpor of the Union commander. We are not able to see anywhere evidence of a master mind during the conflict which followed. We still held the point where the roads converged at Chancellorsville, but our position promised more for offensive than defensive battle.

We had seventy-five thousand men posted between the severed wings of the Confederate army, who did not number forty-five thousand, and from these converging roads as a pivot, we could have directed a terrible blow upon either one or the other of these severed wings of the enemy before they could be united.

On the other hand, the plateau was a cramped space and the number of its defenders was necessarily limited by its size. The numerous roads running thereto enabled Lee to converge his forces to crush its crowded defenders. Had its possessors been relieved constantly by fresh men, however, the result might have been different.

Meanwhile the Sixth Corps, under Sedgwick, still confronted the rebel position at Fredericksburg. It is a question among military men whether or not Hooker should have ordered Sedgwick to join him on Saturday. Without entering into the discussion, it seems to the writer that that procedure would have been needless, as neither Reynolds's nor Meade's corps had as yet fired a shot. Hooker was not so much lacking in men as in the ability to use them. The common sense of the situation would rather have justified him in sending the two corps (which during the entire battle he did not use) to the assistance of Sedgwick. Such a procedure would have transferred the offensive to the left wing, and enabled us to hold Marye's Heights, which had been captured by Sedgwick.

When disaster fell upon the Eleventh Corps, Hooker ordered Sedgwick to seize the heights and advance by the plank road with his twenty-two thousand men to deliver him from the clutches of the Confederate devil-fish which was crushing him in its embrace.

This order could be successfully executed only by the continual activity of Hooker. A passive position, on his part, would enable Lee to concentrate a force sufficient to crush Sedgwick. It seems reasonable that if, instead of like a pair of horses where one stands still while the other pulls, they had acted in unison, some of the bones of the Confederate army must have been broken.

On Sunday morning Sedgwick put his forces in motion to obey the order of Hooker, which he received at midnight on Saturday.

With this remark we turn to the battle about to open at Chancellorsville. During the night of Saturday Hooker had, in the darkness, when he could not fully understand all the features of the ground, laid out a new line to which he ordered the different forces to fall back at daylight. Here occurred the fatal mistake which lost us the Chancellorsville plateau.

Outside of the line to which our army was commanded to fall back, was Hazel Grove and the bare hillock occupied by the artillery, which had so bravely contested its possession the previous evening, and where Birney's division was in possession of the woods. The hill of Hazel Grove was lower than that of Fairview opposite, but it was the key to the battle-field, and as it commanded the roads converging here from Chancellorsville, it would, if crowned with artillery, threaten every force approaching Sickles. When its importance was understood a request was sent to Hooker for permission to hold it. General Doubleday says Hooker was asleep, and the member of his staff in charge positively refused to awaken him until daylight, and that being the hour the new line was ordered to be occupied would be too late.

The batteries, with the exception of the First Ohio, had retired at sunrise. This battery, commanded by the gallant Huntington, was supported by two regiments of infantry, one on the right and one in the rear. Just in the rear, where the guns stood, the ground descended by an easy slope, back of which was a marsh. By putting the guns just behind this crest, their recoil threw them under cover, where they could be loaded and pushed to the front.

As all of their canister had been expended the previous evening, and the work was close, fuse shrapnel, with the fuse hole left open, allowing them to burst in the gun, were fired.

This intrepid commander held the position, firing rapidly upon the advancing rebels, until his attention was called to the precipitate retreat of his infantry supports. Finding that the right of Archer's brigade overlapped his flank and was compromising the safety of his guns, he coolly retired by piece from the left, keeping up the fire of each gun until the instant before it was limbered, and crossed the little creek on a bridge made of rails, with the loss of only one of his pieces.

The drivers and horses of this piece were killed, and while the enemy closed in on them, Captain Huntington dismounted to attempt to extricate it, "when my horse," says Huntington, "thinking he was at the wrong end of the battery, started off at a gallop, and fell into his accustomed place at the head of the battery," leaving his master to retire by crawling on all fours. He was the only man with this piece who was lucky enough to escape.

It illustrates the affection with which an artilleryman regards his guns, that Captain Huntington says: "Regarding the loss of the piece we mourned bitterly." Thus was abandoned this strong position which commanded the field. The enemy soon occupied it, for Stuart recognized it as the master's seat, from which he who held it could hold the field.

The new line was formed perpendicular to the plank road on the ridge occupied by Berry's division on Saturday evening; Williams's division extended to the left, connecting with Geary, while Hancock still held his old position. Birney's and Whipple's divisions strengthened the line in front of Fairview, while the batteries of the Third and Twelfth Corps, with part of the Eleventh Corps batteries, covered this line. The Eleventh Corps was now at the extreme left, while Reynolds's corps, supported by Meade's, was covering the United States Ford on the Ely Ford road. These three corps were practically out of the fight.

This, roughly outlined, was our position at daylight on Sunday morning. At the same time the Confederates pressed forward to possess Hazel Grove a furious attack was made on Sickles by Jackson's men who, with fierce yells and cries of " Remember Jackson !" charged our lines. Mott's brigade met the attack and made a counter-charge, capturing colors and prisoners, but Sickles was attacked in front and his lines enfiladed by artillery fire from Hazel Hill, now crowned by Stuart with thirty pieces of artillery. Under this destructive fire Sickles fell back to another line, and then to another. At the same time, on the right of the woods, Hill's brigades came screaming over the works, and our men, though fighting stubbornly, fell back. French's division arrived and advanced to charge, driving back the exulting enemy in the greatest confusion, breaking their line and swinging it back upon its centre. They rallied and made another attack, but our men fiercely drove them down the hill and even advanced and seized again the old position from which they had retired at daylight. O for the possession of Hazel Hill to make these successes fruitful ! No force can hold its own, battered in flank by artillery and assaulted in front by infantry.

Stuart's guns at Hazel Hill were mowing the plateau. The rebels were attacking Fairview on every side. Lee had partially united his severed wings and was directing the attack. Geary, almost surrounded by foes, was fighting fiercely, but was dislodged from the earthworks at the summit of the plateau where the plank road descends on the south side. The Confederates soon reached the plateau on every side.

The ammunition of the Union men was exhausted. Sickles sent to Hooker for reinforcements and ammunition, but Hooker had been

stunned by the concussion of a shell which knocked away a wooden
pillar of Chancellor House. He was impotent from the first. He
had previously declared, in response to a similar call, that he
could not make men nor ammunition, and that, too, when two corps
had not yet been called into action. To the supreme cry for aid
there came no answer. The army was without a head.

The artillery of the Confederates, now posted on the heights,
struck the ranks of Hancock, who was holding McLaw's division
by the throat in his front, with his second line faced to meet the
attack from his rear. He held on with his usual dogged and heroic
firmness. The plain of Chancellorsville was soon covered with flying
men, batteries, wagons, and the disordered fragments of the fight.
The abatis, filled with the dead and wounded of both armies, was
in flames. Chancellor House was on fire ; the trembling women
concealed in its cellar barely escaped with their lives, while the
Union wounded perished in the flames.

Pressed on three sides, the Union forces were falling back.
Sickles, who had called up all his reserve, appeared wherever danger
threatened his lines. Berry was wounded. Mott was killed, and
Revere, next in rank, took the brigade command. All was disaster
and confusion, and he ordered a retreat. Sickles halted them, but
too late. His artillery was crushed and had fallen back, and the
Confederates rushed in from every direction. The field was lost
and the Confederate wings were now fully united.

Hancock, who had maintained his position to the last, retired. It
was ten o'clock in the morning, and the victorious rebel army was
fully united and in undisputed possession of Chancellorsville. The
Union army retired from the ensanguined field to a new line, while
dense volumes of smoke from the burning woods rolled up between
the contestants.

The centre of the new line was at the Bullock clearing, about a
mile from Chancellorsville, with its left wing resting on the Rappahannock and its right on the Rapidan.

While the Union army was falling back to their new position,
Lee straightened out, as it were, his disordered and entangled
columns. We turn again to Sedgwick before Fredericksburg. He
had been slow, but he had so arranged his lines as to keep Early's
defensive forces stretched out in attenuated line, not knowing where
the threatening blow would fall.

At eleven o'clock the columns for attack were formed by the Seventh Massachusetts and Thirty-sixth New York, led by Colonel Johns of the Seventh Massachusetts, while Colonel Spear, with the Sixty-third Pennsylvania and Forty-third New York, advanced on Cemetery Hill, north of the plank road. This movement was supported by four regiments deployed south of the road.

The storming column was within three hundred yards of the stone wall which stretched out on either side of the road. As it advanced, its lines were enfiladed by grape-shot from two cannon; but this did not stop them. The enemy, under their old defender, Barksdale, held the hill, reserving their fire until they were within a hundred yards, then opened with a terrible effect, which drove back the head of the assaulting column. Again it rallied and again was driven back, but they had almost scaled the intrenchments. The regiments formed again and swept up the hill with resistless valor. Nothing could stop them. Johns was wounded and Spear killed. Their colors went down, but the columns went on over the wall into the enemy's works. They captured the heights, four cannon, and several hundred prisoners.

Colonel Grant had meantime captured Lee's Hill after a sharp struggle. In twenty minutes these heights, deemed impregnable since Burnside's failure, had been seized.

The time until three o'clock was consumed waiting for Brooks's division to come to the front line. When the Sixth Corps arrived in the vicinity of Salem Church they found Wilcox with a small force using this building and a small schoolhouse six yards from it on the edge of the road, to hold the advancing column in check.

We return again to Hooker, who had taken up his new line, partially intrenched with strong abatis work, and all its approaches commanded by cannon. He hoped Lee would attack him in this strong position. Lee was about to gratify this desire when he received, with astonishment, the intelligence of Early's defeat and Sedgwick's advance on the turnpike. In a moment he formed his resolution. Relying on the defeat Hooker had received to keep him passive, and leaving only three of Jackson's divisions and three brigades of Anderson to hold Hooker's whole army in check, he turned with the remainder to wipe out Sedgwick from the slate on which he was solving this problem of war.

Sedgwick opened the fight by planting artillery near the toll-house, and soon silenced the enemy, who were short of ammunition. Two brigades captured the schoolhouse and its defenders, assaulted Wilcox's line, and routed it. Wilcox led his one remaining regiment forward. At this critical moment McLaw arrived and occupied Salem Church; then the whole Confederate line of five brigades advanced, and the menacing movement of Sedgwick was checked, for Hooker had not made the slightest diversion in his favor.

The news of the capture of Marye's Heights had restored confidence to the army. Hooker's new position was so strong that he could have held it with one army corps. Communications were now open by way of Banks's Ford, and Hooker could have ordered the Sixth Corps to join him, or he could, by a twelve mile march in the night, have joined Sedgwick, with his seventy-five thousand men, at Salem Church. The Federal army would then have been in an advantageous position. The heights of Fredericksburg turned and his army posted in an open country, he could have availed himself of his superior numbers, his fresh troops, and his out-numbering heavy guns.

On Monday Lee recaptured the heights around Fredericksburg and Anderson attacked Sedgwick, attempting to cut off his retreat to the river. Sedgwick stubbornly resisted, but yielded ground on the left, where the main effort of the enemy was directed. Night intervened, and under cover of partial darkness (the moon shone) and the heavy fog, Sedgwick recrossed at Banks's Ford.

Gathering up his forces, Lee now turned to attack Hooker in his intrenched lines. Hooker's position, now that Sedgwick had been forced to cross the river, no longer had any great advantages. The rations of the army had partially given out; ammunition was scarce; the time of service of many of his men had expired. The game was lost!

During the night of Tuesday, in a heavy rain, the Army of the Potomac recrossed the river. They left behind their dead and wounded, twenty thousand muskets, fourteen pieces of artillery, and their confidence in Hooker. Their loss in killed, wounded, and prisoners was 17,197 men.

Stoneman's cavalry operations during the campaign served no other purpose than to frighten the non-combatants in the interior of the country, as he did not get fairly to work until the campaign was over.

Thus ended the campaign which Hooker opened as with a thunderbolt from the hand of Mars, and ended as impotently as an infant who has not learned to grasp its rattle.

The wonder of the private soldiers was great. How could they have been beaten with so little fighting? How had one half of the army been defeated while the other half had not fought? "Uncle Joe," said one, "has bit off more than he could chew, and in attempting to swallow it has got choked."

Their muttered curses were prolonged and deep as they plodded back in the mud to their old camps. "How is it we have been so licked?" said one. "What was the matter with Pap Hooker?" said a second. "He hopped out of the wilderness like a parched pea."

"I know," said one of the jokers; "when Uncle Joe got to Chancellorsville it was such a success that the recoil kicked him over, and he waited until Bob Lee came along and kicked him back!" "Oh, pshaw! that ain't it," said another. "When Uncle Joe got to Chancellorsville it was such a big thing it made him feel like a dozen men, and he stopped to 'treat' the whole dozen."

This opinion tallies somewhat with a saying reputed to President Lincoln. He is said to have advised Hooker, when he sent him West, "not to go by the way of Bourbon County."

Whatever may have been the cause of Hooker's mental condition, it was certain that he missed all the brilliant opportunities presented by his first great move in an incomprehensible failure to take advantage of them.

One of the features of the fight which seemed to strike the boys with peculiar horror was the burning of the wounded. One of the wounded narrated to me, some months afterwards, how he watched the flames and counted the moments when it would strike him, when the progress of the flames were arrested by a little stagnant pool of water.

A comrade in the hospital afterwards related the following: "I was among the wounded just outside the abatis when it got afire. This leg you see was as limp as a dish rag, but I couldn't see the poor devils burn up in that way; so using my musket for a crutch, I began to pull away the burning brushwood, and got some of them

out. I tell you it was hot ! Them pines was full of pitch and rosin,
and made a fire as hot as a furnace ! I was working away, pulling
out Johnnies and Yanks, when one of the wounded
Johnnies, pale as a ghost, toddled up and began to
help. He allowed he wa'n't goin' to have a d—d
Yank beat him at anything. The underbrush
crackled and roared, and the poor devils howled
and shrieked when the fire got at them ; and

Unionists and Rebels trying to save the Wounded.

by and by another reb (I guess he
was a straggler) came up and began
to help too, and we fought the fire
all together. We were trying to rescue a young
fellow in gray, — the fire was all around him.
The last I saw of that fellow was his face.   It
was a handsome face. His eyes were big and blue, and his hair

like raw silk surrounded by a wreath of fire, and then I heard him scream, ' O mother! O God!' It left me trembling all over like a leaf. After it was over my hands were blistered and burned so I could not open or shut them, but me and them rebs tried to shake hands. Them two fellers wer'n't so bad ; one of them helped me down to the crossing the next night and got a darky to set me across the river."

" What ? " " Well, yes ! I expect that leg's a goner, but what's a leg if we'd only whipped them ! "

Another comrade told me an incident of the rebel habit of stripping the dead of their clothing. " We left one of our men out there for dead. I thought I saw a shell come along and take his head off, but he was only stunned, and by and by he came running into our lines with nothing on but his shirt and hat, and I don't see how the Johnnies missed them."

" The funniest thing I saw," said another, " was one of those aides. The concussion of a shell tore all his clothes off of him, but didn't seem to have hurt him any. He was running around almost stark naked trying to find his pocket-book ! "

The Eleventh Corps was the butt of many jokes. One of Hooker's aides, after the battle, could not speak above a whisper, he had shouted so loud and long in trying to stop the stampede. Some one asked him the next day what the matter was ; he responded, " That d—d Eleventh Corps ran away with my voice ! "

The sober, mature opinion of the army, however, was that some one besides the Eleventh Corps was to blame for the disaster which overtook it.

When the men reached their old camps at Falmouth they were tired and low-spirited.

CHAPTER XVI.

THE ARMY MULE.

I BELIEVE it was General Hooker who first used the mule as a pack-animal in the Army of the Potomac. As the mule was an important factor in army life, it does not seem out of place here to depict some of the characteristics of this animal, and the part he took in its affairs. Animals, like men, are moulded or modified by their surroundings, and hence the mule who adapted himself to army circumstances became unique.

The army mule was dun-colored and sad. His countenance was extremely solemn, and in length rivalled his ears. The sentimental in his nature was wafted from the ends of his ears, while his humor worked out at his heels. His voice was of unusual compass and pitched mostly in the minor key, harmonizing with nature in a remarkable degree. It had in it the rush of waters, the sighing of winds, the filing of saws, the grating of slate pencils, and as a whole resembled a clap of thunder drawn through a coarse sieve.

When a mule brays he throws up his tail, and not infrequently his heels, in a sort of ecstasy. The darky drivers solemnly declared that a sure preventive of the second was to tie a weight to the first; that if a mule couldn't throw up his tail 'twas impossible for him to lift his voice. The difficulty of applying this knowledge to practical use, was that the veteran army mule allowed no trifling with his personality, and while his tail was being weighted his heels were disastrously busy. Woe to any unthinking midnight marauder who approached his provender with evil intent! At such a crisis his voice was ominous of danger, and the victim, overtaken by the cyclone of his heels, got an astronomical perspective not outlined in the books. He saw stars, if he retained sufficient consciousness to do so, which if he did would be by no good will of the mule.

The step of the veteran army mule was deliberate and indicative

THE TROUBLES OF A MULE-DRIVER. Page 166.

of both decision and patience, though these qualities were never exercised on trifling occasions, and showed themselves to the best advantage by his coming to a dead halt when everything else evinced a disposition to move; at such times he seemed to have a monopoly

Reveillé

The Army Mule.

of all the patience in the army. A veteran mule disdained so trifling an incident as musket firing. I've seen him, while nibbling at his neighbor's tail, whisk his ears in modest disapprobation of musketry, but never lift his voice or heels to emphasize his dislike at so trifling an interruption as the buzz of a bullet. Shell and shot, if they struck the vehicle to which he was attached, sometimes called out from him tones of disapproval, resembling a steam whistle with the hiccoughs.

His manner, like that of all personages of decision, was usually quiet and patient. When provender was scarce he ate rubber blankets, rail fences, pontoon boats, shrubbery, or cow-hide boots, with a resignation worthy of praise. His firmness was a quality much derided, but of inestimable value in the miry clay of Virginia, where firmness was much needed and not usually found.

His merits have been but little understood. The army could never have floundered through its oceans of mud but for his indomitable firmness to back it. Not least among its martyrs and heroes was this unpretentious, plodding, never-flinching quadruped.

One of our colored drivers had in his team a mule of unusual size, — fat, sleek, and of inky blackness, of whom he was accustomed to say, "dat ar mewl knows mos' as much as folkses!" At one time when the driver was separated from his team, the black mule was unhappy and refused to be comforted. He did not eat with his accustomed appetite, and kicked viciously at all who approached from front or rear. The mule at last became so unmanageable that Jim was sent for. Upon his arrival his muleship became quiet, and allowed himself to be harnessed and driven, with a humility quite touching to those who had seen him in his refractory mood. After this who says an army mule is incapable of friendship?

One of our teamsters used to remark that one of his mules wouldn't go unless he did use the whip, another stopped "right plumb" when struck with one, while still another wouldn't pull a pound unless yelled at in a peculiar manner. I asked him if he knew the reason of this, and his answer was, "It's de way dey's been druv, sah!" Profanity was considered indispensable in mule driving.

At different times when I attempted the difficult study of its peculiarities, the philosophical calmness necessary to such a task was broken by various demonstrations from this incomprehensible hybrid.

A grim humor, at times, seemed to be his predominant trait, and the suddenness of its exhibition was very disturbing to reflective moods. Near approach brought out a great many qualities of which I had previously but little conception.

The mind of the army mule seemed to pervade not only its brain, but its ears, tail, and heels. He was subject to sudden transitions from joy to sorrow, which were punctuated in his own way. Sometimes this was done with a full stop, and at others with a prolonged note of exclamation, while his commas were put in with deliberation and dignity at every step. He had an accent peculiarly his own.

I don't know who it was that during the war invented the pack-mule system. The pack-mule, when loaded with a cracker box on each side and a medley of camp kettles and intrenching tools on top, was, to express it mildly, grotesque. At times, when in an over-loaded, top-heavy condition, I have known him to run this side load into a tree, and in this manner capsize with his load, and it was comical to see him lying on his back with a cracker box on each side, and his heels dangling dejectedly in the air, a picture of patience and dignity overthrown ; and in this atti-

Army Mules on Duty.

tude looking like a huge grasshopper. Pack-mules were used for working squads in the winter of 1864, on the lines before Petersburg.

One night, a mule heavily laden and bristling with shovels, picks, and axes, broke loose from his company, and with a terrible clatter and clamor, went charging into the enemy's lines, undaunted and alone. The enemy, believing they were being charged by cavalry, were in considerable consternation, and hastily formed to resist. They fired in volleys and at will, when the mule, not fancying his reception, wheeled, threw up his heels, brayed, and amid shouts and laughter, came prancing back to his allegiance, unhurt. The boys declared that a braver charge than that of "thet er muel" was seldom made.

The value of the mule in the army was very great, on account of his being less liable to injury than the horse. A fracas which would kill a horse would leave a mule unscathed. Sometimes two or more teams coming from opposite directions became entangled in such a manner that it seemed impossible to tell to which team the harness and mules belonged. In these intricate, trap-like entanglements the mule seemed to have the instincts of self-preservation to such a degree as to extricate himself from them unhurt. I have known a team to be overturned down a steep hillside, and wagon and mules to roll over each other in a confusion of harness, wagon, and mules, and yet the beasts escaped uninjured.

Said a veteran soldier, "It didn't seem to hurt them any more than it would a lot of kittens rolling over each other in play." The mule was more hardy and could adapt himself to circumstances better than the horse.

An old Virginian once said to me, "Before the war I never saw a dead mule. I sometimes thought them kind of brute beasts lived forever!" Dead mules were plenty in the army. They would live on meagre fare with a humility and patience almost pathetic. Under adverse circumstances, to his usual severe simplicity and melancholy reserve, was added an air of defiance.

He was hard to kill, yet there were, sometimes, circumstances under which even this resolute creature died. When Burnside was in Knoxville, it was at one time impossible to get enough provender for the mules. The hardy hybrids, thus deprived, made a resolute struggle for life, and gnawed at the poles of the wagons, and the wagons themselves. To prevent their destruction the poles were wound with hoop iron, and trees and brush were dragged in front of the wagons, for the mules to feed upon. The line of march from Camp Nelson to Knoxville was strown with dead mules, and a veteran soldier declares that in the darkest night he could thereby smell out his way over that route.

The hardihood of the mule is illustrated by a saying of one of the drivers, "There is one of three things you must do at the end of a journey with your mules, let them roll over seven times, wade in a stream, or feed them."

He bore hard usage and the scoffs and sneers at "thet ar meul" with uncomplaining heroism and was found dead on all the battle-fields of the war. He was of inestimable value to the army, and it is doubtful if its varied operations could have been conducted without him.

Is it too much to say that to him, above some other claimants, should be given the credit of having saved the Union?

CHAPTER XVII.

THE ordinary drill was resumed at once upon our return to the camps. Great sanitary precautions were taken to prevent disease and to preserve health. The terms of service of nine months' men and two years' men were constantly expiring. Five thousand of these were mustered out from the Army of the Potomac in May and ten thousand in June. In this manner the army was constantly diminishing. On the other hand, the Army of Northern Virginia, under General Lee, was filled up by recruits and conscripts, while every available rebel regiment was consolidated with that one army.

The sad experiences of the war had failed to induce our authorities to abandon a useless and wasteful scattering of troops. They had not learned, with all our reverses, to discontinue or reduce the useless number of posts and consolidate their men into one army. As an illustration of this, at the beginning of the Gettysburg campaign, when men were so much needed, a whole army corps was left at Port Royal, one division at Newbern, two at Suffolk, with no army in their front except one of mosquitoes. There were six thousand cavalry at Manassas and Milroy's division in the Valley receiving orders from Halleck, Hooker not even knowing what orders they received, or but vaguely. Under this shiftless system of "how not to do it" our superior numbers effected but little.

Another reason, it seems to me, for the greater efficiency of the Southern army was that they were nearly all veterans. When the Southern army had made a soldier they kept him. There was no "expiration of term of service" among *their* men.

A hundred veterans, accustomed to hardship and battle, are worth more than a thousand untried or partially tried men, because it is known almost to a certainty what can be done with them. With raw troops this can never be foretold.

172

Good officers, as a rule, make good men. Poor officers will make the best of men inefficient and worthless. An officer must command confidence if he cannot secure love and enthusiasm. The men will then do much more than under one on whose wisdom they do not rely. When soldiers are once assured that an officer commanding them will exact no needless or vexatious service they can be depended upon for an unusual effort on the strength of this confidence, whether they understand its purport or not. If he proves to be brave and cool in battle, his men forget all minor faults, which they would otherwise deem inexcusable weaknesses.

At one time one of our regiments had an officer assigned to it who was such a martinet about military minutiæ as to render him very unpopular; he was dubbed by his men "Old Fuss"! During the first fight into which he went with the regiment he preserved all his characteristics. Unmindful of showers of bullets he aligned his men with as much precision as if on dress parade. After that fight the boys of the regiment loved him enough "to eat him up." "I tell you," said one of them, "he's the bulliest old fighting cock you ever saw! He got us out there in the fight, gave orders to 'right dress!' when a thundering old nail keg of a shell ploughed the dirt up and burst not a foot from our front. One of our men brought his head around with a jerk. That old bull-dog yelled out to him, 'Eyes right, there! you're always gaping at some little thing!' He's the stuff, he is! He didn't mind the bullets mor'n if they were huckleberries! I'm sorry we called him Old Fuss! You bet your bottom dollar he's fitin' breed!"

Such officers, when once known by their men, can do anything with them. During the war much was said about the demoralization of regiments. The demoralization usually began among officers before it got to the men.

Men who fight don't like to salute or pay respect to fine dandy officers who remain in the rear during a battle. The Third Army Corps (one of the finest in the field) after the Chancellorsville fight was reported by the Inspecting General as demoralized and therefore received no furloughs. This report was in consequence of the contempt felt by many of them for those they termed "well-dressed cowards," and their failure to salute them according to the tactics.

"It makes me mad," said one of the bravest of these veterans, "to have them dressed-up gingerbread soldiers who never see a battle come riding around criticising fellers who've just come out of a big fight! Hang me, if one of them fools didn't give me jaw because my musket was battered with bullets! It's 'nuf to make a hoss sick!"

The fighting men despised those showy officers who were full of war during the intervals of peace and parade, but absent when actual fighting was on hand. Officers who were never seen during a fight were often very particular and fussy with their men after one. If their cartridge-boxes were empty they were censured, while to those whose cartridge-boxes were full they said, "You coward, you didn't fire a shot!" Such officers had demoralized regiments. They inspired only contempt.

The active infantry force of our army was reduced in June to eighty thousand men by the causes before mentioned. As summer advanced our camps were decorated with green shrubs and young trees for the purpose of shade, and presented a real gala-day appearance. Drill, baseball, glee clubs, besides the inevitable and never forgotten or omitted "bluff" occupied our time. Hancock was appointed to the command of the Second Corps, and was very popular.

The campaign of 1863 was about to open. We constantly carried three days' rations in our haversacks; were subject to rigorous inspections and drills, and were in consequence not unprepared for marching orders.

The adjutant came with the orders about one o'clock, June 15th, and in twenty minutes we had struck our tents, packed our knapsacks, and were on the march. The camps we left were blue with rejected overcoats and strewn with garments left behind. Men, women, children, negroes of the region, and whites began to gather them as if in a harvest field, when we left.

It was intensely hot. We marched to a point near Acquia Creek and halted; on the 16th to Wolf's Run Shoals, and next day to Sanger's Station. Arrived at Gainesville June 21st; marched through Thoroughfare Gap to Gum Springs, and camped here until June 23d.

The weather was suffocating, and in the temporary rests given us on the march we sometimes fixed bayonets, thrust them into the ground and hung upon the muskets our ponchos and blankets to shield us from the terrible heat.

Gum Spring, from which the place takes its name, was an ever-flowing spring of pure, cool water. An ancient, weather-beaten gum tree stood like a sentinel, with its dead branches extended protectingly over it. One of the citizens, an old man and very garrulous (about the Revolution and subjects which were safe to talk about from the distance of half a century), told me that the name was given by General Braddock, who bivouacked his army here while on the march to Fort Du-quesne. When I mentioned the present war, he looked far away, as if he had never heard of it and was living in another century.

We crossed Edwards Ferry June 26th, and the next day marched through Poolesville, Maryland, and halted at Barnesville.

Not one general in fifty knows how to march troops prop-

Cooking under Difficulties.

erly, so as to make them cover long distances in a short time without needless fatigue. Officers, unencumbered with baggage, with good horses and well-filled flasks, thoughtlessly marched men to death. The reason of this was not so much in the distance covered in a day as in marching without frequent halts. A general who understands how to move troops properly, halts them often, and by this method makes long distances, and yet brings his men in comparatively fresh.

I have several times, in this narrative, spoken of little Day. He was not a handsome boy, but as brave a patriot as ever fired a gun. His face was bronzed by long campaigning, but he was hollow-cheeked, and his eyes, dark and expressive, seemed the largest part of his face. Joe said there didn't seem to be much to him but his pluck, yet he had never reported sick, and was in every fight with his regiment. He had been slightly wounded twice in battle, but had told me that he was hoping to come out of the service rugged and strong and afterward to complete his education. "Then," said he, "I shall be proud of having fought through this war." The marching, since leaving camp, had been very hard, and our brigade had been marched in such a manner as needlessly to exhaust the men. One night, after one of our long marches, Joe came to me and said: "Little Day is kind of petered out! I guess you'd better come and see him!"

I roused myself from a sleep and went. Little Day clasped my hand and said, "I knew you would come!"

"What's the matter?" I inquired.

"I'm all marched out!" was the reply.

"Don't lose your courage," said I, "and you'll come up all right!"

"I never have lost my courage, but there is no more march in me!"

He was completely exhausted, and there was no more endurance in him. There is little you can do for a sick man on the march except to give him sympathy, so I stayed by him during the night. When I awoke it was broad daylight. Little Day lay with his eyes wide open, looking wistfully as if he would make a request. "What is it? Is there anything I can do for you?" I inquired.

"Yes, turn me over so I can see the sun rise!" he faintly whispered.

When I returned from roll call, rough, stalwart Joe, with tears on his cheek, touched my arm and softly said, "Little Day is dead!"

He had fallen asleep to wake, I trust, to a more glorious sunrise than this. The verdict of the boys, as they crossed his thin hands over his breast and closed his mournful eyes in their last sleep was: "Marched to death!"

Long marches without judicious intervals of rest are a potent cause of so-called straggling. Thus poor officers, not inclination, often made stragglers of brave, true men.

On the 28th we marched through Liberty to Uniontown, and were once more among God's people, as the boys not irreverently termed the Marylanders, — schoolhouses, neatly dressed children and women, children who smiled, and courteous men who intelligently answered our questions ; — they knew how many miles it was to any point, and answered you when asked. We halted under shady trees growing by the roadside ; broad, cultivated fields stretched out on every hand, and flowers grew around the houses. The Marylanders were almost as much disgusted with rebels as any one at that time, and much preferred " Greenbacks " to Confederate money.

There was a certain hospitality and openhanded liberality among these Marylanders which presented a pleasing contrast to the Pennsylvania Dutch farmers whom we subsequently met. We found the grist-mills

Death of Little Day.

grinding grain on Sunday, as all their flour had been baked to make bread for the Union soldiers.

"Well!" said Joe, "aint I glad to get out of the wilderness?" as he threw himself down before our stacked arms at Uniontown ; "but they make everything awful hot down here, water and weather." "Yes!" said Wad Rider, remembering Antietam, "and the fighting, too!"

We heard vague rumors of the doings of the rebels ahead ; of requisitions they made upon towns ; and when we got into Pennsylvania the people told us, with absolute horror depicted in their faces, of hearing that the rebels were buying everything they fancied and paying in Confederate money.

"One of my neighbors over there," said a Marylander to me, "was as big a rebel as I ever saw. He preached it and sung it until the rebel cavalry came along here and bought out his horned cattle, horses, potatoes, and general truck, and paid him in Confederate money; then he sung a new tune. He's been cursing them ever since. He sits up nights to swear about them. Nothing like that to bring a man round right good, stranger!" And the Marylander haw-hawed!

As we marched over the borders of Pennsylvania the region grew more and more fertile. Nature seemed to smile on every side. The only mean product of this fruitful country was the Dutch farmers — selfish, greedy, and unpatriotic.

One of them on the border, near Taneytown, was whining and saying fierce things about Yankees because one of our men had taken a few ears of his corn. "What would your corn be worth," said I, "if Union soldiers did not protect your State from the rebels?" With a stolid look, and with as little patriotic glow in his face as one of his pumpkins, he replied : "If der rebs pays for vat dey has in goot moneys I have dem here as soon as Yankees!"

"Well, I guess," said an officer who overheard the conversation, "we'd better leave, and let such fellows as this do their own fighting!"

"I pays mine taxes and you fights for mine land!" said one of them, as if he had settled the national debt.

"Why don't you shoulder your gun and come and help fight?" said one of my comrades to him. "I tells you some tings," was his reply; "I gets hit and gets killed, who takes care of der childers and mine vife?" This language expressed that prudence which many a man felt during the rebellion, but lacked the patriotic glow of the men of New England, of New York, and the West. The grasping selfishness evinced by these men to the defenders of their soil, at a time the rebels were overrunning it, I have not yet forgotten.

Many of them were "Copperheads" of the worst stripe, and Wad Rider said they believed "Stonewall Jackson" to be the veritable "Sheneral Shackson" for whom they had been regularly voting during the last half-century.

As we marched from Taneytown over the broad, well-kept roads towards Uniontown and Gettysburg, July 1st, we could hear in the distance the sound of artillery, which showed that our advance had encountered the enemy. Squads of prisoners now and then passed us, and the usual exchange of compliments, "How are you, Johnny Reb?" "How are you, Blue Bellies?" were received and given. Citizens in farm wagons and hay carts, piled with furniture, bedclothes, and children, accompanied by horses, cattle, and hogs, not alone on four feet either, passed us *en route* to the rear. A few of them, mostly women, manifested some patriotism, and said: "Drive out the rebels; we don't care if you do destroy our houses!"

An officer belonging to a Pennsylvania regiment said: "These Dutch farmers care for nothing but their hogs and cabbages." Even after the fight they took money for bandages used for the wounded, charged a dollar for a loaf of bread, or a quart of milk, even set a price on water, and asked exorbitant prices for carrying wounded men to the railroad depot in their hay carts.

Then came news from the front that a battle was being fought at a place a few miles distant called Gettysburg. The incidents of hard marching were forgotten as every man recognized that at last there was to be a death struggle for our homes and land.

The transfer of the command of the army from Hooker to Meade (then almost unknown) was not a popular one to most of the army. We believed it unwise to swap horses while crossing a river. This dissatisfaction was immediately counteracted, by a general circulation of the report that McClellan was about to take command. This bogus news was publicly proclaimed, and at that potent name men worn out with marching rallied, cheered, and joined again in the march. General orders were read from the head of some of the brigades, particularly those of the Fifth Corps, to the effect that McClellan had been reinstated in command of the army, and was already upon the field. No one that has written a description of the battle of Gettysburg has as yet mentioned the fact that McClellan's name, and not Meade's, was freely used to inspire the soldiers.

Thus McClellan's reputation and name helped to win that victory, though without this the soldiers would have done their best. The feeling was intense that we must win this battle or our country was ruined. Said Joe, who had been promoted to be corporal and felt

his stripes, "We've got ter lick them blasted rebs, boys; I say it as
an officer, this time or never. If they git us whar the hair is short
this nip, it is all up with us. They'll be cutting up like mad down in
Boston, and call the roll of their niggers at Bunker Hill and Beverly."
(This last was Joe's native town.) It very well expressed the feeling
most of us had, but we roared at Joe's speech just the same.

The Pennsylvania regiments in our brigade were full of fight.
"Mad all through!" as Wad Rider said. They talked of the rebels
devastating their State, and Joe said sympathetically, "It's tew
darned bad!"

"No worse," said Hartshorn, who liked to set Joe going, "than
for us to devastate Virginia. I don't feel very bad about the rebs
skinning these Dutchmen!"

"It's dog eat hog!" chimed in Wad.

"There isn't the leastest resemblance," said Joe wrathfully;
"them all-fired cusses in Virginny ain't got anything ter devastate.
I wouldn't give my dad's shoat for every hog in the State. It's a
darned pooty country where all the farming land is growed up with
brushwood!"

"Now just look at this country!" said Joe, spreading out both
hands oratorically.

It was truly a beautiful and fruitful one; a delight to the eye, —
broad, cultivated fields, overflowing granaries, fat cattle, neat houses;
such a contrast to that country which Joe declared, with a show of
justice, was not worth devastating! In Maryland the people gave
food; here in Pennsylvania the greed and avidity with which the
people took pay for everything was a contrast.

Near Gettysburg we met a Dutchman running away who had his
pockets and hat full of Confederate money. "Vil der United States
takes dis and gives me goot moneys?" asked the Dutchman. We
assured him it would not bring its weight in cord wood.

"Der rebs dey takes mine horse and cow and potatoes and says
we pays you well, and gifs me dis. If der govment at Vashington
don't gives me goot moneys for dis, mine Gott, I'm ruined!" blubbered the Dutchman.

"Buy Copperhead votes with it," said Wad suggestively, as we
marched by him.

We bivouacked during the first part of the night on the Taneytown road, and then, the night being moonlight, we were marched to Cemetery Ridge, where we arrived at about seven o'clock, on the morning of July 2d, and looked down upon the smiling valley. Herds of cattle were grazing, flocks of tame pigeons hovering about their cotes, hens clucking with their chickens around the comfortable farm-houses, and all had an air of serene peace as we were drawn up in line and came to an "Order arms!" with the quiet town of Gettys-burg at our feet. The prelude to the grand battle had been fought the day before.

Leaving individual experiences, let us return to the Rappahannock and trace some of the principal features of grand manœuvre which precede every fight, and which are often as interesting and important as the battle itself.

CHAPTER XVIII.

THE success of the Confederate army in defeating Burnside and Hooker had determined the political leaders at Richmond to adopt a more aggressive policy. By carrying the war into the North, one victory like Chancellorsville, they believed, would enable them to finish it by dictating terms of peace on Northern soil. There was much in the situation to justify this belief. A large party in the North was obstructing the prosecution of the war. Increased taxation, the suspension of the writ of Habeas Corpus, the mistakes of the administration at Washington, had created discontent in the large cities. A faction of Copperheads were anxious to make common cause with those who were fighting the Union armies, when they could safely do so.

An invasion of the free States would relieve the South from a grievous burden; and, if successful, transfer the support of the invading army to its enemies.

A victory gained on Northern soil would be more decisive in its results than any hitherto fought. The capture of Baltimore or Philadelphia would almost cut in twain the Northern States, isolate the capital and lead to its abandonment by the government. Recognition by England or France or both, would possibly follow.

The Confederate army, with an almost unbroken record of victories, was anxious to be let loose on Northern soil. Its undevastated territory would support and compensate them for toils and hardships hitherto unrequited.

The bold offensive in war is often the best defensive policy. It was by not allowing themselves to be reduced to a simple defensive attitude, that Frederick the Great and Napoleon I. had both made head against overwhelming combinations. Hence as a measure of defence the invasion was dictated by sound military precedents.

The Commissary General at Richmond, at this time, it is said, answered Lee's requisition for rations by endorsing upon it, "If the general wants provisions let him go and look for them in Pennsylvania." And thus was echoed the universal demand of the South, that the theatre of war should be transferred to the soil of the free States.

In answer to this, and to strike a decisive blow against the seemingly tottering fabric of the Union, Lee set his army in motion. His first manœuvre was with the purpose of disengaging Hooker from the Rappahannock. The corps of A. P. Hill was left to occupy that line, while on June 3d, 4th, and 5th the largest portion of his force was concentrated at Culpeper.

Hooker, observing that some movement was taking place, sent forward a cavalry force to attack Stuart, who, he was aware, had been for some time concentrating his force at Culpeper. The engagement which followed revealed the presence of Lee's infantry, while captured correspondence disclosed his design of invasion.

Hooker on the 11th threw forward his right to Rappahannock Station and Beverly Ford to meet this menace. It was expected that Lee's line of march would follow the course previously adopted against Pope. Instead of this Lee had, by a rapid march of seventy miles in three days, thrown his left into the valley of the Shenandoah; Hill was at Fredericksburg, Longstreet at Culpeper, Ewell rapidly advancing toward Winchester.

Lee's army was thus divided into three parts, separated from each other by a distance of thirty-five miles on one side and sixty-six on the other, and stretched out over a hundred miles. In this daring situation Hooker planned to interpose a large force between Hill's corps and Longstreet, and overwhelm the former before Longstreet could come to his support. This bold and eminently proper move would naturally result in destroying Hill, or, if not successful in that, in recalling Lee from his designs of invasion.

Before this movement was developed, Hooker asked authority for the execution of such a plan and was denied. President Lincoln voiced the objections of Halleck in this quaint and striking allegory: "I would not take the risk of being entangled upon the river like an ox impaled upon a fence and liable to be torn by dogs in front and rear without a fair chance to gore one way or kick the other!"

Thus Hooker's hands were tied by Halleck's interference, at the very inception of the campaign, and the surest way of recalling Lee from his design of invasion rejected. Instead of treading upon the tail of the Confederate serpent, stretched out a hundred miles along the Potomac, to make him turn his head in defence, Halleck proposed that the Union army follow in its wake, and at the same time cover Washington.

No one could guess the direction Lee might take, and the impossibility of doing both will be seen by any military novice. Hooker had thus no alternative but to modify his action. He wisely asked, however, that all the troops available for the defence of the free States be placed under his command. This was denied, and the country in the midst of her peril witnessed the spectacle of wise measures defeated by those who should have been their chief supporters.

The forces under Milroy at Winchester, and Tyler at Harper's Ferry, occupied posts of no strategic value. The enemy could pass around these into Maryland, as had already been demonstrated. Halleck refused to be taught by the disaster of Miles, or the defeat of Fremont. When, on the 13th, the unlucky Milroy found himself threatened by a Confederate force, he naturally concluded it was simply a raiding expedition of the enemy. How should he imagine it possible that he was confronted by a portion of Lee's army, outnumbering him three to one, without Halleck having been informed and notifying him? Yet Milroy has been blamed on the one hand for the feeble defence he made, and on the other for not retreating before he did.

It was not until he was actually engaged that he learned, by prisoners captured, that he was confronted by a corps of Lee's army. On the night of the 14th he retreated, and succeeded by accident in saving a portion of his command. His loss by this mismanagement (to be credited to Halleck rather than Milroy) was not far from four thousand men out of nearly seven thousand, with twenty-three pieces of artillery.

Hooker was left no choice but to manœuvre so as to cover Harper's Ferry and Washington. He had to guess at Lee's movements and wait for them to be developed, meanwhile managing so as not to be taken in the rear or allow himself to be drawn too far from Washington, where Lee could concentrate his entire force to attack him.

Hill and Longstreet moved forward and relieved Ewell in the Valley, who, preceded by Jenkins's cavalry one week previous, on the 24th, passed into Maryland. Jenkins had already penetrated as far as Chambersburg, throwing the country into a turmoil of excitement and consternation. The roads leading to the Susquehanna were crowded with vehicles, people and cattle, fleeing before this prelude to invasion.

On the 24th and 25th Longstreet and Hill crossed the borders into Maryland. Hooker speedily followed, and on the 27th his army was admirably concentrated at the foot of South Mountain, in much the same position it occupied before the battle of Antietam. Lee was meanwhile in ignorance of Hooker's movements. Pleasanton had succeeded in masking the movements of the Federal army by driving Stuart beyond the Blue Ridge.

It is thought that the chagrin produced by this repulse led Stuart, directly afterwards, to make a circuit of the Union army by passing between it and Washington, from which raid he did not arrive in season to be of service to Lee at Gettysburg. Lee was thus deprived of the eyes of his army at the most critical period of the campaign. It proved one of the weights which finally turned the scales of victory against Lee in the battle which followed.

Hooker was admirably posted to march to the defence of Washington, or strike a blow at Lee's communications, and was anxious to gather the forces needful for the movement.

Heintzelman and Schenck had ostensibly been put under his orders. One was in command of the defences of Washington, now covered by the Union army, the other of the forces at Harper's Ferry. When, however, he attempted to use two thousand of the former command to hold the passes of South Mountain, Heintzelman refused to obey, as the service was outside of his department. Hooker had ordered the temporary abandonment of Harper's Ferry that he might add its twelve thousand men to a column under Slocum, for operating on the rear of the enemy. He hoped thus to compel Lee to return from the invasion, or to capture his ammunition trains and bridges.

He was met by Halleck at once with the objection that Harper's Ferry had always been regarded as an important point, and much expense and labor incurred in fortifying it. Thus Hooker's power over the troops placed under his command proved a delusive myth rather than a reality.

In vain Hooker urged that Harper's Ferry did not defend anything, and that the earthworks remained after the troops were withdrawn; that the public property could be secured and the troops marched to points where they could be of service. Like Nero, fiddling when Rome was burning, Halleck quibbled and obstructed while the destinies of his country were imperilled by his inaction.

These objections may have been made to compel Hooker's resignation, or they may have been the result of stupidity. They were, in any case, ill-timed. Hooker saw that Halleck's enmity was perilling the national interests, and patriotically resigned rather than prove an obstacle to its success.

Hooker has been blamed for resigning at this critical period, but obstructed in his action on every side by Halleck's interference, he preferred to sacrifice his own military career rather than the interests of his country.

Halleck, on the other hand, seemed determined that the army should fail rather than succeed with Hooker in command. It is shown that Halleck's objections were made for the purpose of obstruction, as he allowed Meade to do the very things to which he objected with Hooker. Hooker resigned because he recognized, with Napoleon, that one poor general was better than two good ones. Let it always be remembered of Hooker that he sacrificed his own career in the interests of his country, and that he was unwilling the personal animosities, of which he was the victim, should again compromise the army. It was the bravest act of his life.

Though Hooker's judgment was apt to become clouded and muddled during the turmoil and confusion of action, he had shown the highest conception of what was proper to be done in all the preliminary movements which he proposed or acted on, preceding the battle of Gettysburg. Though he is not to be judged by what he did or did not do, tied down and hampered as he was by the malice and the meddling of Halleck, yet he had shown great qualities as a commander.

Meade was appointed to the command and all the power withheld from Hooker quickly placed in his hands. The wisdom of Hooker's design in operating on Lee's communications is shown, in that it was this very menace which led Lee to turn back to Gettysburg from his forward march. Hooker's manner of handling his troops from the beginning of the campaign was deserving of the highest praise.

Meade, who was appointed to succeed him, was an officer who had so far filled every position he had held with steadfast bravery and cool ability. If he had not the dash of Hooker, he was eminently safe and cautious. He rejected the project of operating on Lee's rear, retained Butterfield as his chief of staff, and concentrated his forces in such a manner as to enable him to fall back on the line of Pipe Creek, and fight a defensive battle upon ground of his own choosing.

CHAPTER XIX.

THE Union army was moving forward to occupy Emmetsburg, Hanover, and Gettysburg, with no other purpose than to mask the concentration of troops proposed by Meade along the left bank of Pipe Creek. Buford's cavalry, on our left flank, was thrown out as a feeler over the route by which it was supposed the Confederates were advancing.

Meanwhile the threat on Lee's rear had, on the morning of the 29th, caused him to recall his columns from Harrisburg.

Gettysburg was Lee's natural point of concentration. It was the first point eastward that enabled him to control direct lines of retreat south, and was the centre of all the roads traversing that part of the country. The roads radiate from this point much like spokes from the hub of a wheel.

Lee did not know, meanwhile, that Meade was moving to intercept the road from Chambersburg to York. Thus we find the two armies approaching each other by chance, like men groping in the darkness. It was a gigantic game of blind man's buff. Buford, however, by information gathered from prisoners, and other indications, quickly saw that the enemy were about to concentrate at Gettysburg. He said to General Devin, in command of one of his brigades, "The enemy will attack us in the morning, and we shall have to fight like devils to maintain ourselves until the arrival of the infantry." Thus anticipating, he ambushed his cavalry on Willoughby Creek, which runs south, about a mile west of the town.

Here he awaited their approach. About nine o'clock in the morning, preceded by a close line of skirmishers, the Confederate columns descended the slopes of Willoughby Run. A fierce encounter at once took place along the banks of this stream. Buford, meanwhile, anxiously considered whether he would be able to hold

the outnumbering enemy in check until the arrival of the infantry.
At last the signal officer on the belfry of the Lutheran Seminary,
between him and the town, signalled the approach of the First Corps.
He hastened to the belfry to corroborate, with his own eyes, this joyful
intelligence. He had no sooner reached the belfry than he heard the
voice of Reynolds
calling to him be-
low. That officer
had ardently hur-
ried forward in
advance of his
corps.

Buford went
down the stairs
from the Seminary
on the run, ex-
claiming, as he
approached his
superior, "The
devil's to pay, but
we can hold on till
the First Corps
gets up!" It was
about ten o'clock
in the morning.
Reynolds ex-
changed a few
words with Buford,
went to the belfry,
at a glance under-
stood the situation,

Reynolds and Buford in the Belfry of the Lutheran Seminary.

and sent messages to hurry up his command, and to hasten Howard,
who was at Emmetsburg with the Eleventh Corps. Through a shower
of bullets the two officers then rode forward to encourage the men
and direct the fight. At a little past ten two brigades of Reynolds's
corps arrived. They were Cutler's brigade, and the "Iron Brigade"
under Meredith.

The Confederate soldiers, who had not anticipated encountering anything more than militia at this point, recognized the distinguishing black hats of the Iron brigade, and were heard to exclaim, "There are them d—d black-hatted fellers again! Tain't no militia; it's the Army of the Potomac."

The two brigades went into action on the right and left of the Chambersburg road. While they were deploying into position they were savagely attacked. The Fifty-sixth Pennsylvania Regiment delivered the first infantry fire at this battle of invasion, on the soil of the free States, July 1st.

A small triangular piece of woods, its base resting upon Willoughby Run,

Buford's Cavalry at Willoughby Run.

lay along the western slope of Seminary Ridge. This was known as McPherson's woods. If the enemy could possess it they would gain a foothold in the centre of the Union lines. If, on the contrary, it was held by the Federals, it stood like a projecting bastion from which a flanking fire might be delivered upon all forces approaching the lines extending from it, north and south. While the men were going in at this point General Doubleday urged them to hold the woods at all hazards. Full of patriotic fervor, as they filed by him,

Death of General Reynolds.   Page 191.

they proudly answered, "*If we can't hold it, where will you find men who can?*"

General Archer, of the Confederates, had crossed the stream south of the Chambersburg road, while a brigade, under Davis, was advancing on the north side. Archer was rushing his men into the woods described, in order to reach, under its cover, the slopes of Seminary Ridge, between him and the town. On the Cashtown road, Reynolds in person was leading his men to a point in this wood where the Confederate skirmishers lay hid in the brushwood. While thus encouraging and directing them, turning occasionally to see if reinforcements were in sight, not sixty paces from these ambushed Confederates, he was struck by a bullet, which passed through the back of his head and came out at the eye. He fell without a word, dead, in this first encounter with the enemy, on the soil of his native State. He was forty-three years of age, and was regarded by his associates as the most remarkable man of the army, and one destined, had he lived, to the greatest measure of fame. His quick eye and cool military judgment had, no doubt, comprehended the advantage of Cemetery Ridge as a defensive position from which to arrest the invasion.

One of Reynolds's aides has asserted that in his instructions to Howard he had designated Cemetery Hill as the point to be occupied by him. This is plausible and probable, as, no doubt, he designated some point to which Howard should bring his troops, and that officer, like a good soldier, would naturally obey instructions.

Howard saw its defensive advantages, but it was Hancock who selected the position finally for a battle-field, for he was the only one authorized to so act.

Meredith's brigade had driven the enemy from McPherson's woods at the point of the bayonet, and captured Archer and most of his brigade. At the same time the right of our line had experienced a check. It was outflanked, and fell back to a ridge which connects Oak Hill with Seminary Ridge.[1]

---

[1] Even General Doubleday, who was not present on this wing, represents it as falling back to the village, by order of General Wadsworth. This statement is disproved by General Cutler's report, which General Doubleday does not seem to have read, and by members of the different regiments with whom the writer has corresponded. A comrade of the Seventy-sixth New York says, " Being there personally, of course I know there was no falling back except a few rods to the ridge, first to the woods and then back of them. We changed front four times that day."

As but scanty justice has hitherto been done to these brave men, it seems proper here to digress and to chronicle somewhat more in detail their part in the action, where every man was a hero. The Ninety-fifth New York and the Fourteenth Brooklyn having been despatched to the left by General Reynolds, the right wing was composed of three skeleton regiments, the One Hundred and Forty-seventh and the Seventy-sixth New York, and the Fifty-sixth Pennsylvania, whose entire force at the beginning of the fight aggregated only 957 men.

This small force, formed in a single line, soon found itself engaged with vastly superior numbers, advancing at short range, in double line in front and on its right flank.

In thirty minutes the One Hundred and Forty-seventh New York Regiment lost 207 out of 380 of its men. While under this fierce and murderous fire, the Seventy-sixth New York, in the same time, lost eighteen officers (two-thirds of their entire number, nine only being left), while 151 enlisted men had fallen. This regiment was commanded by a captain, while some of the companies were commanded by privates. The color-bearer of the regiment fell, but still thinking of his charge, cried out, "I'm done for, boys, take care of the flag!"

On the right of the Seventy-sixth was the brave Sergeant Hubbard, who commanded the Provost Guard of eighteen men. In the same time his eighteen men were reduced to six, who fought until the battle closed.

The loss of the Fifty-sixth Pennsylvania was proportionally about the same. Here these devoted men stood, unwaveringly closing up their bleeding ranks, and fighting as only veterans can fight, until ordered to fall back, then retreated a few rods to a wooded ridge, and then back of the woods.

Even then the One Hundred and Forty-seventh, not receiving the order on account of the fall of its commander, remained almost surrounded by the enemy.

Here the Sixth Wisconsin rushed from the Seminary to the front, overtook the Fourteenth Brooklyn and the Ninety-fifth New York, and with a battery drove the enemy into the railroad cut, captured almost all of Davis's rebel brigade with their colors, and rescued the One Hundred and Forty-seventh New York from the terrible fire under which it had been melting away.[1] The color-bearer of the One Hundred and Forty-seventh had fallen, but the colors were caught up by Sergeant Wyburn, who brought them from the front, and exclaiming, "We've saved the flag!" fell with them to the ground.

It is noteworthy to say that these regiments, though reduced by the loss of half their number, moved back again to their old position. Here they discovered the enemy putting a battery in position on their right flank, and moving forward a large body of troops, when General Cutler, leaving the Fourteenth Brooklyn and the Sixth Wisconsin to support his battery, changed front to the right with these regiments, and fought until two o'clock, with no support on either their right or left flank.

Immediately after this, finding a column of the enemy moving on the Second Division, the brigade pushed through the woods, came in on its flank and opened so hot a fire that a regiment of the enemy surrendered. Finding the enemy too close to its left flank, the brigade again changed front, and took position on the left of Robinson's brigade (which had arrived while the fight was progressing) where it remained until it was out of ammunition.

Afterwards, when the Eleventh Corps was retreating in disorder and rout through the town, these regiments, with the Fourteenth Brooklyn, exposed to a fire on both flanks, assisted in repelling a charge of the enemy, then getting the order to retreat, steadily and without excitement, exposed to the enemy's fire on both flanks, acted as the rear-guard. Their steady conduct brought the enemy to a halt.

"That this," says a comrade present in the fight, "was no pleasure excursion is shown by the fact that General Cutler had a horse killed on the railroad embankment, and another wounded while passing through the town." It was to the steadiness of these men, who had fought with such undaunted bravery, that a panic and a rout were

---

[1] The large number of killed and wounded had almost destroyed the Seventy-sixth and One Hundred and Forty-seventh New York and the Fifty-fourth Pennsylvania, and many men had been sent to take the wounded back to the village, and then joined the line in the grove. This hegira of wounded and their assistants may have given rise to the rumor that the brigade had fallen back. In the afternoon, when out of ammunition and temporarily relieved, they fell back under the hill. That is the farthest back they were until the final retreat at night, when what there was left acted as a rear-guard.

prevented in the retreat. There is no brighter instance of personal heroism, or the bravery of private soldiers known, than is found in the history of this one brigade on the first day of Gettysburg. It might well be the foundation of an epic, and a simple statement of its heroism reads like a prose poem.

General Abner Doubleday, on whom the command of the First Corps devolved after the fall of Reynolds, was an officer of great ability and firmness, as marked by his management of that corps that day. But Howard had, meanwhile, arrived at Gettysburg, and from the Seminary belfry saw the First Corps struggling with the enemy. Without making his presence known to Doubleday, or consulting him, he sent a message to Meade, saying that the First Corps had fled at the first contact with the enemy. This was unworthy of Howard. It would have been more becoming to one in his position to have first ascertained the facts. It was a great injustice to the four weak but heroic brigades of the First Corps, confronting six large Confederate brigades, and grandly struggling with outnumbering foes.

About eleven o'clock the rest of the Eleventh Corps came up. The enemy had meanwhile seized all the commanding heights west, and crowned them with artillery. The Chambersburg road was the centre of the enemy's line. Doubleday desired to hold this road. The enemy were advancing on both sides of it. Artillery was formed behind a crest, firing over it into the advancing lines. Colonel Roy Stone, with the Pennsylvania Bucktails, went into the fight on the left of this pike. Deeming it an important position to be held, they exclaimed, "We've come to stay!" General Doubleday expressively says, "The greater portion did stay!" They never left the ground alive. At eleven o'clock Schurtz entered Gettysburg with his division. To him Howard had turned over the command of the Eleventh Corps.

Other forces were, meanwhile, advancing to take part in the fight on the rebel side. The divisions of Rhodes and Ewell were coming north of Gettysburg, on the roads from Carlisle and York. Rhodes, unperceived, was about to seize Oak Hill, northwest from the town, a position which menaced the right of the Union line.

Howard stretched out the Eleventh Corps north of Gettysburg, and sent word to Doubleday to hold his position, as the Eleventh

Corps could repulse all attacks of the enemy on the right. It was easier said than done. A gap of a quarter of a mile had been left between the Eleventh and First Corps, by Howard's faulty arrangement of troops. Doubleday was obliged to weaken his already weak line to fill this gap.

The enemy, advancing north of the town, seized Oak Hill, and the first intimation Doubleday had of the fact was an enfilading artillery fire on his lines from this direction. Schimmelfennig's skirmishers, moving in that direction to take position here, encountered the enemy in possession. Ewell's whole division struck the Union right.

It was half-past two o'clock, and Howard found the enemy swarming on the right. He did not venture to attack. Schurtz pushed his force out where it was taken in flank by Oak Hill, and exposed to attacks on the right from the Harrisburg road.

At half-past two the Confederates attacked all of Doubleday's positions, while the enemy were about to penetrate between him and the Eleventh Corps. To meet this threat Doubleday sent two brigades to prolong his line on Cutler's right. The Confederates hurled a brigade against their flank. Behind the stone wall our men skilfully changed front, and repulsed the enemy. Meredith, meanwhile, with Biddle on his left, tenaciously held McPherson's woods. The Union line on our right was meanwhile extended, making a wide curve north and west of the town, in the vain attempt to cover and hold all the approaches thereto.

A long line is a weak one, and it is the general opinion of military critics that Howard's mistake was in trying to hold a line so thinly drawn out, instead of massing a heavy force of the Eleventh Corps on the right of the line already engaged. In this way he could have commanded the plain north of the town.

Oak Hill commanded the right of the field, and when, at three o'clock, the general advance of the rebel lines took place, Rhodes broke through the right of the First, and left of the Eleventh, Corps, entered the breach and disrupted the entire line.

It was not until the Eleventh Corps was in disorderly flight, and the enemy was closing upon the west, north, and south, that the order came for retreat. This order, if it came to the Eleventh Corps at that time, must have seemed ironical. Howard, urged by Doubleday to order his retreat, or to send him reinforcements, left the First

Corps to struggle against overwhelming numbers. The unfortunate Eleventh Corps was routed, while the First Corps was bravely maintaining itself in the position it had so tenaciously defended.

At the risk of sacrificing Doubleday and the magnificent First Corps, he did not for some reason issue the necessary command. When at last an officer was sent with the order, he lost his way and did not reach the commander of the First Corps. Fortunately, Doubleday understood his peril, recalled Meredith and Stone to Seminary Ridge, and with this excellent support, gathered up his force and retired amid the confused masses of the Eleventh Corps, in comparatively good order, but leaving, as we have seen, two-thirds of his numbers in dead and wounded on the field.

It seems to the writer that the fighting and management of the First Corps was beyond praise.

As the First Corps retreated through the town, it encountered the flying fragments of the Eleventh, while pale, frightened women came out from their houses and implored them not to desert them. As the screaming Confederates came in by the roads at the north and west of the town, they encountered the rear-guard of this corps and the rabble of the Eleventh, and according to Lee's report, took five thousand prisoners! The only semblance of order preserved was by the First Corps, who leisurely marched from the town to Cemetery Hill, where Howard had thoughtfully left a reserve of Steinwehr's two brigades. This officer had made good use of his time and men, by constructing earthworks behind which he had posted artillery to afford a last rallying point to those fighting in front.

It was not far from four o'clock when the defeated Federals were climbing Cemetery Hill. At this critical moment, General Hancock arrived on the ground. He had been sent forward by Meade to take command of the field. His clear head, zeal, and magnetic presence, put a new soul into the fragments of the Federal army. He soon restored confidence, and made such a disposition of the forces at his command as to impress the enemy with the belief that a large force confronted them on the heights.

Hancock saw at once the advantages of the ground. He pointed out to Doubleday the position he was to occupy at the foot of the Emmetsburg road ; detached Wadsworth from the First Corps and placed him on Culp's Hill, and at five o'clock order had succeeded chaos in the Union lines. They had, however, been an hour in forming under the eye of the victorious Confederates. Why was it that the Confederates, usually so prompt, did not attack while the Federals, just repulsed, were in confusion? Various reasons have been assigned. One of them is that the Confederate commander believed a much larger force was confronting him on the hills opposite than there really was, and did not wish to attack until his entire force came up.

This is a popular reason and one flattering to the Federals, but the author believes the real reason to be behind this. When a cat is amused with a mouse she will not abandon it for a string. The Confederate cat could not be induced to leave the mouse she had just seized. In other words, the Confederate soldiers were amusing themselves with the town. They were scattered through the village, pillaging its houses, buying out its stores and people with Confederate money at their own price, and could not be induced to leave this amusement in sufficient numbers to attend to the less interesting affairs of Cemetery Ridge. We believe this is the reason why the Confederates did not follow up their advantage. It was not every day the cat caught such a mouse! Sheridan owed his victory in part to the same cause, when our army was overwhelmed in the morning, and defeated the enemy in the afternoon. On such small circumstances in war often rests the fate of empires and the reputation of great soldiers.

Amusing scenes were occurring in Gettysburg. General Schimmelfennig was hidden under a wood-pile. Some of the Eleventh Corps were in the houses under feather-beds, while the rebel soldiers were racing through them from cellar to attic. The women remaining in town were doing their best to propitiate the rebel soldiers with the best they could give them of eatables and drinkables. The chivalrous Southerners had struck a bonanza, and were not in a hurry to leave it. They were feasting and rejoicing in a land of milk and honey. Here let us leave them while we return to Cemetery Hill where the bright moonlight glistens on the tombs and marble monuments of the cemetery.

CHAPTER XX.

THE early morning hours of July 2d were cloudy, and a heavy vapor overhung the valley. By ten o'clock the threatening clouds vanished and the green meadows were bathed in sunlight, with here and there the shadow of transient clouds flitting across the sunlit valley and hills. Cattle were grazing in the fields below; the shrill crowing of chanticleer was heard from neighboring farmyards; tame pigeons cooed on the hillside, and birds sang among the trees.

The crest, as far as the eye could see, glittered with burnished arms. On our right was the cemetery with its white monuments, among which shone the burnished brass pieces of artillery and the glittering bayonets of the infantry. Beyond this were seen the spires of the town, while farther to the left and rear was Culp's Hill. Running across our front, obliquely, was the Emmetsburg road, while farther beyond was Seminary Ridge, on which the enemy was posted. On our left, over a mile distant, rose the sugar-loaf summits of the Round Tops.

Our men were in their usual moods. To the observant eye there was perceptible beneath the mask of rough humor and careless indifference an undercurrent of anxiety and gloomy foreboding. The look of earnestness which gathers on soldiers' faces before a battle was, perhaps, now deepened by the thought that the impending battle was to be fought on our own soil, and of the consequences if we met defeat. This expression was no more obvious among the men of Pennsylvania regiments than those from other States. At no time had there been such intense feeling shown among all ranks as then. It showed itself in earnest glances and tones of voice.

The general feeling was well expressed by a sergeant of a Pennsylvania regiment, who said, "We've got to fight our best to-day or have these rebs for our masters!"

Long lines of skirmishers were stretched out on our centre and left, where in the green meadows the blue and gray confronted each other. Here and there along the line little puffs of smoke curling up and drifting away in thin blue vapor told that the skirmishers were firing upon each other. Occasionally a lightning-like glimmer on the opposite hills showed the reflection from the burnished arms of the enemy, who were moving into position. With a glass, the rebel soldiers, clad in butternut and gray, as well as the skirmish line in front, could be distinctly seen. The Confederate soldier wore a slouch hat, short jacket, and blanket strapped over his shoulder and under his arm. This light marching order, so invariably a characteristic of the Confederate, was one of the features of their army which made them so fleet of foot. Their poverty had its compensations, as all poverty has. As individuals, they had but little to lose and much to win.

A sarcastic Greek of olden times said of the Helots as soldiers, "They fight well because they had rather die than go back to their black bread!" The same might be appropriately said of the rebel soldier and his fare. Devotion to a cause and desire for better rations and Yankee plunder furnished a powerful motive to make them fight. A victory gave them Yankee boots, jack-knives, overcoats, and "Yankee fixin's."

Occasionally a shell would burst after hurrying over our heads from the opposite hills. At times the Confederate skirmishers would rush upon our lines with a yell, and then a shell from our batteries, in a curved line, would go spluttering and hoarsely whispering, like an absent-minded man talking to himself, and burst in a seeming exclamation of recognition on their front. In rushing thus upon our lines it was doubtless their intention to develop the position of our artillery.

Our prospects never looked darker than at the opening of this battle. Even the government, in whose defence this army was to pour out its best blood, seemed to have conspired against it.

The general commanding was untried in his position, having been appointed only three days previous. He had not been long enough in command to gather the reins of control into his hands, and could not, therefore, exercise that quickness of perception and readiness of decision so essential to success on the battle-field. On the other side, Lee had held command for thirteen eventful months, and, with victory upon victory, had won the supreme confidence and the enthusiastic devotion of his soldiers. He intimately knew the temper and composition of his battalions, and this knowledge and mutual confidence was in itself worth forty thousand men to him.

The Union army on these hills was the only barrier between them and the large cities of the North. This battle was to decide not only the future character of the war, but of the nation; whether the wave of invasion was to break upon this rocky barrier and recede across the border, or sweep unchecked over the fertile fields and rich cities of the North; whether we were to have an undivided country, vital with liberty in all its parts, or one broken into puny groups of States, warlike and despotic, fighting against each other.

The common soldier recognized dimly that this was the pivotal battle of the war, and hence every man's hand was nerved to do his best. The wonder is that with ninety thousand available men, inactive and useless, at different posts, one-half or two-thirds had not been summoned to this army to make the overthrow of the invaders certain instead of doubtful.

From the first this battle was an illustration of the superior directing power which men call Providence or Fate. The armies had met without design on the part of either of their commanders. If, on the 1st of July, the Union army had not been driven back, we should not have taken position on the line of heights which gave us so great an advantage. If, after a victory, we had fallen back on these lines, Lee would have stood on the defensive at Seminary Ridge, and Meade would have attacked and probably been defeated.

It has been asked why Lee fought the battle under so many disadvantages. The answer is that fate or circumstances compelled him. The temper of his army was such, and its confidence in its ability to defeat the Yankees at all times and under all circumstances so great, that Lee himself, with all his equipoise of character, caught something of this over-confidence. He felt obliged to fight a battle to preserve his communications, threatened by Slocum, to send the wounded and sick which encumbered his army into Virginia and to receive ammunition.

After the victory of the 1st of July he was inclined to attack rather than await attack. He was subsisting on the country and could feed his army only by scattering it, hence could not afford to delay. It was a necessity with him to deal the Army of the Potomac a decisive blow before his movement into the free States could be converted into a positive invasion. It has been thought that Lee should have manœuvred Meade out of his strong position. Had he done so the Union general would have fallen back behind Pipe Creek, or some position equally strong. Delays would constantly strengthen Meade, while they would complicate Lee's problem of feeding a concentrated army. It was not so easy a task as it has been assumed, to manœuvre Meade out of his position. In order to do so Lee must have menaced his base, and this involved the abandonment of Gettysburg and its advantageous converging roads, just won at the expense of a battle, and a flank movement on Westminster, southeast from Gettysburg. This movement, made in an open country, surrounded by numerous spies and a people unfriendly to his cause, would be revealed and perhaps defeated. Every consideration, therefore, impelled Lee to fight.

Meade by rapid marches quickly concentrated his army. The Sixth Corps was marched nearly a hundred miles in three days. During the entire forenoon of the 2d the armies confronted each other in comparative inaction. It was not until nearly four o'clock in the afternoon that the terrible uproar on our left proclaimed that the battle had begun. The Union army during the last part of the second day, and the last day, was formed on the line of heights extending from Culp's Hill to the Round Tops. As then posted the Union line resembled in form the letter **f**. The Confederate army was posted on Seminary Ridge, in our front, while its wings almost encircled ours. Their whole line was not unlike a huge letter **C**, which formed a line of over five miles in extent, with its right and left wings facing each other not three miles apart.

It will be seen at a glance that this concave line of the Confederates made communication between its different parts difficult. The convex line of the Union army made it easy to reinforce one part of the line from another. In this position Lee, having marked out the work to be done by his corps commanders, could do little but wait, without personal supervision, for results. At this time, when it was essential to his success to be able to mass men at some one point to break the Union lines, their form of line presented a great impediment to such concentration.

Lee's plan was for both wings of his army to assault the Union wings at the same time by a flank attack, while threats were kept up along the front to prevent reinforcements to either wing. The want of connection between the different parts of his army is shown by the fact that the attack on our left was over on the 2d before the attack on our right was begun. General Doubleday justly points out in this connection the fact that converging columns on a given point seldom succeed because of the difference in the temper and temperament of those who lead.

The two armies were about a mile apart. Ewell's Corps held the town and the Confederate left, Hill the centre, and Longstreet the right on Seminary Ridge. Meade's army occupied the position on the line of hills already described. At the opening of the battle, and during nearly the whole of the day, our left rested in part on the Emmetsburg road (which ran obliquely from the right of the rebel line to the right of the Union line) and then curved back to Round Top. The Twelfth Corps was on the extreme right and one division of the First Corps on Culp's Hill. The Eleventh Corps was at Cemetery Hill, facing the town. There were two divisions of the First Corps at Cemetery Hill, then the Second, Third, and Fifth Corps were ranged from north to south in the order named. The Sixth, which arrived late from its long march, was posted in rear of Round Top, near the Taneytown road, which runs nearly the whole length of this line of hills in our rear.

A word explanatory of our position on the left is necessary to a clear understanding of the position of our line at the opening of the battle. In the morning Geary had been withdrawn from Round Top to strengthen Culp's Hill, as Meade expected Lee would make his main attack on our right. By moonlight, in the early hours of morning, Lee had already marked out Round Top on our left as the position to be captured. This would enable him to enfilade the whole line on the heights beyond with artillery and take our line in reverse. The result, if successful, must have been disastrous to the Union army.

Upon the withdrawal of Geary, Meade had given orders for Sickles to take up the abandoned line. As Sickles did not know this position, and as no one had been left behind to designate it, he could only guess its locality. With the advice of General Hunt

he formed his right, under General Humphrey, along the Emmetsburg road, while his left, under Birney, made a right angle at the
peach-orchard, then curved back to Plum Run, covering the front
of little Round Top. This eminence, which was the real key of the
field, was about a mile in rear of the peach-orchard.

Under the misconception that our left
flank rested at the peach-orchard, Lee
had ordered this attack in order, as he
conceived, to take our line in reverse
and drive us up the Emmetsburg road
in confusion to Cemetery Hill. The
" Devil's Den" was a
sunken spot, filled with
irregular boulders, not far
from the front of Little

Fight in Devil's Den.

Round Top. The brigade of General Hobart Ward rested its flank
on this rocky den, its right extending beyond a triangular wheat-
field to a wooded ridge not far from the peach-orchard.

I have described the place thus minutely as it was by an attack on
Ward's brigade that the battle opened, although the skirmish lines at
the peach-orchard were actively engaged as early as nine o'clock.

With flags flying and with yells and shouts, just before four o'clock P.M., the rebels, under Law, advanced confidently on our long drawn out line under Ward, who fought from behind the rocks to resist the furious attacks made by superior numbers. The Sixth New Jersey, Fourth Maine, and Fortieth New York intrepidly resisted the attack. Hard pressed, at last, however, they lost ground and uncovered Little Round Top. In order to cover their retreat Ward stripped his right, while the Seventeenth Maine was covered by the wall in the wheat-field, near the woods, abandoned by Ward.

The Confederates, having finished Ward, climbed the hill, and took possession of three pieces of artillery.

To show how Little Round Top, which was about to fall into the hands of the Confederates, was saved to the Union army, it is necessary to go back to fifteen minutes before four o'clock, when General Warren, chief engineer of the army, the better to examine the line, had reached its summit.

In the woods between him and the Emmetsburg road he caught the reflected glitter of a long line of muskets flashing among the trees. It at once revealed to him that the enemy were advancing to seize this position, the importance of which he fully understood. He hastened to find troops to defend it. Barnes's division of the Fifth Corps was about advancing to support the now hard-pressed centre of Birney's line. On his own responsibility Warren detached Vincent's brigade and hurried it forward to Little Round Top. It took position on the lower southern projection of this hill.

Warren again sought his elevated position of observation and witnessed the attack on Ward's brigade. The Confederates were hastening on Little Round Top, while our sharp-shooters blazed away from behind the rocks at its western base to resist their advance. He could not see Vincent's men, who were below him, but he saw that this position was about to be lost. The shots of the enemy reached this elevated position, and the signal officer began rolling up his flags to leave. Warren instructed him to continue waving his flags, to disguise the fact that the hill was otherwise unoccupied, and hurried once more to save it.

The first regiment he encountered was the One Hundred and Fortieth New York, commanded by Colonel O'Rourke, a personal friend.

Accompanied by Hazlett's battery it was hurried up the hill. Meanwhile, with volleys, yells, and shouts, the Confederates rushed upon the centre of Vincent's brigade, who, covered in part by the rocks, stubbornly resisted. The Sixteenth Michigan, which held the north side below the hill, was overpowered and uncovered the way to the summit. At this moment, so critical in the destinies of this battle, the One Hundred and Fortieth New York, with the battery of Hazlett's, reached the summit. Without time to load or fix bayonets they rushed down the hill upon the advancing enemy. They captured those in advance and brought the rest to an abrupt halt. Vincent soon rallied to their support, and Hazlett's battery on the summit, though unable to depress their cannon to reach the enemy fighting on the hillside and around its base, opened fire upon their reserve in the valley. The rocks were ablaze with musketry, and in this deadly struggle the young and gifted O'Rourke was killed, and Vincent and many of his brave soldiers fell. On the summit above them, where men were fast falling under the deadly fire, General Weed was mortally wounded; and Hazlett, while leaning over him, was shot and fell dead across the body of his chief. The enemy, foiled in front and on the southwest, moved stealthily farther

Attack on Little Round Top.

around in the valley between the two Round Tops and suddenly rushed with deafening yells upon the Twentieth Maine, here formed. They met their match. This gallant regiment under the intrepid Chamberlain, though twice driven back over the crest, rallied again and again, and finally not only repulsed the enemy but drove them from the valley, and later in the day took possession of the other Round Top. In this struggle Vincent's men captured a thousand stand of arms, seventeen officers, and five hundred men.

Having seen how Little Round Top was saved, and having faintly mirrored something of the valor of its defence, we now return towards the Emmetsburg road and the peach-orchard where the battle had spread and had been for some time raging.

Beyond Little Round Top, towards the Emmetsburg road, and almost parallel to the cross-road, desperate fighting was meanwhile taking place. The Emmetsburg road and the cross-road spoken of may be represented by a cross. Ward's brigade fell back in part to the wheat-field, though some of the men took shelter in "Devil's Den" and were not driven out. De Trobriand, who had been fighting on a tributary about five hundred yards from the road, represented by the upright of the cross, had been relieved by Zook and fell back upon the triangular wheat-field between Little Round Top and the peach-orchard. The Confederates flanked the Seventeenth Maine, formed behind the stone wall which marks the boundary of this field, and compelled Winslow to withdraw his guns to the rear. De Trobriand's remaining veterans were driven back. The Union artillery near the peach-orchard, having retired, uncovered his right, and the whole line, hard pressed, was giving way, when Caldwell's division of the Second Corps came to the rescue.

It drove the attacking forces of Kershaw and Semmes back in disorder. Among those coming to the support was a brigade commanded by the heroic Cross, one of the bravest men of the army, who was soon killed among the foremost of his men. The gallant Irish Brigade under Kelly also was among them.

A more impressive sight is seldom seen than the one which preceded their going into action at this time. The ranks knelt, while above them their chaplain pronounced the absolution of his church, in deep and solemn tones. Prepared for death, these gallant Irishmen rushed upon Anderson's brigade, which was advancing, abruptly brought it to a halt, and then drove it back.

The battle hitherto going on between Plum Run and its tributary then spread to the peach-orchard and the Emmetsburg road. Meade, seeing the peril of the left, was hurrying forward reinforcements. The Sixth Corps came to relieve the hard-pressed Fifth. The Confederate artillery forming on the left-hand upper corner of the cross, converged a terrible fire upon the lower angle of the peach-orchard.

A battery formed across the Emmetsburg road at the position represented by the extremity of the left arm of the cross, enfiladed Humphrey's troops formed on this road beyond. The angle of the peach orchard, represented by the lower left angle of the cross, was defended by two brigades under Graham.

As the artillery slackened fire, Barkesdale with his rebel regiment advanced to the attack at the upper right angle formed by the roads. The brigade of Kershaw had recovered from the defeat inflicted by Caldwell, and now attacked the line forming the southern angle of the peach-orchard.

Wrapped in the smoke on which was reflected the flash of musketry and artillery, the two Union brigades melted away before the converging fire of the Confederates, and the peach-orchard was captured. Barkesdale, followed closely by his artillery, crowded in between Humphrey and Barnes, through this break in our lines, and the whole aspect of the fight was against us.

Humphrey, enfiladed by artillery on his left flank, and furiously attacked in front, was ordered to form a line oblique to the ridge in connection with Birney's division. Following this the rebel general, Woodford, attacked the line now held by Zook and Sweitzer, captured from Kershaw by Caldwell. Barnes's two brigades were soon driven out from their position in the woods and wheat-field. The losses were frightful, and our whole line at this point was soon broken. Humphrey had meanwhile completed his movement.

Hancock, in command of the entire left since Sickles had been wounded, was endeavoring to unite the line. Biglow's battery, without even an infantry support, was in front of the Trostle House, near the left bank of Plum Run, and opened fire upon the enemy, now advancing from the west and south to make this break irreparable, and for a time checked their advance.

The crowding back of Barnes and Caldwell had uncovered Ward's right, and after a loss of nine hundred out of two thousand men, he fell back and formed near the northern base of Little Round Top.

The Union troops, in order to close the gap in our line, re-formed on a rise of land commanded by the Emmetsburg road, abandoned early in the day by Sickles. They must hold this position at all hazards, as its loss would give the rebels possession of our communications, and prove our defeat. The batteries of McGilvery, consisting of thirty or forty pieces, were hurried into position, with their front at the Trostle House, on the left banks of Plum Run. They opened on the enemy, and, together with Hancock's other batteries, got a cross fire upon the advancing, yelling enemy.

Not to follow in minutiæ the kaleidoscopic changes of the fight, Hancock stripped his right and brought up troops to strengthen this line. A part of the Sixth Corps reinforced the line formed from Round Top to the Trostle House. Humphrey had meanwhile fallen back upon the heights and turned at bay.

Anderson's rebel division scaled the slopes along which Gibbon was posted at Cemetery Ridge. Wright had reached the heights on our centre and captured several guns above Gibbon's front. Here a terrible struggle took place with Webb's brigade, which came up to dispute possession of these guns.

The rebels had broken our line in the centre, and had they been reinforced in season, would have secured the possession of Zeigler's Grove, which projects down Cemetery Ridge like a salient where the "f" is crossed. Encouraged by the situation, they fought desperately, but were finally compelled to fall back with a loss of two-thirds of their force.

About dark Early's rebel division attacked the eastern and northern fronts of Cemetery Hill. Here several guns were captured, but the enemy, late that night, were driven back.

Johnson's division of Confederates on our extreme right was isolated by this defeat from the main line, yet as Geary had, in the afternoon, been withdrawn from the works at Culp's Hill to reinforce our endangered left at Round Top, at nine o'clock in the evening Johnson's division, finding it unoccupied, quietly took possession. Thus while our left, through terrible fignting, was in the main successful, and the attack of Wright on our centre had been finally repulsed, yet on our extreme right, at Culp's Hill (represented by the dot at the upper part of the " f ") the rebels had effected a lodgment and formed, with a part of a division, a continuation of our line not far from Meade's headquarters.

Thus, to sum up, while repulsed at every other part of our line, the Confederates held possession of our works at Culp's Hill on our extreme right. Thus ended the second day of the bloody struggle at Gettysburg.

That night Meade called his generals together to determine whether they should continue on that line and fight it out on the morrow, or retreat. The verdict was to fight it out, and Hancock, in giving his vote, pertinently remarked that the Union army had retreated too often already.

CHAPTER XXI.

GETTYSBURG, JULY 3.

A S the gray of dawn crept over the fields of Gettysburg, the storm of battle broke out afresh upon our right and rear at Culp's Hill. All along our front the enemy opened fire from their artillery, though it soon died away. During the night Geary had returned with his division, and was astonished to find the enemy in possession of the works he had left on the afternoon of the 2d, when ordered to support our endangered left.

The Confederates had been unable to get artillery up the steep hill, yet Ewell, having got a foothold, was obstinately determined not to be driven from the position. With this purpose he reinforced Johnston, in command of the forces there, with two brigades from Rhodes's division.

These works at Culp's Hill, if held by them, would seriously menace our rear, and as soon as it was light enough to discern objects our artillery opened fire upon the audacious occupants. Our guns soon demolished the weak barricades. They then slackened fire, and the infantry prepared for a charge; but the Confederates forestalled the movement.

They rushed forward determinedly to seize the road, and a desperate struggle took place among the rocks which cover the ground thickly at this point. The batteries of Meade's reserve concentrated their fire upon the slopes occupied by the Confederates, who had no artillery with which to reply. But Jackson's old soldiers were not accustomed to be driven from a field once won, and continued the struggle. All in vain their obstinate valor! They were pushed back, and finally, finding their retreat threatened by a force of Federals sent to Rock Creek, and being at the same time charged by Geary, they slowly retired beyond the creek, where they remained during the day.

It was now eleven o'clock on the forenoon of the 3d of July, and our lines were once more intact. The battle was over on our left, and as yet the enemy had not attacked our front. This want of concerted action on the part of Lee was due to the concave form of his line of battle, where communication was difficult and the route swept at every point by Union guns.

Shortly after eleven o'clock, the Confederates set fire to some buildings and hay stacks in our front, on the Emmetsburg road, to clear away obstructions in the way of their artillery fire. The pop! pop! pop! of the skirmish lines briskly engaged, was heard on the ridge.

Farnsworth crossing Plum Run.

During this time the Union cavalry made its appearance on our left in rear of Hood's division. Kilpatrick sent Farnsworth forward across Plum Run. He charged the infantry, and endeavored to capture their reserve artillery and supplies. Though unsuccessful, and its leader and many of his men were killed and many made prisoners, yet it proved a useful diversion. It told upon the final issue of the battle by preventing Longstreet from reinforcing the rebel centre, to assist in the final and main attack which Lee was maturing. It also spoiled the execution of a plan Hood had formed to capture our supply trains.

Lee had failed in his projected attacks on our right and left, and it remained for him either to retreat or attempt to break our centre. This was hazardous in the extreme, as our convex lines enabled us to quickly concentrate a superior force to repel the attack.

Our brigade held a position on the right of the grove which projects like a salient down the slopes of Cemetery Ridge.

Stannard's Vermont brigade held post in this grove, and was thereby able to deliver a flank fire on the enemy as he charged up the hill. Webb's and Hall's brigades were on our immediate left; Hayes's on our right. The Third Corps was posted on the ridge beyond the grove, on our left; Doubleday in the rear of the grove.

Two hours had passed with scarcely a sound of battle to interrupt the stillness. It was in the heat of the day, about one o'clock, when the strange silence which betokened the coming storm was broken by a signal gun on the left. A minute elapsed, another signal gun, and then from the whole of the Confederate line in our front, there burst forth the most terrific cannonade ever known upon the continent; a cannonade from one hundred and fifty brazen throats. The solid earth seemed to rock with the terrible explosions. From Oak Ridge to the peach-orchard, hill and valley were a flame of fire; all along the crest in our front a volcano of death.

This fire was converged upon Cemetery Ridge. The enemy fired by volleys in order to obtain a more decisive effect. Right, left, and rear of us, caissons were exploded; scudding fragments of wheels, wood-work, shell and shot sent a hundred feet into the air, like the eruption of a volcano. Eleven caissons were thus exploded.

We were sheltered behind a stone wall surmounted by a post and rail fence, which was struck, splintered, and crushed. The men clung close to the ground, taking advantage of its inequalities for protection. When a caisson was exploded yells of exultation were heard along the whole rebel lines. Only eighty guns of the Union artillery could be crowded upon the ridge with which to make reply. For an hour and a half crash followed crash and "embowelled with outrageous noise the air." The enemy used railroad iron and various other missiles besides the ordinary ones. Shells from the Wentworth guns came with a humming sound like a spinning-wheel in motion. Some of the shot shrieked and hissed; some whistled; some came with muffled growl; some with howls like rushing, circling winds. Some spit and sputtered; others uttered unearthly groans or hoarsely howled their mission of death. If a constellation of meteoric worlds had exploded above our heads, it would have scarcely been more terrible than this iron rain of death furiously hurled upon us. Over all these sounds were heard the shrieks and groans of the wounded and dying. The uproar of the day previous seemed silence when compared to this *Inferno* of sounds.

Cemetery Hill and Ridge were ploughed and furrowed by shell and shot, and every description of missile known to modern war. Holes, like graves, were gouged in the earth by exploding shells. The flowers in bloom upon the graves at the Cemetery were shot away. Tombs and monuments were knocked to pieces, and ordinary gravestones shattered in rows. So the din and destruction went on.

At last, at about three o'clock, the Union guns, by order of General Hunt, gradually ceased their fire. It was to cool the guns and to reserve ammunition for the contest at close quarters about to take place. The enemy, believing they had at last silenced our guns, moved forward upon the plain. Pickett's division of Longstreet's corps, formed in double line of battle, led the advance. It was composed of Virginians who, having up to this time taken no part in the conflict, were full of ardor for the attack. On Pickett's left was Heth's division, under Pettigrew; on his right, Wilcox's and Perry's brigades under Lang. Both of these forces were formed and marched in rear of Pickett. A swarm of skirmishers covered their front. Such was the imposing force, numbering not far from sixteen thousand men, which moved forward to the grand assault on our left centre at Cemetery Ridge.

They had a mile and a half to march before reaching our lines. They came on in magnificent order, with the step of men who believed themselves invincible. The firing of the enemy along our front now ceased, and the bluish white smoke rolled up like a storm cloud when swept from the mountain-side. A light wind sprang up, and the smoke of their guns drifted over the valley towards the cemetery. For a moment it threatened to obscure the charging columns from the sight of those who were about to encounter them in the grapple of death on Cemetery Ridge. It was but for a moment. The smoke drifted lazily away to the westward, revealing to us the gray lines steadily advancing.

The Union guns along the Ridge, silent for awhile, now replenish their ammunition boxes, while injured batteries give place to fresh ones which now open fire on the advancing lines. Solid shot ploughs huge lanes in their close columns. As the enemy approach still nearer, shell burst upon their compact masses. Their shattered lines do not waver, but steadily closing up the gaps of death, come on in magnificent order.

With banners waving, with steady step they sweep on like an irresistible wave of fate. In their tread is the fate of empire, the destinies of the great Republic !

The Union soldiers on Cemetery Ridge clutch their muskets confidently. On each face rests grim resolve and the nervous pallor of suspense. They believe they will at last be avenged for former defeats. On come the rebel lines with bayonets glistening like the crest of a mighty wave. Now the Union guns open with canister at close range upon this line of human targets. Pickett changes the direction of his march obliquely towards our left, while Pettigrew is far off on the right, and Wilcox, keeping straight on, disappears in the smoke to the left of the grove where Stannard is ambushed. Pickett's men are alone.

As they come on they leave behind them a trail of dead and dying, like a swath from the scythe of a mower. Now they are at close musket range, and from behind the stone wall a wave of flame, perceivable even in this noonday light, springs from the muzzles of the line of Union muskets. Volley after volley is poured in with deadly effect upon them. We see them halt and align their men, like a shadowy column through the smoke. They return our fire and rush upon the wall. As they are about to close in upon us they are met by a volley. On they come over the wall ; the shock is terrible and its full strength falls upon Webb's brigade. Our men are shot with the rebel muskets touching their breasts. A fierce encounter now takes place. Great God ! the line at the stone wall gives way!

Before their first line reaches a second fence and stone wall, where our second line is posted, Stannard's Vermont brigade and the Twentieth New York State Militia, form perpendicular to the rebel line of march, and open upon them a flank fire from the grove. This, and the deadly fire in their front, cause them to surrender in masses. The heroic rebel, General Armistead, determined to conquer or die, waving his hat on the point of his sword, jumps the wall, followed by his men, rushes forward and seizes a Union battery.

Troops are now rushing in upon them from every side. The cannoneers fight with their rammers and hand spikes. Armistead falls mortally wounded among the artillery he has captured, at the foot of a clump of trees. Near him lies our young and heroic Cushing who, while mortally wounded, has fired his only serviceable gun, exclaiming, "Webb, I will give them one more shot !" and falls dead by his guns.

Groups of Federals are surrounded by Confederates, — Confederates surrounded by Federals. Shots, shrieks, imprecations, shouts and yells ; fierce calls for surrender with defiant answers, all mingle together in a devilish uproar of sounds. Men fight with clubbed muskets, rifles, pistols, bayonets, and color staffs.

A few regiments from Pettigrew's command of Archer's and Scales's brigades reinforce Pickett. There is soon no order in the ranks of invaders or defenders. At last the rebels surrender and give way at every point. A hoarse shout of triumph goes up from the confused groups of Union men.

Fifteen terrible minutes, which seemed as many hours, had passed since the attack at close quarters began, and Pickett's rebels, who so proudly marched over the plain, were dead or wounded, had fled or surrendered. Two-thirds of Pickett's command were killed, wounded, or captured, and every brigade commander but one fell. It did not retreat, — it was annihilated.

While yet Pickett was fighting, Pettigrew, with his command, attacked Hayes's impregnable lines on our right. The fight was at short range and the Confederates were swept away in masses by the deadly fire.   They attempted to retreat, but the terrible fire scattered them in disorder.   The four brigades of the Third Confederate Corps were thus repulsed and overwhelmed, leaving fifteen stands of colors and two thousand prisoners in our hands.   A few of their regiments had joined Pickett as mentioned.

Meanwhile Wilcox, who had diverged from the line of Pickett's march, attacked on the left of the grove occupied by Stannard's Vermont brigade, and had met the same fate as those on the right. After Pickett's defeat he reached the foot of the hill on the left of the

grove where Stannard's men were ambushed, and where, in front of him on the crest, our Third Corps was massed.

Here he deployed and advanced, ignorant of Pickett's fate, whom he supposed was still fighting on his left.   Stannard repeated the manœuvre in this direction which in another had been so fatal to Pickett's men.   He opened a terrible fire on Wilcox's flank, while our batteries rent and tore his

Hancock Wounded.

front at short and deadly range.   His guns had no ammunition for reply, and his men not captured by Stannard were scattered in flight.

Hancock was the very soul of the defence, and his cool head and animating presence rallied, and preserved the line even after he was severely wounded.   The importance of the actual presence of Hancock cannot be over-estimated.   He did not leave the field until victory was assured, and then from his couch dictated a note to Meade, imploring him to make a counter-attack upon the enemy already weakened and almost destroyed. Meade, however, was in no mood to hazard the success already gained. He had not forgotten the encircling fire of artillery so lately turned upon Cemetery Heights, and which could sweep away his troops in crossing the valley. He was cautiously inclined to let well enough alone. Little more remains to be said of this terrible battle.

A cavalry attack had been made on our right rear, intended to give to the Confederates, if successful in the attack on Cemetery Ridge, a position to intercept our retreat. This sabre thrust was parried by Custer, who drove Stuart back.

The Union loss in these three days' battles is estimated by the Count de Paris as 2834 killed, 13,709 wounded, 6643 missing; total, 23,186. Lee, on the other hand, gives no definite estimate of his losses. The authority cited, however, puts it at a total of 23,000; but if such is admitted by the Confederates to be their loss, it is safe to assume that it was larger.

Thus ended the bloody battle of Gettysburg, which the Confederates began in high hopes and ended in bloody defeat.

Here the last and most terrible wave of invasion beat on Cemetery Ridge and rolled back! Here the tide of rebellion reached its highest limits, and ebbed from that hour!

It is worthy of note that July 4, 1863, the anniversary of our national existence, was the turning-point in the war, and that the government of the people received a new declaration and endorsement by the blood of our soldiers.

CHAPTER XXII.

THE minor occurrences of a fight, as afterward rehearsed around the camp-fire, are too numerous and complicated for repetition, yet no history of a battle is complete without an intersprinkling of characteristic incidents.

Illustrative of the spirit with which our men fought in this battle, Captain Blake of the Eleventh Massachusetts tells, in substance, the following: After Humphrey's division was driven back from the Emmetsburg road, and the rebels were falling back, a cry went down the line, from the private soldiers, "Charge on them!" "Charge on them!" With a shout the First Brigade, unheeding the orders of Humphrey, charged upon the rebels, who fell back before this irresistible advance. As a result of this impromptu movement, several hundred prisoners were captured, and several cannon retaken. The prisoners taken from the enemy cheerfully assisted our men in removing the recaptured artillery to a safe position in the rear.

After the charge, a brigadier-general complained that he could not find his brigade, and sent word to the front to have his men return. The men, wishing to sleep upon the field they had recaptured by their bravery, sent back word that if he would come to the front he would find his colors and men, and if he was not such a d — d coward he'd be there.

When Humphrey's men charged, many of the enemy, and our own men supposed to be dead or wounded, regained their feet on the field over which the charging column had passed. The wounded feebly hurrahed and said, "We don't care for our wounds if you'll only go in and whip the rebs!"

Some of the captured enemy were very doleful over the results of the fight. One of them said, "Doggoned if we've been any match for you'n Yanks to-day anyway. Every rooster fights best on his own dunghill!"

One of them lamented that it was no use to fight now old "Stonewall" was dead. "Anyway he war a powerful fightin' and prayin' man, Stonewall war!" said he.

When the rebels penetrated between Humphrey's and Barnes's brigades, after the peach-orchard fight, as elsewhere related, Barnes's brigade, pivoting on its left, swung back its right to bring its line parallel to the yelling, charging line of the enemy. As the rebels advanced on the brigade our men distinctly heard the order,

My Friend Tom in a Fix.

"Fire!" and instinctively the whole line crouched upon the ground, and the volley went hurtling and zipping among the trees over their heads, bringing down a perfect shower of leaves and twigs.

My friend Tom says not a man was hurt by this volley anywhere in that part of the line, but the enemy were too numerous for them to withstand, and they fell back to a lane, walled on either side with stone. While they were reloading their muskets one of the men, a little behind in arriving, in attempting to get over this wall was shot dead and fell across Tom, who, not understanding that the man had been shot, began to reproach him in language more forcible than polite, as a dunderhead, blunderer, and coward. The limp form and streams of warm blood oozing from a wound soon informed Tom that the man was dead, and he rolled the limp form from him. The incident had, however, so engaged his attention for the moment that he now for the first time perceived that his regiment had retreated. Saturated with blood he was getting to his feet to follow, when a line of rebel muskets was thrust over the stone wall behind which he lay, and a flash and volley followed. Then the enemy jumped the wall and with a prodigious yell pursued the retreating Yanks. The rebel stretcher-bearers following the line, soon came upon Tom, and seeing him covered with blood, naturally thought him severely wounded, and asked him how badly he was hurt. Tom, thinking the *rôle* of a wounded man preferable to that of a prisoner, faintly told them that he didn't think he was long for this life. " Keep up as well as you can and we'll attend to you after we've seen to our own men !" they said. One of them then clubbed and broke Tom's musket over the wall and departed, leaving Tom to make the best of it. "I couldn't tell how long it was," said Tom, "perhaps an hour and perhaps ten minutes, before I heard the sound of battle approaching me from the direction of the Union lines." Not ambitious of being shot by his own comrades, or taken prisoner by the rebels, he crawled between two boulders, where he was likely to be unobserved and comparatively safe from the volleys of musketry. In this position he awaited results, until the Pennsylvania reserves, like a lot of game cocks repelling invading roosters from their dunghill, came driving the rebels over him like a flock of sheep. In a half hour more Tom had picked up a good musket for the morrow's fight, regained his regiment, and reported for duty, where he was welcomed to life by comrades who had thought him dead.

Night came, and silence, interrupted only by the groans of the wounded, succeeded the uproar of battle. The moon rose and looked down with her silvery, kindly light upon the upturned pallid faces of dead men lying upon this field of strife.

The triangular field of wheat over which the battle had raged on our left had been trampled in the ground, and the dead lay thickly strown upon its life-giving grain, all reddened by their blood. Behind every rock in front of Little Round Top lay the Union and rebel wounded.

An acquaintance of mine, who had lost a comrade in the fight at Little Round Top, had, in the comparative darkness, advanced beyond our pickets among the rocks to find him. While cautiously advancing and stepping over the dead, thickly strown at this point, a rebel officer whom he had thought dead, spoke in a low tone and said, " Be careful, or you will be shot! My men are out there just beyond!" My friend, who had at that moment no very pleasant feeling toward the enemy he had been fighting all day, replied crisply that he could take care of himself without any help! He continued to advance, looking into the faces of the dead to discover his friend, when he was brought to a halt by the challenge of the rebel picket and the crack of a musket. Crouching behind the rocks he again crept back to our lines. Arriving at the group of dead where the wounded officer had warned him, he determined to see if he could return the timely warning by some kindly act. He asked the man if he could do anything to help him. The rebel officer replied that he was lying in a painful position with a stone under him. Gathering some blankets from the dead, my friend fixed a comfortable couch, lifted him to it, and gave him some hardtack and water.

The officer said, " You must have had a powerful line there to-day. We Texas chaps have never been so roughly handled since we've been in the service."

My friend inquired of him what officer it was on a white horse he had seen in front of Little Round Top that day.

" I reckon that was Longstreet. He rides a white horse," was the reply.

This simple incident is given to illustrate the good feeling shown the wounded after a fight, and common to both parties. Fighting men are seldom vindictive. It is the non-combatants and skulkers to whom that glory is confined.

Among the mortally wounded on the rebel side, was Barksdale of Mississippi, who was stricken down while, with his long white hair streaming in the wind, he was leading his men in the fierce charge on Humphrey's division. He lay within the second line of Union batteries. He told our nurses, who thought to help him, that he did not need any attention as his wound was mortal. He spoke sorrowfully of his family and home far away in the Southwest. He made but one allusion to the fight, when, with something of his old war spirit he said, "General Lee will clean you out of this place to-morrow!"

General Sickles, who had lost a leg in the engagement, showed constant anxiety about the fight, although desperately wounded.

A little fellow, wearing the rebel gray, was picked up by our stretcher-bearers. He was crying quite boisterously, and when asked what he was crying for, said it was because General Lee had always before put his regiment in the front.

In the engagement on the left, one of our men stopped to assist a wounded comrade to the rear. "Don't mind me," said the wounded man; "go in and lick the rebs; I'd give a hundred lives rather than have them whip us to-day!"

A number of men badly wounded (enough to justify their being sent to the rear) insisted on staying with the line and fighting it out. One of Webb's men, wounded in the arm, was asked why he didn't go to the rear, as he could not shoot with one arm in a sling; he replied, he guessed he could rest his musket on a rail, and with a twinkle of humor in his eye, hesitatingly said, "Besides, it's so near the 4th of July it don't pay a feller who wants to celebrate."

Men who had fought all day requested permission to go upon the battle-field at night and help their wounded comrades. Details took the canteens of those who remained behind, and carried water to the wounded on the field. They extemporized stretchers of blankets, rails, and limbs of trees, and sometimes of muskets, and bore the wounded to the hospital.

The ambulance corps and stretcher-bearers, regularly detailed, who were supposed to attend to their duty, kept themselves in safe positions in the rear, in many cases. In one instance a stretcher-bearer was wounded, and the surgeon spoke in terms of censure, as though he had been out of place in exposing himself while in performance of duty.

Some of the surgeons were unfeeling wretches who always consulted their own comfort and convenience, rather than that of the wounded or sick. I have seen them refuse to attend wounded men because they did not belong to their corps or division, and that when the need was imperative.

Squads of rebels wandered over the plain during the night giving water to the wounded, and one of them who had unwittingly straggled into our lines said: "I'm your prisoner if you say so, but I'm giving water to all alike," and was released on this assurance.

The loss of those engaged on our left was enormous. In some brigades more than half were disabled, killed, wounded, or missing. Webb's division, the second day, was not attacked until sundown, when the rebels charged up the hill on our line. The yells and cheers of the contestants mingled with the crackle of volleys and the roar of artillery. The smoke hung over Webb's brigade, which contested the possession of the guns on the left with Wright's rebel division. Cemetery Hill, which must not be confounded with Cemetery Ridge, was on our right, and the ridge on which we were posted was on its left. We distinctly saw the fight in both directions.

When the rebels attacked Cemetery Hill they got among the guns of Stevens's battery; but the gunners refused to surrender, and

Biglow's Battery retiring with Prolonges.

fought with their rammers and handspikes, exclaiming: "Death on our soil rather than surrender these guns to the rebs!" The Thirty-third Massachusetts opened a destructive oblique fire on the rebels when they were making an attack on the Cemetery in the after-noon. One of the sergeants turned to the men, as the enemy were advancing, and said, "We've got to die here, men. It won't do to let these rebs get up the hill."

The incident is told of Biglow's battery, which was in front of the Trostle House, that it was ordered to continue firing and sacri-fice the battery (which, it will be remembered, was without infantry

supports) in order to give the other batteries with their supports time
to get into position. The men would not give up their guns, but
fought with fixed prolonges (as a sort of compromise with their
instructions) until the enemy were within six feet of them, and then,
with the loss of three officers and twenty-three men, retired.

The rebel report says one shell from this battery killed and
wounded thirty men out of a company of thirty-seven.

General Doubleday gives us the following incident on the authority of Dr. J. R. Wood, a Georgian, who was in the conflict : —

Wright had attained the crest of the ridge, and the brigade of
Wilcox was advancing. "As they approached the ridge a Union
battery limbered up and galloped off. The last gun was delayed and
the cannoneer, with a long line of muskets pointing at him, within a
few feet, deliberately drove off the field." The Georgians manifested their admiration by crying out, "Don't shoot !" and not a
musket was fired at him.

During the long moonlight night of the 2d parts of our line
were being strengthened by breastworks, and there was but little
rest given to the wearied veterans who had fought through the day.

The pluck and patriotism of the private soldier did more to save
the battle to the Union cause than grand manœuvres had done, and
had counteracted the blunders made during the fight.

CHAPTER XXIII.

" JOHNNIE REB has got all he wants of fighting this time!" was the common expression among the soldiers. The feeling was very general among the rank and file that we ought to lose no time in making a counter-attack on the rebel centre or flank. The soldiers said, "We've got them on the run now, let's follow them up!" They believed we had an opportunity of closing the war as if with a thunderbolt.

If Hancock had not been wounded, this might have been done. As it was, Meade was evidently thankful he had not been destroyed, and did not therefore care to further tempt the Fates by an attack. He was slow to understand the damage done to Lee.

The expressions of admiration for the pluck displayed in the attack on our lines by the barefooted soldiers in tattered gray were very common. There was a thrill of pride that these brave men were, after all, Americans.

It is said that the heroic General Armistead, whose brigade was the lance-head of the attack which had penetrated our lines, had, early in the war, fought on the Union side, but had been seduced from his allegiance by the influence of his friends. Before he died, he is reported as having said, "Tell Hancock I have wronged him and my country!"

Whatever may have been his faults, however he may have erred, no braver man ever led in a charge. When he broke through our lines he was followed by not over a hundred of his men, and fell, mortally wounded, near the group of trees which marked the highest tide of the invasion.

It is said that in one of the battles before Richmond, he had dodged behind the trunk of a poplar tree. When he was leading his brigade across the open plain to attack the heights, some of his men who disliked him, sarcastically said, "There are no poplar trees to get behind here!" He replied to their taunts by saying, "Before this charge is over *you* will wish there were some poplar trees here!"

At one time in the din of the fight on the ridge, Hall, of the Second Corps, had ordered the flags of his brigade forward, and the men of two regiments swept on towards their colors as if by an electric impulse, passing completely through Webb's brigade line, and engaging the enemy in a hand-to-hand attack. The brunt of the attack had fallen upon Gibbon's division. Webb's front was the focus of the artillery fire where Cushing's battery and Brown's Rhode Island battery were almost annihilated. Wheeler's First New York battery that took their place proved worthy to succeed them.

The Second Corps, under Hancock, had covered itself with glory by repelling this last desperate charge, and its survivors may proudly say, as a criterion of their bravery, "I fought with Hancock at Cemetery Ridge!"

It was said that Custer, at one time, headed the First Michigan cavalry in repelling the cavalry attack on our left rear, exclaiming, "Come on, you Wolverines!" and with his long hair flying in the wind like a battle-flag, led them into the jaws of death.

The Army of the Potomac, baffled and defeated in so many conflicts and campaigns, had now, at last, won a victory substantial and glorious. It had gained a great victory — but at what cost of human suffering! The smiling valley which looked so peaceful and sweet with homelike scenes on the 1st was now the valley of death. Five thousand dead men and thirty-four thousand wounded lay within a circle of a few miles. Fields of grain were trampled into the ground, and replaced by a harvest of wounds and death. Peaceful dwellings were burned, crushed, and riddled with shot and bullets. The barns were filled with dead and dying. Every shelter was a hospital. The space between Round Top and the peach-orchard and the valley in our front were covered with wounded and dying men.

There are few sadder things in life than the morning after a great battle. The nerves that have been braced and strung to their highest tension are then relaxed, and a depressing reaction follows the overwrought excitement. We then look upon its scenes with different eyes.

Our regiment, says a comrade, lost terribly. The brigade had

CUSTER'S CHARGE AT GETTYSBURG.   Page 226.

lost two of its regimental commanders, while two more were wounded. Among the wounded of our company was my friend, Wad Rider. Down towards the stone wall, on which stood the post and rail fence before mentioned, the stretcher-bearers found him faint from the loss of blood ; Pat Quin afterwards said, "Hobnobbing and sympathizing with wounded rebs!" Wad afterwards told me the following story :—

"When them rebs came piling over that wall the first thing I knew I didn't know anything. My clothes seemed wet with something warm which I found was blood. It made me faintish like. Right side of me was a big reb. He had torn his clothes half off of himself, looking for his wound, and was pale and wax-like, and as ugly as sin. I said : 'Well, Johnnie Reb, how do you like it as far as you have come?' 'You doggoned mean Yank, I'll show yer!' said he, and he drew a long, ugly-looking knife on me. I told him to hold up or I'd fix him, and got my bayonet ready to prod him if he showed any more fight.

"I was awful dry, so with one eye on that reb I took up my canteen for a drink of water. Darn me if it wasn't whiskey! I'd been swapping canteens, somehow, with an officer; but I took a drink just the same, though I'd given the whole canteen full for one little drink of water. I tell you when you are awful dry nothing tastes as good as water! When I was taking a drink that reb was so pale and looked so wistful like towards my canteen, I was so darned sorry for him that I couldn't stand that look of his, so I swung it towards him by the string and said : 'There ain't nothing small about me except my feet! Have a drink?' He took out his chew of tobacco, uncorked the canteen, and gracious ! you'd ought to have heard that whiskey gurgle down his throat! I thought he'd never let up on it !

"At last he finished his drink, smacked his lips, and rolled his eyes, and said, 'Stranger, those is right smart whiskey!'

"Then we 'gan to talk. 'I've got my bellyful of fightin', I have!' said he. I told him we were dreadful willing to fill all the rebs full of them rations if they'd hold still and let us. He kinder chuckled, and said he, 'Well, I reckon so, Yank! but you'll find we'uns have got a powerful sight of fight left. I've a right smart for my use tho'! This is the rich man's war and the poor man's fight.' 'That's so,' said I. 'You don't own a darned nigger, I suppose, and are fighting to keep them for rich men ? '

"'I reckon you'uns ar fightin' over niggers yer don't own either,' said he.

"By and by Pat Quin and Bill Pendleton come along with a stretcher and that darned Irishman Quin, blubbered right out when he see me. 'God bless yer darlint rid hed!' says he.

"They were going to put me on a stretcher, but I told them to take up the reb and I'd walk, with a little help, up to the doctor's butcher shop.

"Pat he growled, and said, ''Twas like lambs trying to help wolves that had just been trying to eat 'em.'"

"Pat was such a lamb, you know!" here interrupted Joe, with a grin.

"Yes," said Wad, "this darned soft-hearted, lunkheaded Joe here wanted to take me up and carry me like a baby! After I fainted I guess you had to, didn't you, old fellow?" addressing Joe.

Taming a Reb.

"Well, that Johnnie and I got to be pretty good friends after you boys marched off. We lay under a fly together. The surgeon most killed me probing around for a bullet — hurt me worse than the bullet did! The sanitary folks were always coming around doing something for us, after the 4th.

"One real kind old maid came around and said, 'Is there anything I can do for you, my poor boy?'

"'I'm pretty well, I thank ye!' said I, 'but ther's a fellow ye might help,' pointing to my reb, who was sick and 'womblecrop' like!

" ' But he's a rebel,' said she. That reb pretended he was sleeping, but I knew he heared every word. ' Yes,' said I, ' but he's a pretty good fellow, tho', and hain't got no friends here, and I have. There's just as much human nature in a reb as in anybody ! '

" So she went over and spoke to him, but he wouldn't open his eyes. So she took out a clean handkerchief and a bottle of some bay rum or something, and began bathing his head and smoothing back his hair and fixing him up. Then she took a lot of goodies out of her gripsack, an orange and other things, and dreadful kind like, said : ' My poor boy, is there nothing more I can do ? Would you like me to write to your mother ? '

" The tears began to come through his closed eyelids, and something like a lump came up in his throat, and he blubbered right out, he did, ' Doggoned if I'd a thought you'uns would be so kind to we'uns ! ' I never heard him say anything ugly or bitter like after that about our folks."

" Well," said Joe, with a sympathetic tear in his eye at this narration, " yer all right neow, Wad ? "

" Yes," said Wad, with a twinkle of humor in his eye, " and I want to catch some more rebs to tame ! "

" What ? "

" Yes, 1 s'pose I blubbered a little, too ! "

" Ye's no more fit to be a soldier than the divil's risidence is to keep ice-wather in. Ye's too aisy wid 'um, me bye ! " said Quin.

" Go away, lamb ! " said Wad, and after that we called Quin " the lamb ! "

I have tried to tell this simple story of Wad Rider as I heard it from his lips because it illustrates the inherent kindness among soldiers for each other, whether friends or foes. Soldiering makes men rough, but generous, brave, and kind.

" The morning after the battle, the saddest sight I saw," said a comrade, " was men calling upon me piteously to kill them to relieve them from their terrible agony." " It seems a pity," said Joe, " you can't put a man out of misery as yer can a horse ! "

One of our wounded men was found near a house on the Emmetsburg road. He told us it was his father's house, and when his company fell back he stayed behind to have a little private shooting of his own. " Got the worst of it, too ! " said Joe.

"Well, I don' know," said he. "I wollenteered to fight and it made me mad to see 'um prowling round our house. I plugged some of 'um! Ven they cum on I shust hold de fort. I ain't saw no 'casion to be sorry yet!"

The rebel prisoners seemed surprised at the richness of the Northern country through which they were marched. Said one :—

"I've been totin' round all over this doggoned Yankee country, and you'uns has got a heap more of truck and fixin's to live on than we'uns have!" One of them remarked to me that as the rebel army approached, the Dutchmen ran away, but the women stayed in their houses. "I reckon your women are the best men ye've got up here!" A tribute which the Pennsylvania women richly deserved.

It rained very hard on the 4th, and the day was passed in assisting the wounded, re-forming the lines, and waiting for an attack. We knew when the rebel army had retreated, by the arrival of non-combatants, red-tape handlers, gilt-edged brigadier-generals, sutlers, and regimental bands.

On the 5th we got marching orders. All through Maryland we were welcomed with enthusiasm by the loyal people, and treated hospitably by all.

There has been much discussion as to why the Union army did not attack the rebels at Williamsport. It is unquestionable that Meade's timidity prevented it. Nature herself seemed to fight on our side.

The retreat of Lee was cautious and masterly, but circumstances, so often averse to our army, seemed to invite the Union army to win another victory. Meade was slow in pursuit. The 5th and 6th of July were wasted.

It was the 6th before he was convinced that Lee really was retreating, and learned that his head column had passed beyond Hagerstown. On the 6th the Potomac, swollen by rains, had risen seven feet. Lee was blockaded. The bridge at Falling Waters was destroyed by our force under French.

Meade knew these facts, and it seemed as if Providence was urging him to attack by stretching out a hand filled with opportunities. He simply followed step by step, with his cavalry. Lee was meanwhile watchful to know when he was to be attacked, in order to select a strong defensive position.

Halleck, who had been surprised into promptness, placed at his disposal the garrisons of Washington and Baltimore. With the swollen condition of the river, why could not this, or some other force taken from our superior numbers, have been sent by the way of Harper's Ferry, and confronted Lee on the south side of the Potomac, cut off his ammunition and supplies and checked his retreat?

Lee was defeated and in retreat, with a swollen, impassable river between him and his base. The Union army was well equipped, flushed with victory, superior in numbers, confident, and anxious to put an end to the war. It might have been defeated; that is possible with an army at any time, but the probabilities were much in favor of its being victorious. Was not the promise worth the risk?

Kilpatrick kept close upon the heels of the enemy, leaving two regiments and one battery at Harper's Ferry to delay the rebel cavalry. Stuart was on his track. At four o'clock P.M. of the 6th Kilpatrick arrived in sight of the Potomac, and advanced against the Confederates there formed. He boldly attacked, but was repulsed. Meade left Gettysburg the same day. He was informed of Kilpatrick's repulse as well as of the rise of the river.

On the 8th Meade had pushed his infantry to South Mountain. He was in no hurry, and did not intend that the battle-field should be left to chance. Meade had men enough. The corps of eleven thousand, under Baldy Smith, was fresh and well equipped. The garrisons of Baltimore and Washington, besides four thousand men under French, were placed at his command.

But, after learning Lee's situation, Meade allowed him five days in which to choose a position, fortify it, and renew his supplies. The manner in which Meade should have attacked Lee may be always a question of an honest difference of opinion, involving special tactical knowledge, but that he should have attacked him before he was able to cross the Potomac upon one single pontoon bridge is a matter of common sense. He had no excuse for hesitation, since he had received repeated orders from President Lincoln to attack at once; the responsibility, therefore, in case of defeat, would not have been his.

On the 9th our left advance was on Antietam Creek, and the

right near Funkstown. On the 11th our left advanced to Jones's Cross Roads. On the 13th it was in front of the position occupied by Lee, to cover the passage of the Potomac. On the 14th, when Meade had determined to attack, it was discovered that the rebel army had crossed the Potomac into Virginia. Thus ended the invasion.

CHAPTER XXIV.

VIRGINIA AGAIN.

THE contrast between the loyal and disloyal States was fairly presented by Virginia and Maryland. "That sounds dreadful natural!" said Joe, as a frowsy red-headed woman came to the door of a dilapidated mansion, where we were drawing water from the well, furiously exclaiming, "If I was a man I'd git a gun and shoot bullets inter your heads!"

"And if ye was a man an' sure I'd knock yer head off, or knock some sinse inter it!" wrathfully growled Pat Quinn, exasperated at such uncalled-for bitterness.

The contrast between Maryland and Virginia was so great as to be noted at once by the most obtuse observer,

Welcome back to Virginia.

upon crossing the borders. At one place, where the boys were pumping water, the burly owner removed the handle of the pump and carried it into the house, and then asked the commanding general for a guard to protect his property!

The change in sentiment and manner, from courtesy to crustiness, surly disrespect, and hate, was as noticeable as the change in condition from thrift to shiftlessness.

The women manifested more bitterness than the men, perhaps for the reason that they had learned by experience how tolerant our men were to disloyalty when simply manifested in words. It was natural, after all, to hate those whom they had been taught to consider the impersonation of every mean quality possessed by mankind. Yet it seems singular to me, even at this day, that those so little capable of appreciating generous treatment should claim for themselves all the qualities of chivalry, and stigmatize their enemies with every epithet of meanness known to their vocabulary.

I have assisted in issuing rations to destitute Southern families, and have afterwards, when marching by their homes, under other circumstances, been taunted with hateful, envenomed epithets. These viragoes of the Virginia borders, who scolded so furiously, were, perhaps, entitled to respect as mothers of brave and tenacious fighters, and no one will deny to them the quality of being good haters, whatever other virtues they may have lacked.

In Maryland or Pennsylvania it was unusual to put guards over property, and the citizens of Maryland seldom complained of our men. Upon our arrival on the Virginia side of the Potomac the owners of property clamored for guards.

At one time, during the marches in Virginia which followed Gettysburg, our men were prohibited from using fence rails for firewood. This order was finally qualified by allowing them to take the *top* rails. This was interpreted in so liberal a manner by our boys, that each man took the rail he found on top, until the *bottom* rail was the top one.

Passing through the Virginia towns, along the base of the Blue Ridge, we noticed a great many cripples, who had evidently been in the Southern army. Some good-naturedly avowed the fact, or at least did not deny it.

"Where did you lose yer leg?" inquired Joe (who was in pursuit of all kinds of information), of one of these maimed men.

"In a thrashing-machine!" was the reply. "Yis," said Quinn,

"and it is quite a number of your gintlemen who have lost their legs, bedad, in that same kind of a Yankee thrashing-machine at Gettysburg."

"Well, stranger," said the reb, "I reckon we uns have helped run a right smart of them machines up hyer!" Joe looked crestfallen in having his friend Quinn outwitted by the reb; but candidly said in an undertone, as if to himself, "I guess that's so!"

Blackberries grew abundantly by the roadside and in the fields, and at every halt our men exhibited an amusing anxiety to break ranks for the blackberry patches. The berries were certainly very refreshing, and contributed not a little, at the time, toward preserving the health of men whose diet was confined usually to a few articles of food.

While it was next to impossible to buy food of the inhabitants, there was one form of persuasion they were not proof against. The most hardened secesh would trade for coffee, and I believe the women would for a little snuff have sold even their right to abuse Yankees. It is not impossible Joe was right, when he declared that the cheapest way to settle the war was to buy off the women with snuff and coffee.

The safe retreat of Lee into Virginia necessitated our pursuit. Meade's plan of manœuvre was confessedly modelled in imitation of that pursued by McClellan after Antietam. A direct advance up the Shenandoah was not considered practicable on account of the difficulty of subsisting so vast an army by the means available in that direction. By pursuing a line of march which clung close to the base of the Blue Ridge, he hoped to be able to attack Lee's army advantageously before it could break through the mountain barriers. We marched so rapidly that our advance reached Manassas Gap on the 22d, while the Confederate column was still passing.

Meade ordered French to make a flank attack on Lee's long-drawn-out column. The commander of the Third Corps had, thus far, shown very few of the qualities necessary for command, and was, as the sequel proved, unfitted for it. He was almost universally hated by the private soldiers serving under him, and many of them declared him to be a drunkard and a coward.

His advance consisted of some of Hooker's veterans who, as they moved forward towards the top of the crest where the rebels were posted, loaded and fired coolly, picking, meanwhile, the blackberries which grew abundantly on the side of the hill.

They had driven the enemy from this hill, when "Old Blinky," as some of the soldiers contemptuously dubbed a certain general, was seen riding along surrounded by his staff and a number of non-combatants. The soldiers declared, with the greatest confidence, either that there would be no more fighting, or that their general would be in the rear.

Some of the men engaged in the affair have declared that he was half drunk at the time mentioned. His promotion was said to be due to Halleck with whom he was a favorite. Whether the sayings and opinions of the soldiers were founded on fact or prejudice, it is certain that this general had, by his mismanagement, deprived the hard-marched Union army of all those advantages gained by their legs, to strike a decisive blow at the enemy.

General Warren, in his evidence before the War Committee, says, " He made a feeble attack with one brigade, and wasted the whole day!" He allowed the weak rebel rear-guard to delay him for hours, and did not come at their line of battle at Front Royal until evening.

The army had now been marching and fighting for fifty days. They had been balked by the tardy action of this misplaced favorite of General Halleck, but were now about to enter upon a period of much-needed rest.

The view from the hills at the Gap was one of the most magnificent possible. Fields of grain, forests green with summer foliage, undulating or rugged hills met the eye on every side. The situation reminded me of those lines in the " Missionary Hymn " : —

> " Every prospect pleases and only man is vile."

"The cheek of these rebs!" said Joe; "they sell every darned thing they raise on their farms to the rebel army, or down South, and then we feed 'um!" It was true: those who had sons in the rebel army, and had sold their produce, hay, and grain, South, often called upon our quartermaster to save them from starvation.

Negro servants were not common, and had evidently escaped to the Union lines, or been sent farther south for safety. The estates of noted rebels were protected by the provost guard.

Balked in the purpose of our pursuit, we leisurely fell back to the Rappahannock, and entered upon a season of rest amid the beautiful forests and blossom-laden trees of Virginia.

Men soon began to leave the army by regiments, corps, and divisions. Many regiments were sent to New York to pacify those sportive individuals who, by hanging inoffensive negroes to lamp posts, burning public halls and charitable buildings, and by other graceful acts showed their patriotic appreciation of the draft, and other free institutions. They were endeavoring to imitate their models in chivalry, and needed attention from our boys.

One division of the army was also sent to North Carolina. Thus began again the policy of breaking a noble whole into fragments, apparently for the convenience of those in rebellion.

Meade waited for the return of the different regiments sent to New York, before making any new moves on the chess-board of war. Learning that Longstreet had been sent to Tennessee, Meade, occupying with the army an advantageous position on the south banks of the Rapidan, projected a flanking movement.

He was all ready to move when informed from Washington that the Eleventh and Twelfth Corps, under Hooker, were to be sent to Tennessee to retrieve, if possible, the defeat of Rosecrans at Chickamauga. Lee did not, however, wait for Meade, but by a bold initiative threw him upon the defensive. Aware that the ranks of the Union army had been thinned by the causes already narrated, on the 9th of October he crossed the Rapidan to move around the right flank of our army.

He hoped by this manœuvre to drive Meade from the line of the Rappahannock. The first intimation Meade had of these intentions of Lee, was an attack on his advance post at James City. Finding his right flank turned, he fell back across the Rappahannock, and when, on the 13th, Lee advanced, he found Meade more circumspect than Pope had been under similar conditions, and too quick to be caught in the trap so adroitly contrived. Meade was now north of the Rappahannock, and receiving information that Lee was at Culpeper Court-House, on the 12th, thought his retreat had been premature. He therefore counter-marched the main portion of the army to the south bank of the river, and marched towards Culpeper, where he proposed to fight Lee if he was there.

But the rebel commander had other views and arrangements. While the Union army was marching south, the Confederate army was marching, by parallel lines, northward to cut off Meade's retreat towards Washington. An attack was made, near the crossing of the Rappahannock, on Gregg, by the van of Lee's army advancing towards Warrenton. This attack showed Meade Lee's intentions, and he at once began a rapid retreat. Fortunately for Meade, Lee remained ignorant of the real situation, or the Third Corps, isolated on the north bank of the river, might have been destroyed.

On the 13th the army was again concentrated on the north bank of the Rappahannock. An exciting race then began between the two armies. Lee, on the one hand, was trying to strike in on Meade's line of retreat by the Orange and Alexandria Railroad, while Meade, on the other, was attempting to checkmate by out-marching him. Failing in this, the Confederate general endeavored to reach Bristow Station before his antagonist. He began his march on the 14th, but again the Union army, marching by interior lines, beat in the race.

In this retrograde movement Warren, who was now in command of our Second Corps, was instructed to halt at Fayetteville until the Third, under French, was able to withdraw. Says a comrade, "We were the rear-guard covering the retreat. Our route was by the way of Auburn to Catlett's Station. Kilpatrick's division of cavalry acted as eyes for our force.

"We had reached Auburn, and Warren, suspecting that Lee was at Warrenton, placed three batteries on the hills at Cedar Run to protect our rear from attack. While the men of these batteries were kindling fires to cook their breakfast, at early dawn, Stuart's cavalry, which had been driven off from its regular line of march by French, in attempting to take another route, had marched into the valley of Cedar Run in our rear. The gray mists of the early morning concealed their presence from those on the hill, yet the heights, illuminated by a stronger light, were plainly perceived by them.

"The situation was all the more complicated, because the head of Ewell's advance, moving towards Greenwich, was now on the Warrenton road on the opposite side of the hill, while Sykes's corps, moving up the railroad, formed another Union column on the other side of Stuart. He was like a piece of ham sandwiched in between two pieces of bread, while our corps was sandwiched between the two Confederate forces of Stuart and Ewell.

"Such was the mixed and somewhat amusing situation when Stuart opened with his artillery on the rear of our batteries, posted on the heights. They at once sought to shelter themselves by getting over to the other side of the hill; but no sooner was this done than they were surprised by a furious outburst of artillery from the Warrenton road.

"The situation was critical, but not so bad as at first sight it would seem, as Stuart speedily escaped from his difficult position by the rear, and Ewell's force was simply the van of his columns, composed principally of cavalry. The enemy, under Ewell, was soon repulsed, and when the remainder of his force arrived they were skilfully held in check till the rest of the corps crossed Cedar Run. We then continued our march, Caldwell's division covering our rear. Ewell did not pursue, but moved by Greenwich to join Hill, as prescribed in his instructions. Our escape was timely, as the Fifty-seventh New York was cut off by the rebel infantry, though it succeeded in joining the main column by making a detour to the right.

"Lee's intention of reaching Bristow Station before Meade, caused him to urge on the advance of Hill and Ewell. When we reached Bristow Station we encountered the Confederate force under General Hill, who was just preparing to attack the rear of the Fifth Corps, under Sykes, whom Warren had expected to join at Bristow's, but which had just crossed Broad Run. Our position was extremely critical, as we (the Second Corps) were attacked while marching, by the flank, and were isolated from our own, and were in the vicinity of the whole rebel army.

"The remarkably vigorous, clear-sighted action of Warren, and the confidence and coolness of our men, alone gave us the victory, and extricated us from the position at Bristow Station. Warren, with the eye of a military engineer, quickly comprehended the advantages of the ground on which the battle was to be fought. As the head of our column approached, the Confederates formed a line of battle towards the railroad. Webb's division, moving under cover of the railroad cut, took position along the embankment, while our division double-quicked for the railroad, in the cut of which we were enabled to deploy unseen by the enemy. When the column of Hill advanced, it was raked by Ricket's battery and met by a terrible fire from the embankment, and driven back in much confusion. Our regiment and others were ordered forward in pursuit, and captured two stands of colors, five pieces of artillery, and four hundred and fifty prisoners." Many of the men captured were North Carolinians.

In the pursuit a funny incident happened to our intrepid corporal, Joe. His long legs and his impetuosity had carried him in advance of our main line, when a dozen rebels sprang out from ambush, calling upon him to surrender. Joe was about to comply with this unwelcome request, when he perceived on his left a line of our men of another brigade, who had got beyond him. "Hello, here!" said Joe. "Gosh dang it, you tarnel fools! Don't yer see yer flanked? Surrender here, every one of ye, or I'll have yer shot!" "Most of the Johnnies didn't mind me worth a cent," said Joe, afterwards, "but cut like lightning for the woods." Joe marched three of them in, highly pleased to have *them* instead of being taken by them.

I have given only the outlines of the fight which reflected so much credit on General Warren. Hill had not only failed to close the passage of Broad Run against us, but had been severely whipped, having five hundred men wounded besides losses already mentioned.

Notwithstanding this, our position was critical; for as the battle closed about sundown, Ewell's corps, which had been marching in by-paths and obscure roads, came up between us and Hill, with whom we had been fighting. The entire rebel army was now in our front.

Under cover of darkness we made our retreat; marching all night, we rejoined the main force of our army (now massed at Centreville), hungry, sleepy, tired, but not despondent, for we had outwitted and out-manœuvred the enemy at every turn. Nothing so much helps men to fight or to march willingly as the knowledge that they are commanded by a general of superior intelligence, skill, and courage. Poor officers, when placed in command of the best of men, negative their bravery and discipline. "Who wants to win feathers for such an old devil as Blinky?" said one of Hooker's veterans to me, referring to a certain general.

It is aggravating to feel compelled by one's sense of patriotism to help win, with life or blood, a victory which exalts one whom we consider a coward and tyrant. Such officers seldom showed consideration for their men, but treated them with that cruelty so common to cowards and sneaks.

Foiled in every direction, Lee, now seeking some advantage for all his trouble, turned aside and destroyed the Alexandria Railroad, and then retreated.

While marching and counter-marching in this region, we passed the estate of John Minor Botts, that staunch Union man, whom no inducements could convert into a rebel. His plantation remained in good condition amid the surrounding ruin. The fences were said to have been burned at one time, but a corps of our army had voluntarily spent a day in cutting and splitting rails and rebuilding the fences. The secret of its general preservation was the respect the rebels had for his unflinching integrity on the one side, and his well-known Union sentiments on the other.

It was said that at one time he was imprisoned at Richmond in company with other Unionists, sleeping on the hard boards, and furnished with but meagre food. Some prominent rebels visited him, and said: "Why don't you come over to the side of your State, Mr. Botts? You could have any position you desired!" The old man's reply, as he straightened his bent form, was: "Sir, I have lived nearly sixty years under the flag of my country and was never deprived of my freedom. The Confederate rag has now been raised but a few months and I have committed no offence, yet witness my condition! No, sir! I prefer the old flag!"

On some of the estates in that part of the country was posted this notice: "British Property! Safeguards placed by General Meade!"

CHAPTER XXV.

THE Orange and Alexandria Railroad, destroyed by Lee, was, by the 2d of November, reconstructed.

The amount of work which a large number of men will, under ordinary circumstances, accomplish in the army, was not so great a source of wonder to me as the small amount they, at times, really performed. With regular army officers the ability to attain small results with a large number of men was brought to a high degree of perfection. Anything attempted outside a well-established routine seemed to drag like a sled on bare ground. The same results in civil life would often have been accomplished with one-half the number of men. When the Engineer or Construction Corps got beyond their accustomed routine they made a great ado over very simple matters, which would soon have been settled by a few ordinary mechanics.

On the 7th of November the army, like hurried travellers, took an early breakfast, and started out in two columns to cross the Rappahannock, in pursuit of the enemy. They had started so many times in that direction, and come back again like whipped puppies, with tails depressed, that the thing was getting to be a trifle monotonous.

The left wing was composed of the First, Second, and Third Corps, and was under the charge of that master of "how not to do it," General French. The Fifth and Sixth Corps were commanded by that able but cautious veteran, General Sedgwick. The Third Corps led the advance of the left wing, and soon arrived at Kelley's Ford, the point of crossing. The semi-circular, rugged crests on the north side of the river, here were seized by General Ward, then in command of Birney's old corps. From these hills our artillery was soon enabled to sweep the low and uncovered land of the south banks of the river. Under its cover the sharp-shooters of Trep, and the

brigade of infantry, under De Trobriand, forded the stream and captured the rifle-pits. Meanwhile the right column, under Sedgwick,
had arrived near Rappahannock Station.

Here, on the north banks, the Confederates held two hills,
crowned by forts, a hundred and fifty yards from each other, with
the road passing between the two. Rifle-pits ran back from the forts
to the banks of the river. A pontoon bridge spanned the stream in
their rear, enabling them to communicate with their forces on the
south banks. Early's division held this position. On each fort was
mounted two small pieces of artillery.

The weather was cloudy and a furious wind was blowing from the
southwest. As night came on, the preparations for attack were completed, and under the double cover of darkness and the wind, which
prevented the rebels from either seeing or hearing the approach of
our troops, the attack was made.

On the right the Sixth Maine stealthily approached the enemy's
position, then with a sudden rush scaled the works, attacked the
soldiers of Hoke, hand to hand and muzzle to muzzle, and captured
the works. Further to the left the Fifth Wisconsin seized the fort
with its two pieces of artillery, and dislodged its defenders. It was
a complete surprise, but the Confederates soon rallied and attempted
to recover their works.

On the left of the road, meanwhile, two regiments, under Upton,
advanced within twenty-five yards of the Confederate intrenchments
before they were discovered. The Fifth Maine and the One Hundred
and Twenty-first New York received their picket fire, then rushed
upon them and drove them from the works. Our artillery, though
they could not see the pontoon bridge which spanned the Rappahannock in the rebel rear, were yet, by their accurate gunnery, enabled
to make the crossing dangerous and uncomfortable. The success of
Upton relieved the Sixth Maine on the right, where the enemy had
rallied, and were making furious attempts to retake their captured
intrenchments. They had been driven in part from the works when
two reserve regiments came up and made our victory secure.

The Confederates rallied around their colors planted on the
parapet, and rather than to desert them, were captured — a good illustration of the prevalence of sentiment over sense, oftentimes shown
even among fighters. Our loss in this affair was not quite three

hundred men. The attacking party consisted of three thousand men, and therefore did not much outnumber the defenders. The surprise and success was so great, that General Hayes, in his report, estimated the assailants at twenty-five thousand men.

Preparing for the Charge.

The Confederates were mostly cut off from their retreat to the bridge, and we captured sixteen hundred prisoners, eight flags, and four cannon. " I tell you," said one of the Maine men, who had come from the lumber district, "we boomed 'em good!" A large number of the enemy, attempting to reach the south bank, threw themselves into the chilling waters and were drowned. It was Ball's Bluff reversed and avenged.

Unfortunately, this brilliant opening of the campaign was as much a surprise to the methodical Meade as it was to Lee. The Confederate army, when thus attacked, lay in *echelon* from Kelley's Ford to the west of Culpeper. They had lost their advanced position and two thousand men at this first blow, which had struck them on both flanks like a clap of thunder.

Lee, at the first news of this most painful defeat, ordered a retreat beyond the Rapidan ; Meade could not for a time believe his enemy had abandoned his strong position and his winter quarters. It is thought by military critics that Meade should have at once pushed forward a heavy column towards Culpeper, cut Lee's retreating army in two, and defeated or destroyed it in detail.

"You'n Yanks are gettin' doggoned smart! You'ns have got our winter quarters!" exclaimed some prisoners to some of our men at Kelley's Ford. These winter barracks were constructed in the dense woods near Brandy Station.

Here were found bushels of acorns, collected, doubtless, for food. This was shown by a dead Confederate's haversack, which was examined at the time, and found to contain nothing but acorns and kernels of corn. One cannot repress his admiration for men who were fighting so tenaciously under such conditions. In these barracks were found drinking-cups made by the enemy from tin cans which had contained meats, milk, and other delicacies bought from the sutler by our men, and thrown away while formerly occupying this region. Some of our acute newspaper men saw in this an evidence of illicit trade between the North and South.

No movement of any importance was made up to the 26th of November. General Meade, during this time, seems to have gained very accurate knowledge of the Confederate position and numbers. Their force, which was about forty-eight thousand, was estimated by him at this time as forty-five thousand. This fact is noteworthy as it was the first instance on record where a commander of the Army of the Potomac had ever underestimated the enemy, or approached so near the truth.

Although the so-called Indian Summer was in season, the nights were very cold, and we all looked forward to settling down into winter quarters.

"Well," said Joe, the night before the move to Mine Run, stretching out his long legs to a blazing fire in one of the log barracks which the enemy had so kindly constructed, "we are going to have a little peace and comfort now! We've been having a pesky hard time fur the last three months. When I'm going to fight I like to fight and have it done with ; I don't like this trapesing all over creation, runnin' 'round after the rebs." In most instances I have found the rank and file anxious to come to blows without much circumlocution.

The news of General Grant's victory at Chattanooga at this time was the occasion of much rejoicing and enthusiasm.

Thanksgiving Day was approaching, and many of our boys were expecting the arrival of boxes from home crammed with goodies and substantials dear to the hearts and stomachs of hungry soldiers.

The movement on Mine Run began on the 26th, and as it had been raining for two or three days previous to this time, we private soldiers did not consider it the height of felicity to be "trapesing 'round," as Joe termed it, in the mud, with eight days' rations, and our baggage on our backs.

The campaign of Mine Run was celebrated for the fighting which did not take place, and for its failures. It was a carefully prepared movement, depending for success on the exact execution of its different parts, such as Napoleon was accustomed to plan and execute.

Three columns, marching on different lines, were to concentrate at a given point, and attack the enemy. Lee's right line of defence extended along the left bank of Mine Run; his left along the railroad south to Charlottesville. There was an interval of several miles between these two wings. Meade's plan was to cross the Rapidan by the fords, left uncovered by Lee, and by way of the plank road and turnpike to interpose between these several wings and destroy them.

The Third Corps, under French, was to cross the river at Jacob's Ford, and unite at Robertson's Tavern and Park's Store with the Second Corps, which was to form the centre and cross the river at Germania Ford. Without entering into the elaborate details of this movement, French, with his usual capacity for great failures, and painstaking care *not* to be where he was expected, managed to bungle his part of the programme with consummate want of ability. He did not get started until three hours later than he should, six o'clock A.M. being the designated starting time.

Gregg's cavalry division covered the left of the army, which was Sykes's corps.

A recent rainfall caused the engineers to miscalculate the number of boats necessary for the bridges, and the construction of log trestles to lengthen them was one great cause of delay in crossing. The halt was all the more tiresome at the fords, as the soldiers could not even make their coffee for fear of being interrupted by orders to march.

My company forded the stream up to their necks, wetting our cartridge boxes and ammunition, and dampening our ardor with the cold water.

The bridges being ready, Sykes on the left, the Second Corps forming the centre, and with the Third on the right, crossed at sunset. They reached Flat Run, four miles from the Germania, that night. Outposts of rebel cavalry were seen in the vicinity when we were crossing the river.

The next morning at eleven o'clock we reached Robertson's Tavern on the turnpike. Sykes performed his part of the programme with his usual energy. French lost his way in the thickets of the woods. Prince's division marched through a tangled and unbroken forest and, as he termed it, soon "found himself in the bowels of the enemy." Weary and out of temper, the men retraced their steps.

The next morning Meade, who accompanied Warren, ordered French to come to Robertson's Tavern, as he did not dare to attack the enemy unless supported by the thirty thousand composing this force. French returned for his answer the self-evident falsehood that he was on the turnpike waiting for Warren.

It was eleven o'clock ; the enemy were concentrating, and the game slipping from our hands, while French still delayed. His soldiers recognized his incapacity. Derisive laughter and epithets greeted his tardy arrival from the rear. "Tap old whiskey barrel with a bullet !" "Give his horse some seidlitz powders." "Hope a cannon ball will knock his head off !" are specimens of the epithets of contempt that greeted him on every side.

On the morning of the 28th the Third Corps at last came up. It rained all day persistently. The enemy, whom Meade expected to surprise, had disappeared, and the valley of Mine Run was flooded by the rains. When we arrived we found the Confederate Army occupying a line of hills on the opposite banks. Meade had been baffled by his incompetent lieutenant, not by the enemy.

The Southern army, now behind Mine Run, presented everywhere a formidable front. Their artillery was displayed on all the heights beyond, yet Meade was reluctant to give up the game. A few shot and shell were exchanged with the enemy, and the exclamations from our recruits, as the shot shrieked over their heads, were a source of great amusement to the veterans. "That shot went right over me !" "That shell went within twenty feet of my head !" "Gracious, wasn't that a rusher ?" were samples of the exclamations with which they greeted every shot and shell. They evidently thought it the great battle of the war.

Says a comrade: "A group of recruits were boiling coffee ; one of them was stooping down over his tin cup, with his legs apart, when *whiz!* went his coffee cup into the air like a shot. 'Who in thunder did that?' yelled the recruit angrily. One of the enemy's shot had passed between his legs and knocked his tin cup far above party con- tentions ; at least he was made to believe so, and told the incident to me as an actual fact."

While on picket in the lowland, our drummer gathered some pieces of shell, watched his opportunity, and when one exploded in mid-air, threw these pieces down between the legs of one of the recruits who was standing in some water. I never saw a man jump quite so high. "Heavenly kingdom! what's that?" "A shell burst right between your legs," exclaimed the drummer carelessly, as if that were a common occurrence. The recruit stooped down, pawed around in the water, and fished up the pieces ; was convinced that Johnnie had told the truth, and afterward sent them home. We had forgotten our own raw-recruit-hood.

It was cold, frosty, shivering weather, and each of us who had thrown away his overcoat on the march now bitterly regretted the improvidence. My friend Tom witnessed a curious freak of a shell from the enemy. It struck the frozen ground, went below the frost, and underneath a man who was sprawled at his full length, its con- cussion tossing him four or five feet into the air, killing him instantly without leaving a mark of any injury upon the body.

To have carried out faithfully the plan of his campaign, Meade should have manœuvred still farther to the south, but the roads were mere foot-paths running east and west, soaked with rain, and his instructions from Halleck necessitated his covering Washington.

The enemy, while we were lying in their front, were throwing up earthworks and slashing trees for abatis. It was folly to assault them here. On the morning of the 29th we began another march to turn the valley of Mine Run, while approaching its source. Warren directed the left wing while making this move.

"What place is this?" we asked an old man at a mud-chinked cabin.

"Ringe County," was the reply.

We moved forward on by-roads, the turnpike being crowded with trains and troops. After a long and tedious march that afternoon

" Whiz ! went his coffee-cup into the air like a shot." Page 248.

we arrived in front of Hill's corps on Mine Run. Warren's first important manœuvre was an attempt to outflank the Confederate right. Hill answered to the movement by prolonging his line of battle. The attack could not take place until the next day.

Knapsacks were unslung, fires kindled, and coffee boiled. The night was cold; near the fires the ground was wet, at a short distance away from them, frozen. A few slept in a sitting position near their fires. Among these was one of our recruits with a large red moustache. Occasionally, as he dropped to sleep, he would pitch forward and that ornamental appendage would catch fire, and the *fu! fu! fu! fu!* of blowing out his ignited moustache was ludicrous. Pat Quin declared it a genuine case of spontaneous combustion. "And faith, I expected to see him go up like a rocket!" said Quin jocosely.

At last the long, cold, weary night was over, and morning dawned. With blankets and clothing covered with frost, and the water frozen in our canteens, we roused ourselves and attempted, by exercise, to get up warmth and circulation in our half-frozen limbs. Several wandering pigs were pursued, and speedily converted into pork to comfort our hungry stomachs. Some of our men found persimmons, now made delicious by the frost. Joe, who had once been unfortunate enough to attempt to eat an unripe one, could not be persuaded that they were eatable. Pat Quin offered him one, and when six-foot Joe declined, exclaimed, " And the devil take your squeamishness; faith, ye can afford to shrink a yard better than any man in the regiment."

As it grew lighter, we discovered that the enemy had been at work all night throwing up breastworks on the heights beyond Mine Run, and were closed in mass behind these formidable intrenchments, completed during the night.

As the sun came up, revealing the muddy-looking works on the crests beyond, gloom and apprehension settled on every face. The word ran down the line that we were to attack at eight o'clock. " B'ys," said Pat Quin, " and we moight as well say our prayers." And then kneeling he began to tell his beads. Watches, money, valuables, and keepsakes were placed in the hand of the chaplain and quartermaster and other non-combatants. Some wrote their names and pinned them on their coats or placed them in their pockets; a precaution not uncommon, however, when going into a desperate battle. It was so cold that the skirmishers on both sides stuck their muskets into the ground by the bayonet, and ran up and down, slapping their hands to keep warm.

"We all felt," says a comrade, "that an attack would be useless and murderous ; but, if not willing, we were ready uncomplainingly to be offered as a sacrifice, trusting that in some way it would not be useless."

Such was the feeling as the cannonade opened at eight o'clock, and the men were expecting to hear the order given every moment, " For ward ; guide right ! " The enemy, from their works, defiantly shouted out invitations, and beckoned to them to come on.

Meade had planned to attack on both flanks, leaving the main attack, however, to the Second Corps. He therefore waited impatiently for Warren's attack. Warren had examined the enemy's position, found it impregnable, and, though he had previously declared it possible to succeed in the attack, now believing it to be useless, conveyed to his commander the resolution he had taken not to assault. This act of Warren's was real courage, more to be commended than reckless disregard of life.

Meade soon joined Warren and confirmed his judgment. When the soldiers understood this resolution, they felt that a great burden had been taken from their anxious but not irresolute hearts.

Meade now resolved upon an attack on the enemy's left, and with this purpose concentrated anew on the turnpike. The Confederates were, however, found impregnable all along their lines.

But for positive orders to the contrary, Meade might now march on Fredericksburg, take possession of its heights, and thus derive a substantial success. But a preposterous order from Halleck forbade, and there was no choice left but retreat.

On the morning of the 3d of December the army re-entered its old camps and did not again take the field until the summer campaign opened under Grant.

The headquarters now occupied by Meade were the same previously occupied by Lee. The telegraph office was said to be occupied by the same operator for the fifth time.

CHAPTER XXVI.

OUR winter hut was very comfortable. It was built of logs, the chinks filled with mud, while the roof was made from split pieces lapped one over the other. A capacious chimney, built of sticks and mud, formed a picturesque turret at the end of the hut. Its interior was in keeping with its unpretentious exterior. On each side, at right angles with a spacious fireplace, and a door, were two bunks, one above the other, each wide enough for two men to sleep in. The floor was of earth beaten down hard and smooth. A rude shelf was fixed above the wide fireplace. On this were pipes, matches, tobacco-pouches, and other conveniences. A small rough table, the top made from cracker-boxes, with a rubber blanket for its cover, and with knotty oaks crossed for its legs, occupied the centre of the hut. Our burnished muskets, brasses, and bayonets were hung around the interior on pegs, with picturesque effect. The knapsacks were at the head of each bunk for pillows, while leaves, and in some instances grass and straw, covered by the blankets, formed the beds. Eight men occupied this habitation, and were proud of their quarters. A small aperture over the door, and another at the end near the chimney, over which were stretched pieces of white cotton cloth, admitted light and air.

Let us look at the group in the hut on a winter evening. At the rough table described, four of the inmates are playing bluff, with sutlers' checks and small change for stakes. Two or three are sitting on the edges of the bunks, with their legs dangling over the sides. One sits with his back to the side of the hut near the fireplace smoking, his eyes half closed in deep revery. A knock is heard at the door, and two visitors from a neighboring camp enter. The card-players abandon their game, while all welcome the visitors with the rough but hearty salutation common to soldiers, " How are you,

Tom?" "Where did you come from?" "Have a pipe?" "Sit down," etc.

Tom and his comrade, both from the ——th Massachusetts, are soon chatting and smoking, and have agreed to stay all night. The conversation turns on Mine Run; each gives bits of his individual experience. Referring to the attack at Rappahannock Station, Tom, a beardless boy, but an old soldier, says: "You fellows attribute the success of that affair to its being made under cover of the darkness and the strong wind blowing from the rebel works. I'll tell you how it was. Our brigade was commanded by Colonel —— of the ——th Massachusetts. We drew the fire of those forts by marching in the open field, in line of battle, directly for the forts, as if we were the only attacking party, while those who made the real attack were masked in the woods to our right and rushed upon them and carried the works in the dusk of the evening.

"At Mine Run we had only two days' rations, and not big ones either. Whew! wasn't the weather cold there! Where were we? Why, our corps, Sykes's, was massed in the woods near the enemy that night before the charge was to be made. We could see them, and they could see us. If they hadn't been so confounded busy building fortifications, they could have thrown us into confusion with shot and shell, we were so huddled together. We were not allowed to build any fires during that night. Some of our pickets were frozen and had to be brought in on stretchers. I don't know how it was where you were, but the rebel position in our front was stronger than it was at Fredericksburg. We were told that we were to attack those works in the morning at eight o'clock. That night there was fought in men's hearts the hardest battle of the whole war. I know some fellows who made their wills that night, and some whose hair turned white. Look at my hands" (showing them cramped and frostbitten), "that's what I got there! The next morning our artillery was mostly in position. It was as cold as Greenland, and there was but little said, and not a bit of flinching, but there wasn't a man who felt that he had any business to find himself alive the next day. It was a great relief when we got word that the plan for attacking had been abandoned."

"Well," said Joe, "I don't like to go inter a fite when there's no show at all. I tell yeou, some of the fellers in my squad had faces as long as hoe-handles!"

"Yis," said Quin, "and Joe was so in love with his divilish long face he wouldn't eat a p'simmon fur fear it might pucker it up sum!"

"Darn ye! you are always full of jaw and jack-knife, Pat!" said Joe, half in anger at Quin's joke.

"And did I iver tell ye, bys, that I was one ov the first prisoners this divilish rebellidn iver tuck?" queried Hanley, an acquaintance of Pat, who had dropped in to smoke a pipe and chat. "Tell us about it!" "Give us the yarn!" was the request.

Hanley, who was an old regular, loaded his pipe afresh, pulled his hat down in regulation style, and began:—

"I'm not much of a man fur a story; I can't git in any fine pints, but here's the substance of it. I was a corporal in the Second United States Artillery, stationed at Fayetteville, North Carolina, in 1861. We were commanded by 'Blue Jim Anderson.' The officers were all rebels from the first. They tried to coax us *non-com's* and privates, and offered some of us commissions to come over and fight on their side, and the divil take thim!

"Of course it was managed so it was useless for us to resist. So we surrendered (to the militia and citizen authorities) thirty-eight thousand stands of arms, two batteries, and ninety tons of ammunition. The terms of our surrender were that we should bring away the company property and our own personal rigs. They put us on board of the *Charles Dennis*, of Marblehead, a schooner they had captured. They had stolen the flag and even the halliards.

"Blue Jim tried to get us to join their divilish Confederacy, but only one man, a private, was at all inclined to do so. We kept him drunk two days for fear he'd disgrace us by enlisting in the rebel army. He was the biggest drunkard I ever knew. And faith, I'v been sorry iver since I didn't let him join with thim. He would have drank the Confederacy dry in a week! Why did they call our colonel Blue Jim? Well, bys, his name was Jim Anderson to begin with, and at the battle of Moliney del Ray, in Mexico, he put on a soldier's blue overcoat to cover his uniform, so he would be in no danger of being picked off as an officer. After that the bys called him Blue Jim! An' the nickname stuck to him divilish toight!—An is there anything else ye can ask me to interrupt me story? Well, then, I'll tell ye the rist. After we got away on the *Charles Dennis* (which was a rattle-ter-bang old fishing-schooner, and leaked like a sieve), and sure the rebels fitted out another craft to capture us. But to make a long story short, our captain was a Marblehead Yankee, and was too smart for thim ribs, and we got away. We had our garrison flag with us. We had smuggled that so the ribs shouldn't disgrace it, and we tied rope yarns together and hoisted it at the peak.

"The last of March, half-full of water, we sailed into New York harbor with our flag flying at the peak. There Commander Winslow, who reported us at Washington, gave us transportation. We arrived in Washington somewhere the first of May, 1861 ; marched the men up by the Capitol; halted them, and then Sergeant Bradley, and meself, with the American flag under me arm, went hunting all over the city to find the United States government. Did ye iver hear the loikes of that, bys ? Well, finally we found the government, way down by the Washington Monument, in a little old yellow building."

"You mean the War Department ?" interrupted Johnson, whose acquaintance with the city gave him the situation.

"Stop your botherin'! If yes know the story bitter than meself, till it, will yez! An' phat the divil is the War Department but the government? an' sure, ye blockhead!" said Hanley, indignantly. "We found it, as I tould ye, and the bys who was waitin' to hear from the government was glad enough to know that we had found it. We had a divil of a time, especially in finding the government! So you see, bys, that's how it was that I was one of the first men who surrendered to this murtherin' rebellion!"

The winter was passed with picket duty and the usual routine. But very little drill was exacted from the veterans, but they were put to the duty of drilling the recruits and conscripts. Visiting friends in different regiments was one of the pastimes.

Says a comrade : "In a large hut, with a capacious tent belonging to the sanitary commission forming the roof, I attended, at Culpeper, an exhibition which was advertised as 'A grand entertainment by the Star Troupe.' Singing and dancing were interspersed through a farce, which gave more unbounded delight to those who listened than to any audience ever before gathered under one roof.

"I have forgotten, after the lapse of years, what the so-called play was all about, but have a remembrance of an unlimited amount of burnt cork on the stage, and enjoyment among the audience. It was said the agent of the Christian commission finally removed the canvas from the top of the mammoth hut, because an innocent dance of enlisted men was held in it.

"A field-officer, after Mine Run, showed his authority, and gained the contempt of the soldiers, by dispersing a meeting of privates and non-commissioned officers who had come together to devise ways and means of sending home a comrade killed during that movement."

Large numbers of substitutes, conscripts, bounty-jumpers, and enlisted ex-rebels went through the army during the winter months. I say went through; for very few were detained. Those who had served in the rebel army were sent West on the frontiers to fight the Indians. The bounty-jumpers deserted, helping to fill other quotas for communities not given to love of country or fighting. Many, unfit for the service, were sent to hospitals. Some were shot for previous desertions. Of all who came to the army at this time, the drafted men were generally the best war material. They were often very homesick, but made good soldiers.

Courts-martial were quite common during the winter. One of these tribunals tried and convicted a chaplain for horse-stealing. For some reason the chaplains of the army, speaking generally, were not a great success. Their intercourse with whiskey-drinking, profane superiors soon contaminated their piety, and little acts, such as selling postage stamps given them by the sanitary commission, at a large advance on the regular price, and similar speculations, brought many of them into contempt among the rank and file. I think properly drilled and selected men of mature years, in this grand vocation, would have exerted a moral influence much needed. They would also have contributed an element not to be despised, and much needed in an army.

There were many exceptions to this rule of worthlessness, and many noble men "filled the bill," as the boys termed it. I remember at one time overhearing a general officer introduce a new chaplain to some brother-officers as a "d—d good fellow for a chaplain." I could not help thinking that the chaplain might render good service to his country and the army by rebuking the unbecoming manners of his superior. A gentleman, whatever his opinions are, will not show contempt for religion.

A certain Brooklyn regiment was the particular rival of the ——th New York. What was well done by one, the other was anxious to do a little better. An earnest chaplain had been preaching with good effect to the Brooklyn men. Knowing the rivalry between the regiments, he shrewdly thought to score a point in this way. With this in view, he went to the colonel of the ——th New York and requested permission to hold divine services. "It will not do any good," was the gruff reply. "You might just as well preach to the horses. They are good fighters, but make dreadful poor saints. We are a godless crowd, but can fight like devils!"

The chaplain replied, "But, Colonel, I held services several times at the ——th Brooklyn and had quite a number of converts; baptized thirteen of them last Sunday."

At mention of the ——th Brooklyn the colonel was all attention, and his eyes sparkled with emulation as he gave his consent to have religious services. "Draw my regiment up in a hollow square for divine service, at once!" was the order given to the adjutant. "If one of them dares to wink, laugh, or move, put him in the guard-house."

The order was obeyed to the letter, for the colonel was a magnificent disciplinarian. The men listened with automatic silence and devotion. The services over, the last psalm sung, the colonel astounded the good chaplain by the following order : "Adjutant, detail twenty men and have them baptized! This regiment isn't going to let that d—d Brooklyn regiment beat them at anything!"

Such were the bluff manners of the army ; and, though the story may be a myth, yet it illustrates both the commendable rivalry between regiments, and the disrespect of the army for ordinary services held by its chaplains.

Yet, on the other hand, I believe there never was a class of men who held proved piety in such deep reverence as our common soldiers. One man, consistently religious, exerted a marked influence for good in the company or regiment which was so fortunate as to possess him. I have already spoken of two men of this character. They had the confidence and respect of every man in the regiment. It was only a few months ago that a former comrade, now a confirmed scoffer, said, when referring to them, "Those men made a man almost believe in religion." Such is the influence of consistent piety.

FISHING FOR A FURLOUGH. Page 257.

Many of our bounty-jumpers exhausted a great share of their mental force in ingenious devices to obtain a discharge. The various methods resorted to for getting away from the army, would in itself make a chapter but little creditable to human nature. But this was the chaff among a mass of patriotic men, and was soon sifted in the whirlwind of battle.

One incident occurs to me of a conscript, who was apparently demented on the subject of fishing. With a pin hook and cotton line and a pole, he would sit or stand, with a blank look of simplicity on his face, before a mud-puddle in the road or by the camp, in rain or sun, the butt of many a joke and jeer. He was examined by a board of surgeons and pronounced insane. His discharge was finally ordered, and so little was he esteemed capable of taking care of himself, that a comrade was put in charge of him to see him safe on his way to the cars. As his comrade got him safely on the train, he said, "Now, Jim, go home to your mother." A new light filled the blank in Jim's eyes as he made reply, "That's what I've been fishing for." He had humbugged not only the whole camp, but an able board of surgeons. However funny, one can but despise such a man.

"My term of service," says a comrade, "expired in the winter of '64. As large inducements of bounty and furlough were given to such as would return to the field, I, like many of my comrades, re-enlisted and went home on a thirty days' furlough. Joe and Quinn were among the number, and nearly all our veterans were thus retained in service.

"It is not my intention to tell of the scenes of home; how the veterans were questioned, petted, and lionized by the patriotic people of the quiet villages to which they returned. Strange as it may appear, many of them missed the excitement of camp life."

"Gosh!" said Joe to me afterwards, "wasn't I lonesome for my company! Seemed liked Sunday at home."

Says a comrade : "On our return, as we passed through Baltimore, a large number of other veterans were on their way to rejoin their regiments. A lieutenant-colonel from Providence had in charge a lot of them, who were somewhat drunk with Jersey lightning. After getting them on board he was anxiously discussing with the surgeon, on the platform of the station, how they were to get sober men enough to guard the drunken ones within.

"An Irishman, who was 'jes' comferbel,' and hardly able to hold up his drooping hand, languidly thrust out of the window, to arrest attention, exclaimed, 'Kernel, dear! Kernel! put the surgeon on guard! Divil a man iver got by him alive.' The surgeon did not enjoy the joke as much as the colonel did.

"General Grant took up his headquarters with the army, March 24, 1864, at Culpeper Court-House. We had expected to see a

My First View of General Grant.

large man, broad-shouldered and athletic. His appearance to many was a great surprise. 'Of all the officers in the group, where I saw him,' said one, 'I should have selected almost any one but him as the general who won Vicksburg. He was small and slim, even to under size; very quiet, and with a slight stoop. But for his straps, which came down too far in front of his shoulders, on his rusty uniform, I should have taken him for a clerk at headquarters rather than a general. This was the first impression. The second was the look of concentration shown in his quiet, self-controlled face.'

"The mouth, as seen through the closely trimmed full beard, made a straight line across the face, and shut like a vice. The eyes were earnest yet calm ; his face was grave, and in the whole expression a look of calm concentration. He seemed, as it were, to centre all his faculties on the thought to which they were at the moment turned. Such was my first impression of General Grant.

"We had heard of his being a great smoker, but he had neither pipe nor cigar in his mouth at that time, and Quin exclaimed, 'And where the divil is his pipe ?' I saw him several times afterward with a cigar in his mouth, but do not remember ever seeing it lighted."

Much satisfaction was expressed when it was known that General Grant was to take charge of the army. Meade was not very popular with the rank and file, and his plan of consolidating regiments, brigades, companies, and corps, hurt the pride of men who had fought together and had a regimental, corps, or brigade history. It was like breaking up families, and did more mischief than would have been done by returning ten thousand men to private life.

" 'Old Spectacles' is nothing but an upper-adjutant now," said Wad Rider, who had just returned to duty, with his wound healed, and full of good-natured, odd fun as ever. Joe and Wad Rider now wore non-commissioned officers' chevrons.

I must have been somewhat fond of authority, for I won a sobriquet from the recruits at that time, more enduring than any of my previous military titles. I was in the habit of saying to the men, somewhat sharply, " Turn out here promptly!" as I passed down the company street to call the morning roll. One morning one of the waggish recruits said, " Here comes ' Promptly ' ! " and the nickname stuck with the tenacity of a burr to a long-haired dog.

They called Joe " Lengthy," having no reverence for his exalted rank. " Gol darn 'em ! " said Joe, indignantly, " I'll pump drill and thunder and lightning inter 'm if they don't stop their nonsense ! "

False alarms were quite common as good weather came on. On the 6th of February we were ordered to prepare rations for another movement.   We crossed the Rapidan on the 7th, recrossed at night, and returned to our camps on the 8th.

Several balls, in which men were dressed to personate women, with other amusements, took place in large log buildings constructed by the soldiers.   Our principal and standard amusement during the long winter months was writing to the girls at home.   It was a poor letter-writer that did not have several lady correspondents.   Another amusement was fishing.   My friend Tom was an inveterate disciple of Izaak Walton, and carried hook, bob, and sinker as habitually as he carried his head.   It was a poor day when Tom could fish and didn't.

The Blue Hills were in sight, and the old inhabitants declared that there would be rain once in two days, until the blue ridge took off its snow cap.   The forests of the region were converted into stump lots, and one of the old men of that country declared to me, "After this yer war ther will be no fences nor stuff to build them with."

The frequent rains enlarged small streams to a quarter of a mile in width, and the camp of the provost guard of one of the corps was submerged.   Some of them awoke to find the water two feet deep in their tents.   As spring came on, we took long tramps up the mountain sides, and caught glimpses of the beautiful country.   Many declared that after the war they would come here and settle.   Lately my friend Tom has informed me, that one of his comrades had returned to Beverly Ford, married the only daughter of a Virginia planter, whose two brothers and father were killed in the Confederate army.   He married the plantation with the daughter, and by his Yankee thrift had restored the land to its original productiveness. The blue and gray thus intermixed will, without doubt, make a worthy and patriotic race, and if need be, fighters that will always be found on the right side.   One feature of winter camp life was the presence of real women.   Often these were officers' wives, sometimes wives by brevet.

Thousands of crows, sleek, fat, and noisy, were constantly seen around our camps.   They performed the part of scavengers and grew fat and tame.   The citizens had no ammunition, and we were not allowed to waste it on "nigger crows," as Pat Quin called them.

Reviews, inspections, and target practice increased in frequency as the spring advanced, and many other forerunners of an early campaign began to appear.

CHAPTER XXVII.

MUCH satisfaction was expressed when Grant took command of the army, with his headquarters in the field. The intelligent common soldier felt that Grant's influence and reputation would crush out the small jealousies and wrangles for unearned promotions which had thus far proved a powerful factor in bringing defeat and disgrace to the "Army of the Potomac." We felt that officers must now win promotion by showing the lion-like qualities of the soldier rather than by the fox-like arts of the politician ; that promotions would now be won by merit in the field, and not by cringing flattery or favoritism at Washington.

If Grant was not identified with the history of the army he was to command, neither was he identified in its entangling cliques.

Though a graduate of West Point, and moulded by its military instructions, he was not inspired by its pretence or pedantry. He had faith in success, and in the volunteer soldiers who fought our battles. His presence in the field inspired confidence if it did not excite enthusiasm. While not given to pretentious reviews of the army, he knew all its parts.

He had learned the modesty of a citizen in his struggle with poverty in private life, and was as unpretentious at the head of the army as when driving a wood team from his farm to St. Louis. He had thus far been "lucky," yet deservedly so. He owed his successes to great elements of character rather than to great military knowledge. Had he been subjected to competitive examination with prominent officers of the Union army, he would, perhaps, have stood at the foot of the class and been rejected. He had, however, qualities which made him the peer of any of them. He had that indefinable quality called common sense, a faculty which is so often superior to brilliancy in actual affairs. To this was added a tenacity of purpose which never wavered because of the cost of that which he deemed important to grasp. This concentration and singleness of purpose, which moved inflexibly for the main point to be attained, made him terrible.

It took a battle to wake up his sluggish temperament, yet nothing overthrew his wonderful equipoise. To think clearly and decide promptly, when the turmoil of battle had thrown others from their mental balance, was one of his characteristic qualities. The temper of his mind was such that the most ready syllable on his lips was " Forward," and the most familiar decision of his mind, " Fight ! "

Such was the man called to command the "Army of the Potomac," and direct the general movements of all our armies. Whatever criticism else I may deem it honest to record in these pages, one fact stands indelibly written by the logic of events, — his success, not favoritism, secured for him his great command ; and when this man of iron, this earnest, inflexible soldier, gathered the reins of control in his hands, the defeat of the Confederacy was assured.

It was his good fortune to reach his high position when, instructed by reverses, the people, the press, and the administration were prepared to give him intelligent support. Sustained by a patriotic and devoted people, and with a million of men at his back, he was fortunate in being enabled to direct all our armies in one systematic plan. The destructive incoherence of action hitherto existing between the armies in the field (which he aptly likened to a balky team) no longer stood as a cause of our defeat.

One fact, small in itself, showed his common sense. Most military men would, if called to general command, have made their head-quarters at Washington. Grant seems to have comprehended instinctively the importance of holding himself aloof from its entangling political and semi-military influences.

He had the wisdom to direct and inspire the army with his presence and will. He devoted himself to preparation for the death-grapple about to ensue, yet he had a more difficult task than he conceived of. He had thus far been playing the game with the less skilful players of the Confederacy. He was now about to encounter that master of the game who had checkmated so many antagonists on the difficult chess-board of Virginia. He was about to encounter that incomparable infantry on whose undaunted hearts the Confederacy rested. He was about to meet that heroic army which, with tattered garments and scanty food, for three long years had carried forward, upon its scarred and bleeding bosom, the standard of revolt ; that army which on so many bloody fields had successfully disputed the possession of empire with its superb and brave antagonist. On the one side was discipline and intelligence in the ranks, patriotism

Our Friends the Enemy.

and the resources of a great people ; on the other, blind enthusiasm and devotion — poverty of resource, but confidence in success, with directing skill and steadfast purpose seldom equalled.

It remained to be seen, when Grant should meet this trained ath-lete of the rebellion, whether he would preserve his reputation. Like

Pope, Grant seems to have attributed the failure of the "Army of the Potomac" to not being thoroughly fought. He believed he could grapple with and crush the rebellion out of existence by sturdy, continuous, unrelenting battle.

In selecting the overland route for the campaign before him, it seems to the writer that he did not thoroughly appreciate that elementary maxim of Frederick the Great, that "an army, like a serpent, moves on its belly!" The whole problem of that difficult field of operations, ridged by mountains, crossed by streams, and veiled by tangled woods, was complicated by the difficulty of feeding an army upon it.

The poverty of Virginia — "where a crow in flying over it would be obliged to carry his rations" — was one of its strong defensive features. An army moving through its labyrinth of tangled woods must be fed, and its trains of supply protected. Its superior artillery could not be brought into the "continuous hammering" in this wood-entangled region.

On the other hand, the Confederates were familiar with all its by-paths, its intricate and confusing mazes. Its inhabitants were their spies and scouts.

To the Union army it was like a voyage of discovery made in unknown lands, among warlike enemies lying in ambush. These disadvantages to the Union army were deftly used by its antagonists to destroy and overwhelm it, as will be seen in the narrative which follows.

It is shown that Grant's original impressions were against the overland route. I can but think that he yielded his own pronounced views in this direction to the decided preference shown in its favor by Lincoln and Halleck. He believed it unwise to excite antagonism by opposing long-entertained and pet projects. Had he done so, it is plain to see at this day he would have encountered moral obstacles which, at critical moments, might have proved the ruin of his plans and reputation.

In yielding to these views he, perhaps, was wise. Had the army met the same murderous losses it sustained in the wilderness while carrying out plans contrary to the prejudices and fears of those in high military circles at Washington, the chances are he would not have been sustained and seconded as thoroughly as he was.

Thus that which, viewed from the pure military standpoint, lacked wisdom was, perhaps, wisest and best when viewed as a whole. Grant wisely forebore to antagonize the moral forces at work in the field of politics. He steered clear of the dangerous eddies and quicksands, refusing to mix and complicate the game of war with that of politics.

CHAPTER XXVIII.

THE WILDERNESS.

ABOUT the 1st of May active preparations betokened a speedy move. The log barracks which had sheltered us during the winter were abandoned and destroyed. To prevent delay in marching, the troops were bivouacked in the open fields.

On May 4th, at midnight, the army began its march to open the great campaign of 1864. Breaking camp was like many similar scenes in the history of the army. The march began silently, without call of bugle or beat of drum. The veterans, as a rule, silently following their file leaders, marched forward, reserving their strength, while the recruits laughed and noisily joked. " Laugh while you can," is a wise proverb ; but this had been tempered and modified in the practice of the veteran by many weary marches, many a terrible battle, and humiliating defeat. Their thoughts were moulded by former experiences.

Did their footsteps tend to victory or defeat ? Would its end give them mutilation, unknown graves, or honors and a safe return to happy homes ? A careless indifference outwardly, with an undercurrent of saddened forebodings, often accompany the intelligent veteran soldier, when starting out for the uncertain adventures of the battle-field.

The bravest men known in my experience are those who are neither blinded by hope nor indifferent to actual dangers. Bravery is often a matter of temperament ; often it comes from familiarity with the form of danger encountered. Escaping unscathed from perils often met makes men confident. They become fatalists. The proud soldier says it's of no use to dodge bullets or fate. Napoleon once uttered a maxim well fitted to make brave soldiers. It was this : " Drive death into the enemy's ranks, and you drive it out of your own."

266

Towards daylight the head of our column reached Ely's Ford. Here a light canvas boat-bridge, and a bridge of wooden boats, were quickly constructed by our skilled engineers. A column of cavalry preceded the infantry, to watch every road and path by which the enemy might be advancing to attack. At Germania Ford and the fords above, three boat-bridges spanned the Rapidan. Warren's and Sedgwick's corps crossed by these bridges. The heavy teams crossed on the wooden boat-bridges; the infantry, with the lighter fighting trains, on the canvas pontoons. The column on our right was also preceded by a division of cavalry, while another division was in the rear to prevent straggling and to cover the trains. Such was, in substance, the order of march of this great army, with its enormous trains of four thousand wagons and a hundred thousand men.

During the day each of the three corps marched twenty miles, threw out five bridges without an accident, and with but little delay. "It was the stride of a giant." As the march progressed, the soldiers began to throw away their overcoats and blankets. "I could have marched a mile," said a comrade afterwards, who was with Sedgwick's column, "on these rejected garments." I have an ungratified curiosity even to-day to know what became of this immense waste. Doubtless wherever there was a harvest there were also harvesters.

At eleven o'clock in the morning of the 4th we reached Chancellorsville and bivouacked near the blackened ruins of the old Chancellor House. Weather-stained remnants of clothing, rusty gun-barrels and bayonets, tarnished brasses and equipments, with bleaching bones and grinning skulls, marked this memorable field.

In the cavity of one of these skulls was a nest with the three speckled eggs of a field-bird. In yet another was a wasp-nest. Life in embryo in the skull of death! The sting of the wasp and the song of the bird! One, as it were, defending the skull of the battle's victim; the other singing the hopeful pæans of a nation redeemed by their death.

Here a word of explanation is needful to an understanding of that which follows. When the Union army began this movement, the centre of Lee's line was at Orange Court-House. From this point two roads, the Orange plank road and the Orange turnpike, run parallel to each other and struck our line of march. When Lee found his flank turned, he did not retreat, as Grant confidently expected, and as an ordinary general would have done. By a rapid change of front he concentrated his men so as to compel battle in the dark and entangling depths of the Wilderness. Here he hoped either to ensnare and destroy, or to compel the retreat of the Union army, now hurrying forward to seize his communications with Richmond. It was a masterly conception of genius ; a movement little expected by either Meade or Grant, who believed the rebel army, with its flank turned, had no alternative that was safe, but retreat. Thus it was that they made no competent preparation to meet the enemy in force at this point.

On the night of the 4th, Warren's corps bivouacked at the Wilderness Tavern, which stands near the junction of the Germania plank road and the two roads hitherto mentioned. At the same time Ewell's corps of the rebel army bivouacked on the Orange turnpike, within three miles of Warren. Sedgwick's corps had as yet not moved up from Germania Ford. Warren had thrown out Griffin's division on the turnpike, so that the enemy might not come in on this road and interrupt Sedgwick's column while he was moving upon the Germania plank road. Neither party knew the presence of the other definitely, yet like magnets they were being irresistibly drawn together by the gravitation of war.

Leading our right column on the morning of the 5th, Warren's corps resumed its prescribed march towards Parker's Store, which is on the Orange plank road. The reader will see that a speedy encounter was inevitable. Early in the morning, Ewell began his march on the same road by which Griffin was advancing. They met. The Union skirmishers were driven in. The intelligence of the meeting was conveyed to Grant, and orders suspending the movements prescribed to the different corps were at once given.

Grant and Meade both arrived at the Wilderness Tavern shortly after the initial encounter. Meade was heard to say : "They have left a division to fool us here while they concentrate and prepare a position towards the North Anna, and what I want is to prevent those fellows getting back to Mine Run." Grant, with this misconception, at once ordered an attack to brush away or capture this obtruding force.

The attack was opened by Griffin's division, which at first swept

GRANT AND MEADE IN THE WILDERNESS.   Page 268.

everything in its front. It had simply encountered the van of Ewell's column. Had the situation been well understood by the Union commander, a disposition of forces might have been made which would have proved fatal to Ewell. The means employed were naturally incompetent and in keeping with the misunderstanding.

The disordered van of Ewell's column re-formed on a wooded hill, where it was joined by the remainder of the corps, and resumed at once the offensive. It so happened that the right of Warren's corps was at this time uncovered. Wright's division of the Sixth Corps, which should have covered this flank, had not come up, owing to the dense underbrush through which it was compelled to move. On this exposed flank Ewell directed his attack. On Griffin's left was Wadsworth's division. This advanced, but while beating through the dense undergrowth encountered a terrible fire from an unseen enemy. It illustrates the difficulty that beset troops operating in this tangled region, that there being no other guides, their directions were given them by the points of the compass. The orders were to advance due west. For some unknown reason Wadsworth advanced northwest, and this brought the fire of the enemy on his flank. Under this terrible flank fire the division broke in disorder. The best way to retreat was for each man to get to the rear, and not stand on the order of his going. The division of Wadsworth finally re-formed in the rear and did good service during the fight which followed.

Crawford's division, on the left of Wadsworth's, was nearly surrounded, and was driven back with the loss of two regiments. In this abrupt encounter began the battle of the Wilderness. The opening was not auspicious. Warren had lost three thousand men. The enemy was in force in our front.

In this initial encounter several of my acquaintances were made prisoners. Here my friend Tom, of whom I have often spoken, met the enemy for the twenty-second time, and was theirs at last, and lacking only fifteen days of the expiration of his three years' service. One of my friends had captured a rebel and was marching him into our lines. As he came out into a little cart-path he and his prisoner encountered a rebel officer. "Where are you going?" said the officer, with his revolver turned upon the Yankee soldier. "To the Yankee lines!" replied the prisoner. "Give that man your musket!"

imperiously ordered the officer to the Yankee soldier. "He had me, and I obeyed!" said my informant. No sooner had the officer disappeared than the rebel soldier, to the astonishment of my friend, coolly handed him back his musket, saying, "Here, take your shooting-iron, and march me to the Yankee army. I'm done with this doggoned Confedercy, I am!" On the way into our lines my informant inquired why he had gone back on

Things reversed.

the Confederacy. "Well, stranger, the rich men made this war, and we poor men have to do the fighting, and there's too much fight, I reckon, for my health. I've been fighting ever since this blamed war began, and I can't see no end to it!"

The abrupt encounter of arms already detailed had awakened Grant to the fact that the Army of Northern Virginia was in his front. He countermanded the previously ordered marches, and at once accepted Lee's challenge to battle. Here in the gloomy forest, with dogged resolution, he prepared to grapple with the enemy in this blind wrestle to the death. He at once recalled Hancock's corps from its march to Shady Grove Church. Our corps had advanced about ten miles when the order reached us, and at eleven o'clock we began our return march up the Brock road. The strategic point was where the roads intersect around the Wilderness Tavern. It was this point that Ewell was attempting to seize when the encounter began.

Getty had already begun the fight before our arrival. Cheers went up from our sweat-begrimed, dusty veterans, as they came up at about three o'clock and formed in double line of battle in front of the Brock road. The road was very narrow, and densely wooded on both sides. Here we began to construct rifle-pits, by piling up logs and throwing up the soil against them. For this purpose men used their tin drinking-cups, bayonets, and case-knives, as well as the few shovels and picks which accompanied each division on pack-mules. We had not completed our rifle-pits when an order came to move on the enemy.

The scene of savage fighting with the ambushed enemy, which followed, defies description. No one could see the fight fifty feet from him. The roll and crackle of the musketry was something terrible, even to the veterans of many battles. The lines were very near each other, and from the dense underbrush and the tops of the trees came puffs of smoke, the "*ping!*" of the bullets, and the yell of the enemy. It was a blind and bloody hunt to the death, in bewildering thickets, rather than a battle.

Amid the tangled, darkened woods, the "*ping! ping! ping!*" the "*pop! pop! pop!*" of rifles, and the long roll and roar of musketry, blending on our right and left, were terrible. In advancing it was next to impossible to preserve a distinct line, and we were constantly broken into small groups. The underbrush and briars scratched our faces, tore our clothing, and tripped our feet from under us, constantly.

On our left, a few pieces of artillery, stationed on cleared high ground, beat time to the steady roar of musketry. On the Orange plank road, Rickett's battery, or Kirby's, familiar to us in so many battles, was at work with its usual vigor, adding to the uproar.

"We are playing right into these devils' hands! Bushwhacking is the game! There ain't a tree in our front twenty feet high, but there is a reb up that tree!" said Wad Rider. Two, three, and four times we rushed upon the enemy, but were met by a murderous fire and with heavy loss from concealed enemies. As often as we rushed forward we were compelled to get back. It was in the midst of this uproar that Mott's division gave way, and here the brave General Hayes, in endeavoring to close the break thus caused in the line, fell pierced by an enemy's bullet.

With the intention of relieving this pressure on our front, Wadsworth's division was sent from Warren's Corps southward through the woods, to fall upon Hill's rear and flank. It did not arrive in time to be of use, owing to the difficulty of making its way through the underbrush.

That night the men of this division lay on their arms, so near the enemy that during the night several parties of the rebels, while looking for water, wandered into our lines and were captured, while our men straggled into the embraces of the enemy on the same errand.

The uproar of battle continued through the twilight hours. It was eight o'clock before the deadly crackle of musketry died gradually away, and the sad shadows of night, like a pall, fell over the dead in these ensanguined thickets. The groans and cries for water or for help from the wounded gave place to the sounds of the conflict.

With the green leaves and the darkness for their winding-sheet, and the mournful whisper of the tree-tops, stirred by the breeze, for their requiem, the dead lay thick in this wild and tangled wood. This singular battle was a disconnected series of bushwhacking encounters, illustrating the tactics of savages rather than science of modern war. Thus ended the first day's fighting of the Army of the Potomac under Grant.

CHAPTER XXIX.

OUR lines now faced westward. Burnside's corps had arrived early in the morning, and the formation was north and south in the following order : Sedgwick on the right, then Warren's, Burnside's, and Hancock's corps, in the order named. The orders given for the battle were very simple. They were these : "Attack along the entire line at five o'clock ! "

There was no opportunity for grand manœuvres on this difficult field. It so happened that the commanders of both armies had aggressively determined to assume the offensive early on the morning of the 6th. The plan of the Confederate commander was to overwhelm our left and compel us to retreat to the Rapidan. Longstreet had, however, not yet arrived to participate in the fight, and Lee could not deliver his decisive blow until he came up. Pending his arrival he determined to call our attention from our left by a movement against our right. It thus fell out that Lee began his movement before the hour of attack designated by Grant.

Before five o'clock the roar of musketry on our right told that Sedgwick was attacked by the enemy. Then Hancock and Warren joined in the attack, and the whole line was engaged. Ward's and Hayes's brigades, of Hancock's corps, were supported by the brigades of Owens and Carrol of our division. These advanced on the right and left of the Orange plank road, through the same impediments of underbrush characteristic of previous advances. As Longstreet had not yet arrived, this was Lee's weak flank. Wadsworth's men, whose position the evening previous, on the right of Birney, we have already designated, fought their way across the front of that portion of Hancock's corps which was on the plank road, and began to drive the Confederates up that road. The enemy were at once attacked with such vigor that their lines were broken at all points, and they were driven confusedly through the woods. Their dead and wounded lay thick in the jungle of scrub-oaks, pines, and underbrush, through which we rushed upon them. Squads of prisoners constantly going to the rear exchanged rough but good-natured salutations with our men.

One of them said, "You'ns run over we'uns in four rows, right smart, git! this morning!"

Another exclaimed, "You blue bellies will have red bellies before you'ns git inter Richmond!"

By six o'clock the rebel lines had been driven a mile and a half and were broken and disordered. The advance of our corps through swamps and tangled thickets, in this hot encounter, had broken our own lines. A proper formation of the ranks or any control by the officers in command, in this tangled region, seemed impossible. In this disorganized condition a portion of our lines, under Birney, was brought to a stand by the firm resistance of the enemy. It had encountered the van of Longstreet's corps hastening to the fight. A halt was ordered, and the lines which had become irregular, and the brigades and regiments confusedly mixed, were reorganized.

Longstreet had, meanwhile, begun to form on the plank road, and when a further advance was attempted by the Union lines, they met this new force, and the fighting became fierce and bloody. Hancock had promptly informed Meade of the presence of some of Longstreet's men on his front. Neither was aware that he had met the entire force of that general. Intelligence had been gathered from prisoners the night previous, which led to the inference that he was moving to attack the Union left. Expecting him in this direction proved to be a great hindrance to Hancock. It was for this that he had allowed his left, under Gibbon, to remain on the Brock road.

Meade ordered Sheridan to attack Longstreet with his cavalry as far as practicable, without endangering the safety of the trains, and also notified Hancock that a division of the Ninth Corps would, if required, be sent him. Burnside, who was directed to get possession of the open ground at Chewings, and fall on the rebel general Hill's left and rear, had not attacked. Hancock had been informed of this arrangement, and was anxiously looking for this diversion in his favor.

At eleven o'clock the firing died away. Burnside, though constantly ordered, had not attacked. Longstreet, meanwhile, was preparing for a decisive onslaught on our front. His first blow fell on Frank's brigade of Hancock's command, which was soon swept away by the whirlwind of attack, then struck Mott's division and scattered it like leaves before the wind. Hancock answered to this by attempting to swing back his left to the plank road, and unite with his right, which was still holding its advance position.

On the right of Hancock, Wadsworth's division fought with heroic firmness. It charged the enemy several times, but was finally driven back in disorder. In this encounter General Wadsworth, while in the rear and centre of his lines cheering his men, fell mortally wounded. In the confusion which followed he was abandoned to the enemy, and died next day within their lines.

It was impossible to manœuvre on account of the obstructive undergrowth, where no one could see a hundred paces in any direction. The roar of musketry alone disclosed the position of the foe, and the movements were generally learned only by actual collisions. Under these circumstances, general officers could hold but little control of their lines.

The troops fell back, in the confusion caused by the difficult field on which they fought, and re-formed in two lines behind their old intrenchments on the Brock road. Before this the tempest of the attack had ceased as suddenly as it began.

Longstreet, at the head of the assaulting column, was desperately wounded. He had, by mistake, been fired upon by his own men when the tempest was at its height. This caused the halt in the attack. Lee now took command of this part of the line in person, and cautiously postponed further battle until more perfect dispositions of his troops were made. This lull in the storm lasted until four o'clock. The attack was then resumed. Then the Confederate columns came dashing on through the undergrowth until within a hundred yards of our lines. Here they halted and opened fire. Protected by their breastworks, for a time our men received but little harm.

The attack on the left of the plank road was especially desperate. Here Mott's division and Ward's brigade of Birney's division held the line. Here the guns of the Sixth Maine Battery kept up a rapid and destructive fire upon the enemy, who made no headway until a new ally came to their assistance.

Flames sprang up in the woods in our front, where the fight of the morning had taken place. With crackling roar like an army of fire, it came down upon the Union line. The wind drove the blinding smoke and suffocating heat into our faces. This, added to the oppressive heat of the weather, was almost unendurable. It soon became terrible. The line of fire, with resistless march, swept the thickets before its advance, then reaching out its tongue of flame, ignited the breastworks composed of resinous logs, which soon roared and crackled along their entire length. The men fought the enemy and the flames at the same time. Their hair and beards were singed and their faces blistered.

At last, blinded by the smoke and suffocated by the hot breath of the flames, with the whole length of their intrenchments a crackling mass of fire, they gave way and fell back to the second line of log intrenchments.

Planting the Rebel Flag.

With a shout the rebel column approached the road and attempted to seize the abandoned position. The impartial flames in turn drove them back. The fire soon consumed the logs, and the rebels planted their colors there.

The fire swept on and reached our second line of intrenchments. This, like the first, was soon consumed. The men formed at some places eight and ten ranks deep, the rear men loading the muskets for

BREASTWORKS ON FIRE.   Page 277.

the front ranks, and thus undauntedly kept up the fight while the logs in front of them were in flames. Finally, blistered, blinded, and suffocating, they gave way. The enemy yelled with exultation. They rushed forward and attempted to place their colors on this line of our defence. Their triumph was brief, for the last line of log defences was soon consumed like the first. Then, with a shout resembling the rebel yell, our men charged the enemy, and swept them back from the field. At sunset our pickets were advanced half a mile without opposition.

During the conflict our men had exhausted their ammunition and had been obliged to gather cartridges from the dead and wounded. Their rifles, in many instances, became so hot by constant firing, that they were unable to hold them in their hands. The fire was the most terrible enemy our men met that day, and few survivors will forget this attack of the flames on their lines. It is estimated that two hundred of our wounded were consumed.

We have but little to add to our description of this battle. Burnside, who was to have engaged the enemy at an early hour, did not attack until two o'clock. When he did advance on the enemy, he found them intrenched on the opposite side of a swampy ravine, and could gain no advantage in the encounter. The attack was made too late to be of assistance to Hancock, who had relied on this diversion in his favor, and had made his dispositions with this expectation.

After sundown the Confederates made an attack on the right of Burnside's corps, creating considerable confusion. The night prevented them from following up their success. Thus ended this terrible battle, the full details of which were hid in the tangled woods and darkling forests, where its mysteries will never be disclosed. It was a drawn battle. Both commanders, at its termination, arrived at the same conclusion, — that further attack on those lines was hopeless. The losses on both sides were terrible. Our killed and wounded were 12,484 men ; our missing, 3047.

It is estimated in the "Medical and Surgical History of the War" that the Confederates lost on this bloody field eight thousand killed and wounded, and thirty-four hundred missing. No authority is given for this estimate. In most instances we were the attacking party, and our losses were doubtless much larger than those of the enemy.

Had Grant, at the conclusion of this battle, retreated beyond the

Rapidan, his action would not have been without precedent.   Its results had not, however, shaken his resolution to advance.   The one difference between him and previous commanders of the army was that he advanced when they would have retreated.   It was this inflexible, undaunted temper which made him a great soldier.

CHAPTER XXX.

THE men of both armies were worn out with the two battles just fought. The terrible fighting, the difficult nature of the ground, as well as the heat of the weather, had been very exhausting. Besides this, the reaction which follows the excitement of battle had set in.

The morning of Saturday, May 7th, found the hostile armies confronting each other from behind their intrenchments. Neither cared to assume the offensive. Each was willing to receive an attack with the advantage of the defensive on their side, but neither could see a favorable opportunity on this field, for further aggressive action. Neither could attack without danger of being checkmated.

Grant, aggressive by nature, determined on a move toward the rebel capital instead of from it, as had been the previous action of the Army of the Potomac after undecisive conflicts.

In the report of these operations, referring to his antagonist, he says: "It was evident to my mind that the two days' fighting had satisfied him of his inability to further maintain the contest in the open field." The real position of affairs at that time appears to have been that neither cared further to maintain the contest under conditions then existing.

Grant could not expect Lee, for mere sentiment, to abandon the advantage which the defensive gave him, and attack under disadvantages which he himself thought prudent to avoid.

From the beginning of his military operations in Virginia, Lee had adopted the theory of war known as the "defensive with offensive returns." Throughout the war it was his policy, while assuming the defensive, to watch for opportunities to deliver aggressive blows. Grant's quoted phrase, therefore, seems to have been intended as an excuse for his own position, for the newspaper readers at home rather than for veritable history.

On the 7th, other than an undecisive cavalry encounter on the Brock road, no action took place. Grant had, meanwhile, formed the plan of making a rapid march to Spottsylvania Court-House, thus planting his army between the enemy and Richmond. To carry out this plan successfully, it was necessary first to move his heavy trains, that the roads might be clear for the infantry columns. The distance from the Wilderness battle-field to Spottsylvania Court-House, by the direct route of the Brock road, was fifteen miles.

The trains were set in motion about three o'clock Saturday afternoon, May 7th, by the roundabout way of Chancellorsville. The movement could not be made, however, without attracting the attention of the enemy, and it was doubtless this which led Lee to surmise the plan of the Union commander. It was half-past eight in the evening when the army finally began its march.

The cavalry, under Merritt, was on the Brock road, trying to clear it of a cavalry force of the enemy who were endeavoring to seize it. Preceded by Warren's Corps, the Second Corps under Hancock began its march on the Brock road. Sedgwick and Burnside moved on the pike and plank road, by the exterior route of Chancellorsville. Warren found his march blocked by the Union cavalry force engaged with Stuart's cavalry, before mentioned, who were barricading the roads by felling trees and by other devices. Meade's cavalry escort also got in their way and delayed them. These obstructions, in spite of Warren's well-known energy and clear-sightedness, delayed the whole movement at a time when success depended upon a rapid march.

Night marches are usually slow and tedious, and require much more careful supervision to prevent confusion than marches by day. That night Hancock's Corps made a tedious and constantly interrupted march to Todd's Tavern, which stands half-way between Spottsylvania Court-House and the scene of the Wilderness fighting. The men were wearied and fretful. At every halt they would fall asleep while seated on their knapsacks in the road. Then, moving on a short distance, would be brought to a halt ; again, after waiting and standing and fretting, they would get the order, " In place, rest ! " and then again be called up to hitch along a short distance farther, to be halted again in the same manner.

The atmosphere was close and muggy, and the road narrow and dark. If there is anything that knocks the patience out of a soldier, it is starting out on a march, and then, after being hours on the road, to find that you could have marched the same distance, if not delayed, in a half-hour.

It is scarcely possible to conceive of men being in worse condition for fighting than when morning dawned. There is, to my mind, full as much lost as gained by night marching. Jaded men do not fight as resolutely as fresh ones. A night's rest and a good breakfast are essential to put a soldier in proper fighting condition. The contrary condition makes men irresolute and discouraged. Surgeons bear witness to the fact that among wounded men the shock to the system is less serious among those who have eaten their breakfast than those who have not.

The difference between a hero and a coward is often just this difference in condition produced by proper sleep and food.

Todd's Tavern was not reached by Hancock's tired men until nine o'clock in the morning. Here they found a division of Gregg's cavalry engaged with the enemy's cavalry, in front of the shabby little building called "Todd's Tavern."

The infantry relieved the cavalry, and at once began piling up logs and rails, and digging for defence. At half-past one, we marched up the Brock road, midway between Spottsylvania and our starting-point, to support the troops operating in that direction. Warren's Corps which, as we have mentioned, preceded us, had already encountered the rebel infantry.

The presence of the enemy ahead of Warren was said to be, in part, an accident. Lee, having been informed of the movement of our trains, guessed its meaning and instructed Anderson, then in command of Longstreet's Corps, to be ready to march to Spottsylvania early the next morning. Anderson drew out his men from the intrenchments in order to be in readiness for the march. The forests were on fire all around him, and, unable to find a comfortable camping-ground for his troops at that point, he began his march that night.

On their march his men met none of those impediments which embarrassed our columns. They had rested and eaten their breakfast when they encountered our troops. The Shady Grove road, by which they marched, runs almost parallel with the Brock road, and the distance to Spottsylvania Court-House by this route is about the same as that travelled by the Union troops. Had Anderson carried out strictly the orders received from Lee, Warren's Corps would have been ahead of the Confederates in the occupation of Spottsylvania Court-House.

Warren's advance consisted of Robinson's and Griffin's divisions. They came out of the woods into the clearing at Alsop's, about nine o'clock in the morning. "They were rejoiced," as one of them said, "to get out of the woods into the daylight of cleared land." The road, before reaching Alsop's, forks, and again intersects, a mile from the fork. Robinson's division took the right, and Griffin's the left. They were marching carelessly; had not as yet eaten their breakfast. They had no thoughts of encountering an enemy other than the cavalry which, though troublesome, like flies, is easily brushed away.

When nearly half-way across the open fields at this point, and while ascending a hill, they were surprised by fierce volleys from hostile infantry posted behind the crest. The men had not braced their nerves for an encounter, and at this unexpected assault the line wavered, and the men finally broke, and fell back in confusion like raw recruits. They were rallied with some difficulty in the woods beyond the clearing.

It is a mistake to suppose that in a stampede of this kind the officers do all the rallying. The most intrepid and earnest men of all ranks do this. The men often rally each other, and brace the nerves of faltering comrades by sarcasms which hit as hard as bullets. Sometimes I have known officers kept in their places by the same methods. I have known privates stop the flight of demoralized superiors by force, and turn their unwilling steps towards the enemy.

During the initial encounter just narrated, private soldiers of the Eighty-third Pennsylvania Regiment rushed upon the enemy's intrenchments, pulled Confederates over their barricades, and marched them as prisoners into our lines. While the disordered men of the two divisions were re-forming in the woods, Crawford's division came up. It charged the enemy on the double-quick, and drove them out of the woods on Griffin's left. Wadsworth's former command also arrived on the field and drove the enemy on the right. The whole corps then moved up close to the enemy. Taught by experience in the Wilderness the convenience of intrenchments, the men needed no orders to construct them, but began at once piling up rails and digging up the soil with their tin plates, drinking-cups, bayonets, and knives. Sedgwick arrived in the afternoon with a portion of his corps. An unsuccessful attack was next made by a New Jersey brigade. Crawford's division, advancing shortly after, surprised a part of Ewell's Corps marching by the flank, and captured a hundred prisoners. The day closed, however, with the enemy in possession of Spottsylvania Court-House.

Thus opened the battle along the lines of Spottsylvania, made famous by twelve days' continuous, obstinate, and savage encounter. It was on this field that Grant doggedly said, "I'm determined to fight it out on this line if it takes all summer!"

Early on the 9th, the army was in position in front of Spottsylvania in the following order: Burnside on the extreme left, then Sedgwick, Warren, and Hancock in the order named. Hancock held the high ground overlooking the river Po, and from which could be seen the Shady Grove road. From this position, clouds of dust rising in different directions marked, for three or four miles, the progress of marching troops. At one time a long baggage train of the enemy was seen moving on the Shady Grove road, which ran nearly parallel to the river, and a half-mile distant.

No action occurred on the 9th. The time was spent in digging and building log intrenchments, which in some instances were covered with green bushes to guard against fire, which had proved so disastrous in the Wilderness. Our skirmishers were pushed up close to the enemy, and actively engaged, in order to ascertain or develop, as it is termed, the enemy's position, and feel out his weak parts.

The sharp-shooters of the enemy, with long-range rifles, were unusually busy in preventing our men from obtaining this knowledge. "At one time," says a comrade, "a bullet struck among a party of soldiers playing euchre, made a hole through one of the cards held, and mutilated the thumb of a player. This player good-naturedly remarked, 'I pass!' and the game was removed to a safer place." A considerable number were killed and wounded by these vigilant sharp-shooters. An acquaintance belonging to Sedgwick's Corps lost a finger and a brass ornament on his cap by a bullet from one of them.   The most illustrious victim of this rifle practice that day was General Sedgwick, who was killed while standing behind the breastworks within his lines.   The love his soldiers yet have for him is the best attestation of his worth and soldierly qualities.   General Wright then took command of the Sixth Corps.

The intrenched lines of the enemy on the 10th might be said to resemble, in their general outline, an immense letter A.   The general course of the two lines forming its arms from its apex to its base was north and south.   The west or left arm of this A was two miles and a half, the right or east arm, three miles and over in length.   The dash across the top, to complete this A, is made by the Brock road, which runs northeast from Spindlers' farm to Spottsylvania Court-House,

Confederate Sharpshooter.

Death of Sedgwick.

where it intersects with the Fredericksburg road, a short distance inside these intrenchments. Above this road, towards the apex of the A, and formed across the angle, nearly parallel with the road mentioned, was an interior line of breastworks.

Of course this fortified line which we have represented as forming an A was jagged and sinuous.   It was rendered wonderfully strong by abatis, slashings, curtain works, and all devices known to the military engineer.   To this must be added the fact that the works were mounted with artillery, and had indented lines for flank fire wherever practicable. They were also partially concealed by dense, scrubby woods. Such was the strong position upon which the Union army was soon to be hurled in a succession of desperate attacks.

It is a well-established maxim in war never to attack an enemy's strong position in front when this position can be turned. Did not General Grant violate this sensible and well-grounded maxim by attacking enemies in a position which, by reason of its strength, was equivalent to increasing their numbers threefold? The more probable reason for these attacks is that Grant favored "continuous hammering," and hated the delays necessary to manœuvre the enemy out of his works, as was done afterwards at Petersburg. He believed in his ability to overthrow the enemy by his superiority in numbers, and death-grapple with him whenever and wherever found, and he knew that the people at home were in accord with this method.

Lee took advantage of this disposition by exacting a heavy tribute of blood at every step and throwing upon his antagonist all the perils of attack. While this policy of the Union general might be permitted to one having back of him a people with almost unlimited means, it is easy to perceive that it would soon have proved fatal to a weak country.

In front of Hancock's position the river Po ran east, and then on his left made an abrupt bend and ran for several miles nearly due south, describing almost a right angle. Moving on the enemy in his front, across the angle, would therefore compel him to cross the same river twice. Intelligence was received which indicated that the enemy was moving towards Fredericksburg.

At six o'clock on the morning of the 9th, Hancock's entire corps crossed the river, which was here from forty to fifty feet wide, too deep for fording, and fringed by dense, entangled growths of bushes and trees.

Our division, under Gibbon, crossed without opposition from the enemy. Barlow's force was crossed above us with but little fighting. Three boat-bridges were thrown out across the river in our rear, one near Barlow's crossing-place, the other two near that of Gibbon. From all accounts the men of Birney's division had a rough time in crossing, for here the enemy's opposition to the movement seemed concentrated. Said my comrade who participated in this affair, "The rebs were as thick and as bloody as mosquitoes, and seemed determined we shouldn't cross."

The object of Hancock's movement appears to have been in the nature of a reconnoisance in force, to ascertain the position of the enemy's left flank, and, if possible, to capture the trains moving on the Shady Grove road, a half-mile therefrom and parallel to the river. Possibly there may also have been in reserve a design of turning the enemy's flank.

The difficult crossing and the construction of bridges occupied much of the day. The column was then pushed forward across the angle formed by the river towards the Brock House bridge. The thick woods and the gathering darkness soon brought the column to a halt for the night.

At early dawn it moved forward, and, approaching that portion of the river running south, found the enemy intrenched on the opposite bank, near the Brock House bridge. The enemy were so strong here that it was impossible for the Union troops to force the crossing, and Brooke, commanding the fourth brigade of Barlow's division, crossed a half-mile below.

Pushing forward, he soon encountered the enemy behind their intrenchments. At this moment the whole movement was checked by an order received by Hancock to recross the river with two of his three divisions, to assist in an attack on the enemy's centre.

Under these instructions Gibbon's division, followed by Birney's, recrossed the Po and hastened to execute the order of the commanding general, leaving Barlow's division to hold the position on the south side of the river. The enemy, finding their trains endangered by the presence of our troops, proceeded to drive him from this threatening stand.

It was soon discovered that the enemy was advancing in force to overwhelm Barlow, and it was deemed prudent to withdraw to the north side of the river. The movement to return began about two o'clock. Two of the brigades were in front of the Shady Grove road, and two in the rear of it, facing south. Behind this position were open fields extending to the pontoon bridges on the river, which were swept by the Confederate artillery at Brock House bridge, as well as from other parts of their intrenched line.

The brigades of Brown and Brooke were finally withdrawn to a wooded crest on their right, while the other two brigades formed on a hill in front of their pontoon bridges. The enemy, seeing these movements for retreat, were emboldened to attack. Said a comrade who was in this affair : " The rebs came up yelling as if they'd got a special license to thresh us. We'd have sent them back howling if we'd been allowed to charge! They didn't like our reception, as it was, and got back almost as quick as they came up. You'd ought to have heared the volley our brigade gave them ! They re-formed and 'tried it on again,' though they didn't seem quite so cheerful as they

Barlow's Division holding the Enemy.

did the first time. We drove them back the second time. By this time the woods were on fire on our right and rear."

With the enemy advancing in our front with determined fierceness, a roaring forest fire in our rear, and the plain swept by the artillery of the enemy, we began our retreat to the bridges. "Taken all together," said my comrade, "this was the hottest fight I ever got into. The weather was hot, the fire was hotter, while the enemy in front warmed our faces with their rifles."

Coolly and in admirable order the troops crossed the level plain under the artillery fire converged at this point. The enemy followed, yelling with exultation.   Occasionally our men would face the enemy, and drive them back with a fierce volley.   Our troops fell back reluctantly, notwithstanding their imperilled surroundings.   During this retrograde movement, the horses of Captain Arnold's battery, frightened by the flames, became unmanageable, and ran, wedging one of the guns between two trees in such a manner as to compel its abandonment to the enemy.

General Hancock mentions, in his report, the loss of this gun as the first ever lost by the Second Corps.

In referring to this retreat, Swinton says, "The remarkable coolness of the MEN alone saved them from a great disaster."

Barlow's troops were finally safely crossed, the bridges taken up or destroyed, and the affair ended in the smoke of a fierce artillery duel between the hostile forces on opposite sides of the river.   The enemy were so jubilant over this affair that General Heth, commanding the Confederate forces, issued to his troops a congratulatory order, countersigned by General Lee.

In referring to this report, Hancock grimly says, "Had not Barlow's fine division, then in full strength, received imperative orders to withdraw, Heth's division would have had no cause for congratulation."

This movement had put the enemy on his guard, and resulted in the strengthening of this part of his line.

" Wedged between two trees."   Page 288.

CHAPTER XXXI.

THE point against which the next important blow was aimed by the Union commander is known as Laurel Hill. This hill stood at the apex of the immense A, which we have mentioned as bearing a general resemblance to the form of the enemy's intrenched lines. The top of this hill was densely wooded, and behind the woods were the enemy's works. Its approaches were protected by an abatis, and swept by artillery and musketry. Opposite the right, in front of the attacking force, was a stunted growth of sprawling cedars, mostly dead, with their pike-like branches near the ground, interlaced and projecting.

At a quarter to four, Generals Wright and Mott were ordered to attack. The assault was made at five o'clock, with great determination. The men, passing through the cedars mentioned, were thrown into disorder, and when the attacking column reached the open field beyond, a terrible flank and direct fire swept the whole ground. Some of the men of Carroll's brigade reached the abatis, climbed the exterior slopes, only to be killed inside the intrenchments. The troops failed in this attack, notwithstanding it was made with great resolution and courage.

A soldier, mortally wounded in the assault, was asked by a comrade if he could do anything for him. "Yes; give me a drink of water, and fix me so I can get one more shot at the rebs!" was the response.

General Rice, one of those who had so bravely defended Little Round Top, was mortally wounded in this attack. In response to an inquiry, "Is there anything I can do to make it easier for you, General?" he replied, "Yes; turn me with my face to the enemy."

A comrade says, "When we saw General Warren in full uniform among us, our confidence in him was so great that we felt as if we could go up *two* hills ; but when we came in sight of the rebel works on top, I, for one, wished the hill was greased so I could slide down again."

" I felt," said another, "as if it was a repetition of the charge on the heights of Fredericksburg."

At half-past six another charge was made by our division. This assault was as fruitless as the first. It began at seven o'clock, and was soon over.

Meanwhile, on the left of Warren's position, Colonel Upton of the Sixth Corps led a more successful charge. He attacked that part of the enemy's works which formed the apex of the salient. His force consisted of his own and the Third Brigade, and four regiments of Neil's brigade of the Sixth Corps. The artillery opened on the enemy's lines with heavy fire. The understanding was that when this cannonade ceased, *that* was to be the moment of the attack. During the artillery fire the force formed in four lines and was silently led to the edge of a pine wood, in front of which was open ground, two hundred yards or more from, and leading to, the enemy's intrenchments.

To act in conjunction with this attack, Mott's division formed in the open fields near the Brown House, and was ordered to attack at five o'clock the next morning.

When the thundering cannonade ceased, Upton's troops sprang into the open ground, and with wild hurrahs rushed upon the enemy's intrenchments. The artillery and musketry which swept the plain could not stop them. Without pausing, they pulled away the abatis, and after a moment's hand-to-hand struggle with the bayonet, took possession of the works. The enemy soon rallied and attacked them on flank and in front ; but they held their position resolutely, until, under cover of the night, they were withdrawn.

The division of Mott, which was to have seconded this attack, for reasons not fully explained, completely failed to do so. Mott's column was formed in full sight of the enemy and of Upton's forces, under cover. This undoubtedly converged the attention and force of the Confederates upon Mott, and made it easier for Upton to succeed. A comrade belonging to Mott's division says they were told there were not over a hundred men behind the intrenchments they were about to attack. When, however, they approached the works, the yelling and shouting of the enemy proved that a force superior to their own was there.

Mott's failure will, perhaps, illustrate the folly of attempting to deceive men as to a task to be performed. Experience has repeatedly demonstrated that with soldiers it is better even to exaggerate difficulties to be overcome than to conceal them. No better fighting men than Mott's were to be found in the army, and its commander had earned a high reputation for courage.

With this attempt the fighting on the 11th ended.

HANCOCK'S ATTACK.

The fighting at this point had been just successful enough to lead the commanding general to believe that an attack made at an earlier hour, and with fuller preparations, would be successful. Thus, notwithstanding the failures narrated, it was determined to assault the position with Hancock's Corps, supported by the whole army.

At midnight, during a heavy rain, the Second Corps was moved into the open fields near the Brown House, within twelve hundred yards of the position they were to attack. The details of the works to be stormed were but little known, although, as far as practicable, the ground had been examined by the engineers, and by Hancock in person.

It illustrates the difficulties which beset the fighting on this murderous field, that the order for the advancing columns was given, as if to a befogged squadron on the ocean, by the compass, as the only possible method of direction. The engineers had ascertained that the McCool House was just inside the apex of the salient, the point of attack, and that following a straight line from the Brown House to this building would carry our troops inside their intrenched lines. The co-operating corps of Warren and Wright were to be pushed aggressively close to the enemy's works, in readiness for any weakening of their lines, or to attack elsewhere if ordered. In this manner the whole army was to be combined in action.

The salient to be attacked was inside the open fields of the Laudron Place, and these were connected with those belonging to the Brown House. Hancock's line was formed in the cleared fields, near this house. Barlow's division was formed on the cleared land which

extended up to the enemy's works. Birney deployed on his right;
Mott supported him, with Gibbon's division in reserve.

At half-past four o'clock a dim twilight gave sufficient light to see
the compass, and the whole column moved forward. Barlow's men,
at double quick, overran the enemy's pickets without firing a shot,
and impetuously moved to the works. In their eagerness, the intervals between the lines of the storming columns were closed up, and
in one solid mass, with wild, exciting cheers, they broke into a run
towards the enemy.

The sharp volleys of infantry fire with which they were met did
not stop them for a moment. As they came in sight of the angle of
the enemy's works on their left, the whole mass of men, without
orders, by one common impulse, made towards it. In the twinkling
of an eye those in advance had pulled away the fallen trees forming
the abatis, and were upon the enemy's works.

Fierce yells and cheers, the quick *pop! pop! pop!* of rifles was heard
for a moment, then angry thrusts with the bayonet completed the
work, and the confused column poured like a mighty wave over the
works.

On Barlow's left, Owen's and Carroll's brigades, almost at the
same time, had driven Stuart's men and captured two guns. Birney's
and Mott's troops entered the west face of the salient, and encountered the "Stonewall Brigade." Inside the angle our men were now
mixed in a great confusion, caused by the hurried attack. They pursued the enemy half a mile through the woods towards Spottsylvania
Court-House, but were brought to a halt at the intrenched line
formed across the angle. There were captured, however, thirty
colors, twenty pieces of artillery, and four thousand prisoners, among
whom were Generals Stuart and Edward Johnson.

As is often the case with attacking forces, ours had expended
their energy in the pursuit, and had none left for the attack. The
reserves were soon moved up to occupy the captured works. Every
circumstance had favored this assault. The enemy's artillery for this
part of the line had been sent away to meet an anticipated sally on
their flank, with instructions to be back at daylight. They were just
arriving as the attack was made. The unpropitious weather had
lulled the vigilance of the pickets, and the fog, like a veil, concealed
the advancing columns from sight until they were close at hand.

Wright was ordered to attack the west face of the angle, on Hancock's right. Upon the arrival of the Sixth Corps, a comrade says: "There we were with a picket line thrown out inside of their works, while we were holding the intrenchments from the outside. We weren't proud! It was easier to take the outside of the rebel works than to dig new ones inside. We'd got their log rifle-pits any way they could fix it!"

We now held the woods and ravine on the right, as well as the apex of the salient. Lee seemed determined to re-take his lost position at all costs. Not less than five heavy assaults were made during the day for this purpose, each assault being repulsed by our men with great loss to the enemy.

Comrades have since told me some of the incidents of the fight at the west face of the angle. Here the most murderous fighting took place; by all accounts the fiercest and most deadly of the war.

"There was," said my informant, "nothing but a log breastwork between us and the enemy. They were fighting from the inside, and we from the outside. Our flag was planted on one side, and the rebel flag on the other. At times our men would find a crevice in the logs, and punch the rebels on the other side with a bayonet, or get a hole large enough to shoot through. Then one of our men would creep on top the breastworks and, protecting himself all he could, shoot in among the rebs huddled together on the inside, while his chums outside would pass to him loaded muskets. Sometimes one of our men would be seen standing upon the works, deliberately shooting in among them, while comrades passed loaded muskets, and when he was shot, another would take his place. One reb near me attempted to play the same dodge, when one of our plucky little fellows, with a sudden rush, grabbed him by his collar, and pulled him over on our side, head first. That reb swore like a heathen. At one time, when we were 'going it' hot and heavy, a reb stuck up his gray or white hat on his bayonet, when two or three bullets were put through it.

"'That was a flag of truce!' exclaimed the rebs on the other side.

"'What do yer want, Johnnie?' we inquired.

"'Want to surrender, if we can get a right smart chance!' was the reply. During a lull in the fighting these came over the works and were marched to the rear. But bless yer soul, 'twant a bit of use!

Half a dozen times the rebs stuck up something white to show that they'd got enough of fighting, and wanted to be taken in out of the wet. But others kept crowding up and taking their places as fast as we took them in. They kept the intrenchments jammed full on the other side of the logs all the time. Lively? Well, you jest bet! The rebs had to stop and throw their dead one side to get room to fight in. The logs around them were cut and slivered inter kindling-wood. Trees were cut down by bullets. The bushes and twigs were shot into flinders like broom-corn."

Our men, while sheltering their own bodies as much as possible, would reach over to shoot among the Confederates. One of my chums, with his jack-knife, enlarged a crevice in the logs so as to get a fire on them. Before he could get a chance to use it, the muzzle of a Johnnie's rifle came poking through the hole. Quick as thought, my chum, the proprietor of that port-hole, placed the muzzle of his musket against the intruding muzzle, and with a big yell fired and pushed with all his might. The suddenness of the act dislodged the reb. "Gosh," said my chum, grimly chuckling, "you bet that reb was astonished!"

The spectacle was horrible in the adjacent cornfield and on the road, but in the trenches at the angle the dead men were found literally in piles. The margins of the log works were fringed with them. Thirty were counted within a distance of fifty feet.

The large number of dead on our own side who lay in this vicinity is illustrated by an incident told me by one of Wadsworth's men, belonging to the Seventy-sixth New York.

"We were moving into the fight on the morning of the 13th, when we came upon a lot of men, apparently sleeping, covered by their shelter-tents. 'Why don't these men get up and go into the fight with us?' growled one of our soldiers.

"'They take it mighty cool, to be sleeping under this fire!' said another, advancing towards them to make an attempt to arouse them. He kicked one with his foot, then pulled the shelter-tents from the prostrate forms, only to be appalled by the upturned, ghastly faces of dead men! 'These soldiers will never go into a fight again!' exclaimed Eggleston."

It was literally a bivouac of the dead, who had thus been hastily covered by the rough but loving hands of comrades.

" These soldiers will never go into a fight again."　Page 294.

The Union troops brought up artillery which was well directed close up to the intrenchments near the east angle, while at the west angle it was run up against the breastworks, enfilading the face of the angle.

The terrible nature of the infantry fire is shown by the fact that a tree eighteen inches in diameter was cut down by bullets inside the works of this angle of horror and death, and the whole forest within range was killed by the infantry fire. "An oak-tree, twenty-two inches in diam-

The Sleep of Death.

eter," says a rebel general, "was cut down by musket-balls, and fell about twelve o'clock, injuring several men of the First South Carolina."

It was not till midnight (after being in bloody conflict twenty-four hours, with constant and fierce efforts made for the recovery of the angle) that the rebel troops were finally withdrawn to an interior line which they had meanwhile constructed. Although we had broken through the angle which appeared to be the hinge of their position, the interior lines of Lee proved impregnable. On the right, Warren attacked, but without driving the enemy. General Potter, of Burnside's Corps, attacked the east side of the angle, at one time capturing two pieces of artillery. He could not, however, get possession of the works from which he had driven the enemy, and the guns were finally recaptured and Potter repulsed.

During the week which followed, the Union army moved from flank to flank, seeking some weak spot where it could break through and disrupt Lee's formidable structure of intrenched lines. The 15th, 16th, and 17th were spent in intrenching, opening roads, and examining the country.

The next movement was a turning operation designed to dislodge the Confederates from their intrenchments. The preparations for it were begun on the afternoon of the 19th. The watchful enemy, surmising that a movement was contemplated, delivered one of his sudden counter-blows on our right wing.

Part of the line attacked was held by some foot-artillery under General Tyler just summoned from the defences of Washington. They had never been in a fight before, but were magnificently drilled and disciplined. They knew nothing about bushwhacking, or the methods of fighting now adopted by our veterans. Some of these regiments were as large as our ordinary veteran brigades. When attacked, they boldly rushed upon the enemy, and with regular and furious volleys soon put them to flight. Their loss was very heavy in killed, wounded, and prisoners, but to them, doubtless, belongs the honor of repulsing the enemy.

The Fifth and Sixth Corps soon after came up, pursued the enemy through the woods, and captured several hundred prisoners. One of the prisoners, when told that the troops who had defeated them were never in a fight before, said, "Well, Yanks, I reckon you'ns better bring the rest of yer green sogers up hyer if yer are in a hurry to lick we'uns! We shot lots of 'em, but doggoned if they seemed ter know we'uns were licking 'em at all!"

On May 20th the army finally moving by the left abandoned the lines which it had so long and obstinately maintained, and moved once more towards Richmond.

Thus ended this memorable battle, or succession of battles, along the lines of Spottsylvania, which began on the 9th and ended on the 20th of May. History has rarely if ever presented such a strange, savage, and long-continued struggle.

From the 5th to the 20th of May a bloody and almost constant battle had been waged by both armies. The chance for recuperation and rest was small, and the hardships and nerve strain put upon the troops engaged were terrible.

The losses on both sides were in keeping with the desperate nature of the fighting. The number of killed, wounded, and missing since the campaign opened at the Wilderness is estimated by General Humphrey to have been 33,110 men ; of these, the killed and wounded are estimated at 28,207. Total losses at Spottsylvania, 17,723.

The enemy's loss is surmised to have been large, but is not definitely known.

CHAPTER XXXII.

CO-OPERATIVE MOVEMENTS. — TO COLD HARBOR.

IN conjunction with the advance of the "Army of the Potomac," co-operative movements on James River and in the Shenandoah Valley had been early set in operation. Before proceeding with the main narrative, a rapid survey of these is needful to a general understanding of the situation.

As early as April 1st, an army under General B. F. Butler had been assembled at Yorktown. In placing it at this point, it was intended to convey to the military authorities at Richmond the impression that an advance up the Peninsula was intended.

With Richmond for its objective point, on May the 4th, the larger part of this army, composed of 34,379 men of all arms, was embarked on transports. Two days later, having passed up James River, the main body of the army was landed at Bermuda Hundred, a neck of land which is formed by the meeting of the James and Appomattox rivers.

General Butler had been instructed by the commanding general to move simultaneously with the army under Meade ; to advance on the south side of the James, and gain a foothold as far up the river as possible. If Lee fell back on Richmond, the Army of the Potomac was to unite with the Army of the James. Such, briefly, were the general plans, as shown by General Butler's instructions. After landing the main body of the Army of the James at Bermuda Hundred, a line of intrenchments three miles in length was thrown up across the connecting neck.

On the morning of the 7th, the Fifth Brigade was sent out to destroy the Petersburg and Richmond Railroad, three miles distant. Here it encountered the enemy, and, after a brief engagement, both parties fell back. Another advance on the 9th resulted in the destruction of the railroad and the retirement of the enemy to Petersburg.

Intelligence from Washington was at this time received by General Butler to the effect that Lee was in full retreat upon Richmond. In accordance with his instructions, General Butler abandoned further operations here and began advancing up the south side of James River on Richmond. While advancing, he encountered the army of defence, which had been rapidly formed under General Beauregard, and, after an undecisive conflict, retired behind his intrenchments at Bermuda Hundred. Here the enemy leisurely threw up intrenchments in his front, and, to use Butler's own expressive simile, he was "bottled up."

While his position was now such that the enemy could not attack him advantageously, it was equally impossible for him to emerge to attack them, or further to operate on Richmond from the south side of the James. The one movement still open to him was to cross the narrow Appomattox and seize the city of Petersburg, ten miles distant. This city was the strategic key of Richmond; and had Butler then been successful in taking and holding it, some military critics believe that Lee must have abandoned as vain the attempt to further defend Richmond, and would have fallen back on another line of defence. Its possession by our army would have left the enemy but one line of railroad running south from Richmond, whereby his army might be fed.

While contemplating this movement, Butler received orders from Grant to send all but about fourteen thousand of his command to reinforce the Army of the Potomac.

Meanwhile an army under General Sigel, May 1st, moved up the Shenandoah Valley, encountered the enemy at New Market, and, being defeated, on the 15th retired behind Cedar Creek.

Sigel was superseded by General Hunter, who moved his army to Charlottesville, on the way destroying the railroad. On the 5th of June, Hunter defeated the enemy at Piedmont, and on the 8th formed a junction with General Crook, in command of the infantry, and General Averill, in command of the cavalry, who had moved at the same time with Sigel by the Kanawha, to operate against the East Tennessee and Virginia Railroad. Thus reinforced, Hunter moved towards Lynchburg, which he found well defended. Upon learning that the Confederates were fast receiving reinforcements, and his ammunition and provisions being insufficient for further hostile operations, he determined to return by way of the Kanawha.

Upon his arrival at Meadow Bridge, where a million and a half of rations had been left by Crook and Averill, he found that the two regiments in charge had been defeated and dispersed, and the rations destroyed or carried off by a small band of guerillas. This mountainous and curious line of retreat uncovered the frontiers of the loyal states, and brought great suffering to his troops. He succeeded in bringing them safely through by the route adopted. His operations had no perceptible influence on the campaign in Virginia.

On the 9th of May, a cavalry column of three divisions under Sheridan cut loose from the Army of the Potomac. Its purpose was to raid on the enemy's communications, threaten Richmond, and communicate with Butler on the James. Its first move was towards Fredericksburg as a disguise to its real purpose. Turning southward, Sheridan thrust his column like a lance inside the rebel lines. The clouds of dust rising in the roads soon warned the vigilant troopers of the Confederacy of the movement. Gordon's rebel brigade attacked the rear-guard, but could not stay its march.

Custer's brigade arrived at Beaver Dam Station on the 10th, destroyed locomotives, cars, supplies, and ten miles of the railroad, and rescued three hundred and seventy-five Union prisoners on their way to captivity. On the morning of the 11th it arrived at Ashland on the Fredericksburg Railroad. Here it destroyed the depot, a large amount of stores, and several miles of road. Crossing the South Anna, Sheridan destroyed six miles of track, a railroad train, the station, and large quantities of stores, and then moved forward toward Richmond.

The Confederate general, Stuart, had meanwhile massed his cavalry at Yellow Tavern, between Richmond and the troopers of Sheridan who were hurrying thither. Here the two great cavalry leaders of the Union and Confederacy met in conflict. The enemy was defeated, and the able, brave young Stuart mortally wounded. Sheridan, pushing back the defeated force that fell back upon Richmond, entered its outer line of intrenchments. Then, turning, he crossed the Chickahominy at Bottom Bridge, and reached Harrison's Landing, or Haxall's, on the 14th of May. Here he remained till the 17th and rejoined the army on the 27th, having lost in all his encounters but 425 men in killed, wounded, and missing.

TO COLD HARBOR.

On the night of the 20th of May, Hancock's corps began its southward march in advance of the other infantry corps of the Army of the Potomac. It moved behind the remaining force, which, like a heavy curtain, screened this opening movement from the observation of the enemy.

It was believed that Lee with his whole army might fall upon this isolated corps while on the march. An opportunity to attack Hancock, while so employed, might occur before he could intrench himself. If Lee did not attack, however, the march was to be continued as a turning movement. A cavalry division, under Torbert, preceded the marching column and cleared the way. It dislodged a force holding the bridge across the Mattapony River, seventeen miles from Spottsylvania and near Milford Station, on the Fredericksburg and Richmond Railroad. The movement did not long escape the vigilance of the enemy, as was in fact impossible and not expected. Where men, women, and children acted as spies, and where peaceful-looking old men became guerillas, if need be, to help drive back the hated invaders of their soil, secrecy was impossible.

The country over which Hancock's corps now marched was unlike any on which the Union army had previously set foot in Virginia. This region had hitherto escaped the devastating hand of war, and was virgin to its blighting touch. The country bloomed with thrift, and the contrast with that portion of Virginia hitherto familar to us made it seem beautiful. It was like a garden blooming in the midst of desert places. The rich bottom-lands of the river were green with grass and sprouting wheat. Herds of cattle grazed in fenced pastures. Sleek, blooded horses shook their manes and galloped over the fields at the unwonted sight of marching men with burnished arms. Around the comfortable homesteads of the planters everything was on a broad and generous plan. Hens, geese, chickens, ducks, and turkeys made a joyful sound, which found gleeful echoes in the neglected stomachs of tired soldiers. Men, strained and jaded by incessant conflict, revelled in long unused luxuries and in sights of beauty.

"I could lay down here and sleep and eat a week on a stretch!" said Wad Rider, unconscious of the inconsistency of his statement.

"I could marry a gal and settle here for life! It's tarnation good land!" said Joe, as his practical eye took in a view of the rich and beautiful undulating country.

The perfume of blossoms, the growing corn, the fragrant clover, and the hum of bees gratefully saluted the senses of men long unused to sounds of peace and scenes of comfort. Along the roads, and by the side of the houses, broad, spreading, ancestral elms gave grateful shade to the halting columns. Canteens were filled with water clear and cool from the wells near each dwelling. Sad to say, as the army advanced, and gathered satisfaction, chickens, and creature comforts, the people grew fierce and discontented. They could not sympathize with our glad appreciation and — appropriation of their plenteous stores.

Our army, operating in hostile territory, was like a swarm of locusts, destroying every green thing except the people who had rebelled against the thrift and content conferred by a good government. Where each man of an army takes a little, not much remains. I don't think we were very hard with these people, yet their fences fast melted away into camp-fires, and their chickens and turkeys and geese into goodly messes, to the satisfaction of those who were enduring hardships to restore to such as these the blessings of an undivided country.

The colored people whom we met did not seem overfed, but greedily gathered scraps of fat and beef thrown away around our camps, yet their faces were the most contented ones we saw in this country. Discontent and sullen anger, ill concealed, were written all over many of the white countenances. The few old darkies whom I talked with in most instances informed us that young "massa" was in the rebel army, and that the younger male servants were either beyond Richmond, or had been engaged in digging fortifications around it.

Our column, under Hancock, halted, late in the afternoon of the 21st, at the Mattapony River, near Milford Station. The left crossed the river and intrenched, and the right soon followed. Here we remained until the morning of the 23d. Our unpretentious little dog-tents were pitched in a field near the beautiful wood-skirted stream.

The people at one of the home-like estates claimed to be Union people, and requested a safety guard over their house. I was sergeant of the guard during a day around this place, and had a very comfortable time while so engaged.

While seated, near the house, endeavoring to make a sketch of the picturesque homestead, with its background of foliage and negro shanties, I was interrupted by a shadow falling across my small sketchingboard, and upon turning, was not

Sketching the Homestead.

unpleasantly confronted by a tall, black-eyed miss, who had been glancing over my shoulder. "That's our place!" she exclaimed, evidently in surprise; and then, in apology for the rudeness, said: "You were so engaged you did not hear me speak, and I looked over your shoulder to see what you were doing. Where did you learn to draw?"

I told her; when she replied, "I was at boarding-school near there two years before the war."

I found her more intelligent than most of the Southern girls I had thus far met, and from her inquiries I got the impression that she had a tender attachment for a young gentleman in the North. Her questions were quite searching regarding people whom, as it chanced, I knew by reputation. I finished the roughly executed sketch, and presented it to her with such compliments as a susceptible young man of twenty-three years might make to a young lady, and thought to myself, "Here is one of those unwritten romances of war, the end of which I shall doubtless never know." Her father was an elderly, white-haired man, with courtly manners, and a lurking bitterness of expression towards those who were using his fences for camp-fires, and his chickens for rations.

It was of little use for a small guard to attempt to preserve a large estate from the locust-like swarm of soldiers, all blessed with appetites so disproportioned to their supplies. One of our men, on guard at the time, was reprimanded for allowing his comrades to appropriate leaf tobacco stored in one of the out-buildings, which had a door at each end.

"Well, Cap," was the excuse of the guard, "I can't face both ways at the same time. While I'm walking post faced one way, the boys git inter one door, and before I know what is going on they are leaving with the tobacco from t'other door. I couldn't chase them without leaving my post."

"You could have halted and arrested them!" said the officer of the guard.

"Thunder, Cap, didn't I try to? but they wouldn't halt!"

"Why didn't you shoot the rascals then?" said the officer.

"Well, Cap, I should have shot our own soldiers, and we have none to spare," was the long-reaching reply.

The officer smiled a queer smile, which might be construed into a tacit agreement with his subordinate, but said no more.

While marching beyond the North Anna River, afterwards, I came upon a log shanty, mud-chinked, and with the stick chimney common to such residences in the South. It was occupied by an elderly man and wife of the lower class, such as commonly clustered around the plantations of Virginia. He chewed tobacco, and smoked a cob pipe. She dittoed the latter, and sported a snuff stick in place of the former. When I offered to barter hard-tack for some johnny-cake, he removed his cob pipe from his mouth long enough to explain that the durned Yankees, he reckoned, had stolen his baking-pan, and about all the other fixin's. In reply to an offer to give him some Northern newspapers to read, he informed me that he had no occasion for such fixin's; in other words, couldn't read. Notwith-

A Philosopher in his Way.

standing this ignorance, he displayed unusual common-sense when speaking of the war — a fact quite new to my experience with ordinary Virginians.

Said he : " I tell our people I reckon if we alls hadn't hankered to go to war with the Yanks, durned if I believe you alls would care enough about fighting to come down here to fight we alls. Now we alls are in this blamed war, we've got to fight it out, or tote out of it the best way we can. I've got two sons in our army, and I'd a doggoned sight ruther they'd be at hum. They were right peart ter go though, stranger.   We alls poor folks, who don't own property, didn't help make the war, but we alls do a right smart of fighting, though.   Our great folks, up yer to the house (referring to a plantation near) tell us we alls are fighting for our country.   I had country enough before we alls left the United States, and before this doggoned war cum down yer, and I reckon I won't have a right smart more after it is over ! "

I gave him and his snuff-chewing wife some "salt hoss" and hard-tack in return for some very good bacon, and went on my way pondering why it was that a poor, uneducated white man should have displayed in conversation the only good sense regarding the situation I had ever heard among Virginians.

Three of our men, two of whom were Wad Rider and Quin, had brought into camp the honey of a bee-hive.   The third member of the party, called Hale, was a new recruit, but as sharp as a veteran in all things which had reference to eating.   The planter, to whom the bee-hive belonged, made his appearance at post one day, and asked to be admitted to the officer in command.   Here happened to be posted the identical Hale, and Pat was corporal of the guard. Hale surmised instinctively that the planter's errand had something to do with the bee-hive, and refused him entrance to camp without the countersign.   Finally, after some parleying, he called for the corporal of the guard.   Pat Quin made his appearance, his face bearing marks of the skirmish with the bees.   He, seeing the "lay of the land," peremptorily refused the old fellow entrance to the camp. After a vain endeavor to gain admission, the planter retired.   Pat took pains to inform the succeeding guard of the situation, and bribed them with honey, so when the old gentleman again returned he found the same difficulty.   He was, to use Joe's expression, "Gol darned mad !" and declared that every d—d Yankee in camp had some of his honey, and was in a conspiracy to keep him from getting redress. He finally made a complaint to General Hancock, but it was too late to do him any good, as the foragers could not be found.

On the morning of Monday, May 23d, we resumed our march, and reached the North Anna that forenoon.   We found the enemy ahead of us, and posted on both sides of the river.   It was evident not only that they were aware of our movement, but were marching to obstruct it.   The marching of an army by the flank, in the presence of a watchful enemy, is considered one of the most difficult movements known to war. That we were not attacked, under the circumstances, was attributable either to Lee's weakness or to the skilful manner in which the movement was made.

Hancock's corps reached the North Anna River at a point one mile above the railroad bridge, and found there a redan, built on a narrow tongue of land formed by Long Creek and the North Anna, commanding the bridge and telegraph line. The south banks were fortified in a similar manner.

At ten o'clock on the 21st Warren had begun the withdrawal of his corps from Spottsylvania, following Hancock, but by a more direct route. As soon as the roads were clear of the Fifth Corps, General Burnside followed. Upon the withdrawal of the Fifth Corps, Lee set his army in motion, not to attack it while moving by the flank, but to cover the Virginia Central Railroad, and interpose between our army and Richmond.

The lines on which our army had advanced brought it to the North Anna River near the crossing of the Fredericksburg and Richmond Railroad. Warren threw Bartlett's brigade across the stream, by fording it at Jericho Ford, and under cover of this force constructed a pontoon bridge. In the afternoon the whole corps crossed.

Hancock had, meanwhile, dislodged the enemy from his strong redan, with a loss of not over a hundred and fifty men, and on the following morning it was found that the works on the south banks had been abandoned. The Sixth Corps followed Warren.

Burnside had been ordered to cross at Ox Ford, but finding the enemy in strong position there, made a crossing a mile and a half above. Thus was effected the difficult crossing of the North Anna. Lee was found posted with his left resting on Little River, from thence to Ox Ford on the North Anna, thence backward southerly to Mornsis Bridge.

Lee's army, in the compact shape of the letter V, was easily reinforced from one part to another. The point of the V, forming the centre, rested on the river, dividing our separated wings in such a manner as to compel us to cross the river twice to reinforce either wing. The reason that Lee did not attack Hancock while thus isolated was probably because the latter was intrenched and the former too weak to afford the experiment.   Lee understood too well the advantage which an intrenched line gave in an attack.

General Wilson crossed the North Anna, demonstrated on our right, and broke up the Central Railroad in order to convey the impression that we were about to move by the right flank.   From the 21st to the 26th our losses in the encounters along the line at this point were two thousand one hundred men.   On the 26th the Second and Fifth Corps were secretly withdrawn to the north banks of the river, without opposition, and headed south for the Pamunkey River. The Sixth Corps, led by two cavalry divisions, held the advance, followed by the Fifth and Ninth Corps.   The Second Corps moved behind them as a rear-guard.

Without giving further details, not interesting to general readers, of the movements of troops on the 28th, the Fifth and Ninth joined the van on the south side of the Pamunkey River.   During these movements, since the army had left the Rapidan, its base of supplies had twice been changed, and in the following order : from Fredericksburg to Port Royal, and from thence to White House Landing on the Pamunkey.   After crossing the Pamunkey the army was amid scenes familiar to the veterans of the Peninsular campaign of 1862.

On crossing this river, Lee was found covering the railroad with a line of battle facing northward, on the east side of the Chickahominy. A cavalry combat, to dislodge the Confederate force before crossing the Chickahominy, took place on the afternoon of the 28th.   Sheridan succeeded in gaining an advanced position where a number of intersecting roads converge, and known as Howe's Shop.   This was near the point where the right of our lines rested under McClellan in 1862. The position secured, the whole army was thrown forward in advance of these roads, whereupon the enemy retired behind the Tolopotomy River.

Richmond was now only ten miles distant.   To find out Lee's position, the Sixth Corps moved toward Hanover Court-House ; the Second followed.   The Fifth and Ninth moved up to support these. The Sixth passed around the Confederate left toward Hanover Court-House.   While thus moving, the advance of Hancock was brought to a halt at Tolopotomy Creek, which is a branch of the Pamunkey River.   The strong force here shown by the enemy induced Hancock to bring up the rest of his corps.

During the day following, the Ninth Corps was formed on his left. An attack being made to carry the lines of the Confederates, they were found intrenched behind marshy ground in such a manner as to make it inexpedient to attempt to drive them out.

Warren on the left, in his advance to Shady Grove, found the enemy in line of battle where the Shady Grove road is crossed by the Tolopotomy. The whole of Ewell's corps was found in the vicinity of Shady Grove Church. The enemy furiously attacked Crawford's division, which was moving out to cover the Mechanicsville pike. It was near the Bethesda Church when attacked, and was compelled to fall back to the Shady Grove road with the enemy in hot pursuit. Here the enemy was kept in check by our artillery until reinforcements came up and drove him back.

At dark our left was covering the Mechanicsville pike. These movements, which were in substance reconnoissances in force, found the Confederate army strongly posted and covering the approaches to the Chickahominy. The attempt to break this line and force a crossing, brought on the battle of Cold Harbor.

CHAPTER XXXIII.

COLD HARBOR.

THE battles of the overland route were, in several respects, different in their general character from any that had preceded them.
Both armies had learned to intrench in an incredibly short time, and
rude but formidable field works rose as if by magic wherever their
lines were formed.

Taking place as it did in the tangled woods, the character of the
fighting combined the features of guerilla war, Indian tactics, and
bushwhacking, all on an immense scale. Intrenchments which in
previous operations had been the work of weeks were now improvised in a few hours.

As the Army of the Potomac was the attacking party, it is almost
needless to add that Lee was able to throw upon it all the disadvantage of attack, and retain for himself the advantage of the defensive.
It was a facetious saying often heard at that time among the rank
and file, that "Lee was choosing some unusually hard spots for Grant
to bunt his head against!"

One moral advantage retained by Grant was recognized and
expressed in their own phraseology, — "Grant goes ahead instead of
backing out." After every conflict he advanced and sought new
ground on which to encounter his stubborn and skilful foe, instead
of falling back to old positions.

This fact had its influence in preserving the *morale* of the Army
of the Potomac. Its course since crossing the Rapidan had been
marked by difficult marches, constant battles and sieges, bloody
encounters unparalleled, with murderous losses and sufferings incal-
culable. It now, at Cold Harbor, occupied almost the identical
ground which it had held in 1862 under McClellan at Gaines's
Mills. The same foe was yet in their front, seemingly unconquerable.
The veteran material which composed the army at the beginning

of the overland campaign was fast dwindling away. Many of the bravest had been killed, wounded, made prisoners, or mustered out. The remaining veterans began to say among themselves that Grant was simply "bull-headed and stubborn, not skilful and great"; "that he was lavish of their lives without giving them corresponding victories."

In this respect it was but natural that they should, at this time, compare him unfavorably with McClellan. There are no men who so quicky resent the needless exposure of their lives and comfort as the volunteer American soldier. On the other hand, hardship, suffering, and the perils of battle are met cheerfully where there is a corresponding chance to achieve victory. The truth is, the soldiers of the Army of the Potomac at that time thought that Grant just a trifle more than averaged their stubbornness and fondness for fight.

For all this there were compensations. Their commander's great reputation made them believe that somehow he would finally achieve success. If death mowed down their ranks with a broad swath, yet promotions were correspondingly rapid, and the acknowledgments of merit for bravery and skill, so dear to every soldier's heart, promptly came as a salve for suffering and loss of comrades. The sergeant of to-day was a captain on the morrow, and in the great lottery of battle, where Death threw the dice, if on the one hand there were blanks for graves, on the other there was honor and expectation of victory.

The nearness of the Chickahominy (which Swinton aptly characterizes as "a wet ditch to the outer defences of Richmond"), and the proximity of these fortifications, apparently brought the turning movements in this direction to a close. It was needful to further operations on this line either to force a crossing of the river, now easy to ford, or to break Lee's lines in front and force him to withdraw behind the outer defences of his capital. It was believed that if he was thus compelled to retire across the river, an opportunity to inflict a severe loss upon him while crossing would thereby be presented.

While our army had been securing the roads whereon to advance against the rebel capital and army, Lee was skilfully endeavoring to cover them. Cold Harbor was no harbor at all, and was destitute of water to make one. It was doubtless thus named by English settlers after their former home. It is a point three miles north-east from the Chickahominy, and from it the roads radiate to all the bridges of that river, as well as to White House and other points. As White House was now the base of our supplies, while Lee's army and Richmond were the objective against which Grant was moving, it was an important strategic point.

Lee had thrown himself in the path of our advance, and in part covered these converging roads. Sheridan, after a spirited cavalry encounter on the 31st, had secured Cold Harbor. During the succeeding day Wright moved with Torbet's and Gregg's divisions from the extreme right to relieve the cavalry. Here also General W. F. Smith from the "bottled up" position at Bermuda Hundred was advancing with twelve thousand men from the Tenth and Eighteenth Corps, to take position on the right of the Sixth to co-operate in an immediate attack. Hokes's and Kershaw's rebel forces were also converging thither. Lee, perceiving the movement of the Sixth Corps, and suspecting its object, now also directed Anderson with Longstreet's old corps to this point.

The Federal infantry upon arriving at Cold Harbor found the enemy posted in the dense woods. In their front was cleared land over which an attacking force would be compelled to move. Their first line of rifle-pits or intrenched picket line, on the left of Smith and the right of the Sixth Corps, was attacked and carried under a heavy fire. In this opening encounter, although large losses were inflicted upon the enemy and several hundred prisoners were captured, our loss in killed and wounded was not far from two thousand men. The important point of Cold Harbor was, however, secured to us. Meanwhile General Wilson's cavalry force on the right had gained possession of Hanover Court-House. In attempting a further advance he had been attacked and had fallen back, destroying the railroad bridges.

The cavalry, with Torbet's and Gregg's divisions, had been moved from Cold Harbor to the Chickahominy to cover the left of our army. General Warren had extended his left to unite with Smith at Woody's, and had contracted his right so as to bring it near Bethesda Church. It was thought that this shortening of his front would leave him a force available for attack, yet his lines were now long drawn out, though shortened practically by swamps which he could command without occupying. The corps of Hancock, which after the withdrawal of the Sixth had formed the extreme right, began its march by a circuitous route, early on the night of the 5th, to reinforce the left near the Chickahominy.

The route was long, the roads dusty, the weather not and suffocating. The veterans of the Second Corps will remember it as a most uncomfortable march. As they arrived the next morning, tired and unfit for fight, refreshing showers cooled the air and settled the dust. The main attack was postponed until the next morning.

To recapitulate : the Union army was now formed for battle with Hancock on the left, across the Dispatch Station road, and Sheridan holding the lower crossings of the Chickahominy with Warren, Burnside, and Smith on the right. The extreme right wing was on Tolopotomy Creek.

Lee's right rested on the Chickahominy just below Alexander's Bridge ; his left, among the swamps at the heads of the Tolopotomy and Matadequin — positions which were very difficult to attack. The front of his line was consequently the assailable part.

The whole army was ordered to attack at half-past four on the morning of the 3d. The cavalry under Wilson, reinforced with infantry and more cavalry, was ordered to attack the left flank and rear of the enemy at Hawe's Shop.

The gray, sombre mists still overhung the lowlands of the Chickahominy when the attack began. A lurid fire of musketry suddenly burst from along the six miles of the Union lines. Shouts, cheers, and yells of the opposing hosts, the din of musketry and the roar of artillery, broke, in infernal sounds, the stillness of the morning air. The battle of Cold Harbor had opened. In less than an hour it was virtually over, and the Union army again baffled and held at arms' length.

At half-past four the Second, Sixth, and Eighteenth Corps, under a terrible artillery fire, advanced and carried the enemy's first line of rifle-pits. The rebels seem to have purposely abandoned these advanced intrenchments, as they were found, when occupied, to bring our men in line with a destructive fire from their artillery, which enfiladed them from Smith's right to Hancock's left.

The attack of Hancock's Corps was made by Gibbon on the right and Barlow on the left, with Birney supporting. Barlow's men rushed forward, and, after a terrible struggle, carried a sunken road held by the enemy. Beyond this was Watt's Hill, whose bare crest dominated the whole ground. Here Lee's fortified line rested behind the sunken road already mentioned. If this hill could be captured and held, the rebel line might be taken in reverse.

Barlow's men rushed forward, with enthusiastic cheers, and carried the ridge and works beyond. This position was held, however, but a short time. The force was too weak for it. What might have been the result had a heavy force been massed to have made the formidable captured line secure? Barlow's supports did not come up, and the men sullenly and reluctantly fell back, after sustaining a heavy loss. Taking advantage of the ground, they intrenched within thirty and fifty yards of the enemy's works.

Gibbon's advance was divided by a swamp which projected like a wedge in their front. The separation increased as they advanced. From the whole line, on the enemy's front, there flashed out a long and lurid sheet of flame. The air began, as it were, to rain bullets, shot, and shell. Then the yelling of the rebels from behind their intrenchments, of *hi! hi! hi! hiiiialieeeee!* followed by the *pop! pop! pop!* of firing at will. We advanced close up to the works from which came the *buzz!* and *ping!* of bullets and the yells of the defenders. A part of one of our regiments planted its colors on the enemy's parapet, but were quickly driven back, made prisoners, killed, or wounded.

The attack at this point failed, but so stubborn was the line, so dogged and determined and proud the men composing it, that they refused to fall back, but covered themselves by digging, and by the natural depressions in the ground. Some of our men were so near the enemy that they could be rescued only by digging covered ways to them. The vigor of the defence and attack may be inferred from the fact that in two divisions making this assault the loss was 2217, officers and men. In Gibbon's division alone the loss was sixty-five officers and 1032 men.

Hancock wisely reported that it was inexpedient to make a further attack, as the enemy had been reinforced at this key-point of the field. To many who took part in the affair this fact seemed as apparent before it was stated as it did after. Referring afterwards to this attack, a veteran with sergeant's chevrons on his arm said,

"There isn't much science in a bull-headed attack along a six-mile line; and if there isn't any science, what's the use of generals?"

It was rushing men into the jaws of death without being superior at any one strategic point which it was expedient to carry.

After all, it made little difference what private soldiers thought; they were simply food for powder, and were but the pawns in the game. If they gave their lives in building reputation for their superiors, but little heed was given to their brave acts and heroic endurance. Before and since, those who hold human life cheap have builded their reputations on the bleeding breasts of brave, unselfish, and undaunted men, never in return giving them their meed of praise.

The attack of the Sixth Corps resulted in the capture of the advanced rifle-pits of the enemy. It was, however, soon forced back with a loss of eight hundred men. Smith advanced through a ravine, with Devens to protect his flank, and they, too, carried the enemy's advance rifle-pits, but gained no further successes.

General Burnside attacked with the same result, and a loss of eight hundred, officers and men.

In an hour and a half the attack along the entire line was over and had failed. Grant, by this time, had concluded that it was better to leave the enemy behind their works than to drive them into the defences around Richmond. By so doing, it was affirmed he could better assist Hunter in his designs on Lynchburg. General Humphrey, at least, in substance so declares.

At half-past one o'clock further operations were suspended, and advances to advantageous positions were ordered to be made by siege approaches. The fighting had died away, only breaking out here and there between the pickets and skirmishers. So near were the lines, that an attempt simply to establish the pickets often brought on sharp fighting.

During the night many of our wounded between the two lines, and under the direct fire of the rifle-pits, were brought in by comrades. These chivalrous attempts would, of themselves, make a volume. In one instance, two soldiers pulled themselves along by digging their hands into the soil and grass, and delivered a comrade, wounded and under fire. A little drummer had followed his regiment into the fight, notwithstanding the protest of his officers. He was wounded, and lay between the two lines. When brought in, he clung to his drum, and when in comparative safety began to cry. "What's the matter, Johnnie? Does your leg hurt you?" "No, but they have made a darned great hole in my drum!" was the laughable response.

After remaining ten days before this impregnable line, Grant wisely determined to change his base of operations to the south side

The Wounded Drummer.

of the James. The losses of the Army of the Potomac had now reached the terrible figures of sixty thousand men since starting out on its great adventure across the Rapidan.

The losses of the Confederate army, it is claimed, did not foot up

" What's the matter, Johnnie ? "   Page 316.

over twenty thousand, but I believe it would be safe to add ten thousand to this estimate.

After this addition, may I inquire, without criticism, if the advantages gained justified these disproportionate losses? If not, was not Grant balked and outgeneralled up to this time?

It may, at least, be safely asserted that it is not often that a commander is so situated as to afford such terrible and unequal losses and not feel them.

The overland route and the system of attacking in brute masses, marked out for General Grant by the wise ones at Washington, proved a failure, and, considered as a whole, were fruitless. It may, however, be pertinent to inquire whether, without this demonstration of the futility of headlong attacks, the people, the press, and the government would have patiently endured the long siege operations before Petersburg which finally resulted in the disruption of the Confederacy.

CHAPTER XXXIV.

CHANGE OF BASE.

THE whole period during which the army held the intrenchments at Cold Harbor was one of extreme hardship. Notwithstanding the order was issued that no more assaults were to be made on the enemy's lines, the firing was constant. The nearness of the contestants brought on a collision of arms at almost every attempt to relieve pickets. The difficulty with which these were established, on account of the open ground between the two lines, is thus illustrated by a comrade in Burnside's Corps: —

"The night of June 4th was dark and rainy. Our pickets were within fifty yards of each other. Each man had protected himself by what might be termed an individual rifle-pit, — a hole dug into the ground with the soil thrown up in front. While being stealthily relieved during the night, the vigilant enemy opened a galling fire upon us. The only practicable procedure was for each man when relieved to take care of himself, and stand not on the order of his going. The relief did the same, and in the darkness hunted out the holes where we had been as best they could. . . ."

Here the men lay in cramped and narrow trenches, where cooking our food was almost impossible, until the 12th of June. Exposed to great heat during the day, and with little but muddy surface-water to drink, deprived of sufficient sleep, and with the incessant nerve strain kept up since the campaign opened, they began to lose heart. Added to this, their subsistence had been principally hard-tack, with beef from cattle exhausted and ill-fed.

The ground along which the army lay was for the most part low, marshy, and malarious. Between the two lines unburied dead men, horses, and mules made anything but a wholesome atmosphere. During the whole campaign the sanitary condition of the army had received but little attention, and its health and *morale* was much, if not seriously, impaired.

In the Trenches at Cold Harbor.   Page 318.

"Give men a good camp and plenty of good food," says a practical veteran, "and they soon forget hardships." A demoralizing reaction is apt to follow contrary conditions.

Seldom had it been the lot of any men, even in war, to sustain so constant a strain of hardship and battle as had been thrown upon this army since it crossed the Rapidan. Its killed and wounded alone now footed up the terrible total of not less than FIFTY THOUSAND men. Of these, 44,695 belonged to the Army of the Potomac, the balance to the Ninth Corps, which was not under Meade's command until after the battle of Cold Harbor.

It was evident to the private soldiers of the army that the principle of "continuous hammering" had proved more damaging to the Union hammer than to the Confederate anvil.

Many of them were reading men, and had not forgotten that that great master of war, Napoleon, when speaking of Turenne's campaign of 1855, said, "Turenne constantly observed the two maxims : first, never attack a position in front when you can obtain it by turning it ; second, avoid doing what the enemy wishes ; . . . shun the field of battle which he has reconnoitred and studied, and more particularly, that in which he has fortified and intrenched himself."

The nature of the task assigned to the Army of the Potomac, viz. to destroy Lee, defend the National Capital, and capture Richmond, had led to the violation of these maxims, and consequent defeat.

The army was now about to enter upon a new line of action, as skilful in its execution as it was glorious in its results. In the change of base which followed, Grant displayed those qualities of persistency and moral firmness which made him great. He had thus far followed the plan in part dictated by the semi-political military cabal at Washington He was now about to adopt a line of action which, though averse to the wishes of the administration, was dictated by the highest military considerations, and in the execution of which he showed military abilities of the first order.

Between the 9th and 11th of June a new line of intrenchments had been constructed in rear of the position at Cold Harbor, extending from Elder Swamp to Allan's Mill Pond. The corps of Hancock and Wright took position in this intrenched line.

About eight o'clock on the evening of the 12th of June, the army began its march to the James, Hancock and Wright following as soon as the roads were clear for them to march. The movement of each corps was carefully prescribed so as to prevent confusion. The march of fifty-five miles across the Peninsula was made in two days. To deceive the enemy, Warren had seized and held the bridges over White Oak Swamp, and covered all the roads by which the enemy might disturb or observe the movement. This effectually conveyed the intended impression that the Federals would advance by this direction on Richmond, and "it was not until the 17th," says Humphrey, "that Lee was aware of the real movement." The march of the army to the James was exhausting to the worn-out veterans.

The following from the notes of a comrade will show something of the conditions under which the withdrawal was conducted : —

"We began our march at dark on the evening of the 12th of June. The picket lines were not, however, withdrawn until two o'clock in the morning. We arrived at White House the next morning, having marched fifteen miles during the night. The men were footsore, shoes not having been issued since we started out on the campaign. The next day we marched eleven miles, and bivouacked within three miles of the Chickahominy, crossed that river at Jones's Bridge, twenty miles below Cold Harbor ; the next morning, halted and made coffee, then moved at one P.M., marching until within two miles of the James River (where the Second and Fifth Corps had preceded us), and camped near the Sixth Corps.

"By noon of the 16th the army was transferred to the south side of the James. Here at Douthard's the river is very broad and the channel thirteen feet deep. At this point was constructed the longest pontoon bridge, it was said, ever thrown out for the passage of an army. It was over two thousand feet long, and was constructed with great rapidity, having been begun in the forenoon of the 14th and finished before twelve o'clock the same night."

My comrade of the Ninth Corps says, "We lay within two miles of the river all day, crossed it at eight P.M., and marched all night. The march was a very hard one.

'The order of march seemed to be, as one of the boys said, 'to slue to the left.' The Second Corps was ahead, and we were swinging the left. We arrived before Petersburg at eight o'clock A.M., the 15th, with only five men left in my company to 'stack arms.' Over half the men in the division were stragglers. At three P.M. of the same day we formed on the left of the Second Corps, had a fight, and lay on the battle-field all the following night.

"By midnight on the 16th, Warren's corps halted a few miles from Petersburg, and on the morning of the 16th General Hancock, in command of the troops in front of the city, made a reconnoisance. The intrenchments encircled the city at a distance of two miles from it, and an attack previously made on the 14th, by General Smith, whose corps had been transported mainly by water to this point, had failed through the timidity of its commander. The force defending the city at that time was made up principally of old men and boys. Had the attack been boldly made, Petersburg must have fallen."

The capture of the city was very important, as it would leave in the hands of the Confederates only one line of railroad and its feeders, by which to receive their supplies. The destruction of the remaining line must have speedily followed, or in anticipation of such an event Richmond have been abandoned. Had Hancock or Meade been made aware of Grant's desire or plan for its capture, it must have fallen, so Meade says, in substance, in his report.

Hancock's corps had been ferried across the James, on the morning of the 15th, and, according to orders, there awaited rations from General Butler. The rations not arriving, he ordered the forward march of his corps according to previous instructions, viz. "to where the City Point Railroad crosses Harrison's Creek"; but this place, instead of lying as indicated on the map, was a long distance away, and within the enemy's lines.

While Hancock was in search of this will-o'-the-wisp, he received a despatch from Grant, directing him to move to the assistance of Smith, who had that morning attacked Petersburg. This was the first intimation he had of Grant's design of capturing that place. Had he understood this earlier, he could have easily joined his force with that of Smith, and the capture of Petersburg and the possession of the line of the Appomattox would have followed.

Fate seemed to have overruled the plans of the Union general, in order to make the final overthrow of the enemy more speedy and complete. Had Petersburg fallen at this time, the probabilities are that General Lee would have abandoned Richmond, and retired into the interior, thus prolonging the contest for an indefinite period.

On the morning of the 16th, General Hancock, in command of the troops then before Petersburg, ordered a reconnoissance in his front. Redan No. 12 was captured by General Egan's brigade. Meade having come up, Hancock was ordered to attack at six o'clock.

Behind the Apple Tree.

The assault was made by the Second Corps, supported by two brigades of the Eighteenth Corps on the right, and two brigades of the Ninth on the left. The enemy was driven back along the whole line. At early dawn Potter's division of the Ninth Corps, in a gallant fight, carried the redan and lines on the ridge where the Shand House stood, capturing six hundred prisoners, four guns, and five stands of colors.

My comrade of the Ninth Corps makes memorandum of the fact that his brigade lost twenty-five men in this attack, and that it was shelled by the enemy all day; that during the day a spherical case shot struck in the Sixth New Hampshire regiment, wounding seven men.

"On the next morning, 18th of June," says my comrade, "we advanced as skirmishers to within sixty rods of their rifle-pits ; had a severe skirmish, in which two of our men were killed, and ten wounded out of a hundred that we had. While thus shirmishing we saw the enemy engaged in constructing the redan, known afterwards as the 'Elliott Salient,' the very one we afterwards mined and blew up."

Captain J. N. Jones, of the Sixth New Hampshire, in alluding to the severity of the artillery firing at this time, says, "Within a minute five shots struck an apple-tree behind which I had got for protection."

At one o'clock the next day, the left of the line, under Potter, took up a position about three hundred yards from the Confederate lines and threw up breastworks. Our pickets were within fifty yards of their works.

The attempt to establish an advance line by taking Petersburg had not been bloodless. The total of killed and wounded, when footed up, was 8772. Add to these 1814 missing, and we have as the total of our losses 10,586 men.

Thus opened the fight along the lines of Petersburg ; as a whole, the most remarkable and long-sustained contest known in history.

CHAPTER XXXV.

THE SIEGE OF PETERSBURG.

THE several attacks made on the 17th had resulted in the establishment of a connected line for our army, now gathering like a cloud around Petersburg. On the 18th our skirmishers discovered that the enemy had retired to an interior and more compact line on the high ground around that city.

An attack which followed resulted in great loss of life and a repulse all along the Union lines. Our army, therefore, began strong systematic intrenchments, which enabled a part of the army to hold the front, leaving a large portion available for manœuvre or attack on the left flank of the enemy.

On the 2d the Second and the Sixth Corps moved out of the city, and established themselves on the west side of the Jerusalem plank road, which lies between the Weldon and the Norfolk railroads, south of Petersburg. They connected their line with Griffin of the Fifth Corps, which was established on the east side of the road. The Sixth Corps extended itself to the rear and left of the Second Corps.

The cavalry divisions of Wilson and Kantz destroyed several miles of the south-side railroad track. It was part of the general plan for the Sixth Corps to extend its left to the Weldon Railroad, but in our attempt to do this, the force of the enemy was so menacingly developed that the movement failed. The Second Corps then swung forward its left to envelop the right flank of the enemy's works. The forces of Mott and Barlow, pivoting on the right of the line, were commanded by Gibbon.

This movement having been made without reference to the position of the Sixth Corps, a wide gap was left between the two. While Mott was intrenching, and Barlow was swinging into position, the Confederates, under General Hill, were hurled into the interval between the two corps. Gibbon's force, thus struck on the flank, rolled back on itself in disorder. The remainder of the Second Corps stood firm, while the line was re-formed.

The enemy were repulsed by Miles, whom they attacked, but held the intrenchments which had been taken from Gibbon until the removal of the artillery, when they retired as suddenly as they had advanced, carrying off the captured guns, twenty-five hundred prisoners, and many stands of colors. Our cavalry expedition had, meanwhile, defeated General W. H. F. Lee's cavalry division at Nottoway Station. The divisions united and destroyed the Danville Railroad for twenty-five miles.

In retiring, Wilson was attacked by both cavalry and infantry in such force as to threaten his destruction. Finally, with the loss of his artillery, a large portion of his trains, and a number of prisoners, he reached the Union lines. No substantial advantages had been gained commensurate with our losses, which up to this time had been fifteen thousand men.

These operations had demonstrated that the place could not be taken by assault. The Army of the Potomac, thinned hitherto by futile assaults on desperate positions reconnoitered and intrenched by its foe, now set itself resolutely down to the siege. A year after, and the last great act in the drama of the Rebellion was played, when Petersburg, standing like a fortress thrown out upon the flank of Richmond, and the key to its possession, finally fell with the surrender of Lee at Appomattox.

IN THE TRENCHES.

From a comrade of the Sixth New Hampshire, in the Ninth Corps, the following narrative is drawn : —

On the morning of our arrival before the city, we were ordered to advance our pickets, but found the Confederates had left their advance line of rifle-pits, and had established their lines on higher ground further in the rear. We pushed forward until within fifty yards of their new line, and there saw them engaged in building a fort afterwards known as the " Elliot Salient." This was the same fort that we afterward mined and blew up.

As we went forward over the gradually ascending ground towards the Confederates, we met with a sharp fire, and the *hiss!* and *ping!* of bullets were quite emphatic against venturing further. Finally, as nothing was to be gained by a further advance, the captain gave orders to fall back, which we did, followed by shots from the enemy.

We had lost in this sharp skirmish ten wounded and two killed out of one hundred men. I heard General Griffin express to Captain Jones surprise that we had been able to advance as far as we did, and said he did not intend that we should engage the enemy's pickets. Our lines at this time were not over three hundred yards from the enemy's. The day following we threw up breastworks, and then awaited the next turn of affairs.

Our brigade lay here three days, and during that time kept up an almost constant exchange of rifle shooting with the enemy. We were then relieved, moved to the rear, and refreshed ourselves by washing our faces, and by sleeping. To some degree we were, while there, free from the constant crackle of musketry, the hiss of bullets, and the boom of cannon and mortars.

It was a restless sort of life at the front, where at any moment we were liable to get a shot through the top of our heads if we exposed them above the breastworks. After a day's rest we again went on picket, where the same constant attentions were paid us by the enemy as before.

The firing was incessant. At this time, I remember, we received a supply of tobacco from the Sanitary Commission, for which we were very grateful. If a man ever uses the fragrant weed, he will need it in the trenches, under the constant nerve strain incident to such an incessant fire as that to which troops were there exposed.

On the night of June 26th we had a sharp fight on picket. The constant flash of the enemy's muskets in the darkness reminded one of fire-flies, while the buzz and spat of their bullets sounded, at times, not unlike June bugs flying at lighted candles. The nights were warm and uncomfortable enough, without having one's blood stirred up and quickened by these demonstrations of the enemy.

The next afternoon the incessant *pop! pop!* and *whizz!* of rifle shooting ceased, and they then began shelling us. Their shot could be seen travelling the air in slightly curved lines, while the curves described by the mortar shells were more like those of rockets.

BUILDING ABATTIS.   Page 327.

The shells from these mortars could be seen by observant, keen-sighted men, and dodged as easily as a base ball.

After a short interval of rest, on the 29th, we moved to the front again, and began to strengthen our lines by abatis made of trees thrown over in our front, with the branches pointed outward. We did not attempt to fasten them to the ground as a man's life wasn't worth much when so engaged. As it was, we worked all night under the fire of the enemy, from both cannon and muskets.

Under this constant fire, our men were being gradually thinned out; not many were killed on any one day, but up to July 27th, our regiment, which upon our arrival numbered two hundred and fifty men, had lost eighty in killed and wounded. As we had not lain here forty days, this made an average loss of two men per day in our little regiment.

Since crossing the Rapidan, many of the bravest of the officers and men had been killed, wounded, or mustered out. New regiments had been sent to the front with inexperienced officers. The same men would have been more efficient, if they had been put into old regiments. As a rule, a new regiment lost twice as many men as an old one in doing the same fighting. This was regarded by old officers as very wasteful.

Their practical manner of regarding the value of the lives of men, and the desirability of economy in their use, is illustrated by the following incident : Some new men had needlessly exposed themselves, when our watchful and veteran captain roughly exclaimed, "Get down out of that, or you'll get a bullet through your head; you cost the government a thousand dollars apiece, and I'll be d——d if I am going to have you shot without good cause; you're too expensive ! "

This was said in all seriousness, but it made us laugh. It is wonderful how many things men found to laugh at, while engaged in such serious work. The cracking of jokes was as incessant as the crackle of musketry.

There was more steadfast, earnest devotion among the veterans of many battles than among recruits. This illustrates a fact often recognized, that those who give most generously to a cause are those to whom we can look for still greater sacrifices.

A corporal of our company, who was shot through the breast June 30th, reported back for duty in September, saying, " My time is not out and I can do good duty yet." It is safe to say that none but a veteran, having at heart the cause of his country, would, under such circumstances, have reported for duty again.

Much of the new material sent us since the campaign under General Grant began, was worthless as fighting material. "Substitutes," "Bounty Jumpers," and conscripts replaced the patriotic men who had fallen in the fight.

A great many of them had enlisted under fictitious names, such as "Abe Lincoln," "Johnny Boker," "Jim Crow" — names which they did not always remember themselves. During a roll-call it was not uncommon to see them look into their hats to read the assumed name they had written there, that they might correctly answer to their "*nom de guerre*" when called.

"A man who don't wear his own name," said our captain, "hasn't pride enough in it to make him a good soldier"; a true philosophy, but one not always appreciated.

Some of these men referred to had formerly been in the Confederate service. Among these was one North Carolinian, who was an enthusiastic Union man, and made a good soldier. Another, an Irishman, also proved a good soldier; still another, who had enlisted under the name of "Joe Hooker," shirked active duty, and finally deserted to the enemy while on picket. I had no doubt he intended from the first to desert to his old comrades, and only watched for a good chance.

Though the lines were close, the fire was so constant that there was not so great an opportunity for desertion as one might suppose. A veteran regiment, one which had earned a national reputation for gallantry on many a field, had been filled up with the worthless characters referred to. They deserted in such numbers that the enemy jokingly sent word, that, as they had most of the regiment over on their side, they thought we had better send them over the regimental colors. The desertions were, however, more frequently from the rebel side than ours. At our part of the line was the Second Maryland Regiment.

An Irish private of the regiment ascertained that his son was in a rebel regiment opposite to them; he sent word for him to meet him on the picket line; this was done. While this conference was taking place, one of the rebels called out, "Say, stranger, it's too doggoned bad that you and your son should be fighting each other; you'd ought to be over here with us."

"No," said our patriotic Irish soldier, "he'd ought to be over here with us." That night the son deserted to our lines.

In the winter of '64–'65, on our left, not far from Fort Fisher, the men of the opposing armies were on more friendly terms than at our part of the lines.

There was a piece of woods between the contestants, from which both armies got fuel; it was quite common for the representatives of the "blue" and "gray" to meet here, converse, exchange opinions, tobacco, coffee, and compliments. One of our men, having an unusually heavy load to get into our lines, invited a good-natured rebel to help him a short distance; the two came into our lines with the wood; the rebel glanced around with a satisfied air, sniffed the perfume of coffee and other "Yankee fixin's," and then said, "It looks right comfortable here, Yank, and I guess I'll stay!" Another came into our lines from the same wood with a mule team which he turned over to the provost guard, saying, "I'm done toting fixin's for the Confederacy."

Desertions from the rebel lines were constant; men who had fought gallantly for that cause saw that it was waning, and refused to risk their lives further in hopeless struggle.

The Ninth Corps sustained a more incessant fire from musketry and artillery than any other part of our line. The rebels declared it was due to the fact that we had a division of negro troops. We thought this was rather "rough," as up to this time they had taken no part in the fight.

Among our substitutes were a number of professional gamblers, who had enlisted for the purpose of plying their vocation; some of them were brave men and made good soldiers, and as the whole army gambled, it was not very heartily laid up against them. If they risked their lives as cheerfully as their money, few were inclined to find fault: playing cards was the greatest recreation of the soldiers.

The cooking for the men on duty in our front line was usually done in the rear, and the food brought up to the front.

While some of our men were on this advanced line, a camp-kettle of hot soup had been brought for their dinner. The men had begun a social game of cards, while waiting for the soup to cool, when a sputtering shell from the enemy's guns struck in the camp-kettle and exploded, killing one man and wounding two.

Our brigade took turns with the Second Brigade alternately forty-eight hours on, and forty-eight hours off, in duty at the front.   The incessant firing on this line may best be illustrated by the ordnance return, which, during one quarter, shows that ninety-six thousand

The Shell takes the Pot.

rounds of cartridges, or nearly five tons of ammunition, had been used by this company of little over two hundred men.   A copy of that report is in my possession, and can be verified by those on file at Washington.

The breastworks were eight and ten feet high in places.   They were not thick enough to stand shot and shell, and needed constant repairs.   Timber for this purpose was often brought two miles.

Meanwhile the regular routine of camp life was uninterrupted. Pay-rolls were made, camps policed, descriptive lists of sick and wounded men in the hospital made out, and forwarded.

A redoubt had been for some time in building on the high land near the roads in our rear, and thirteen guns were in position by July 25th ; six of these were thirty-two pounders. By their aid the boys gleefully anticipated expounding their own superiority to the enemy. To their minds the rebs were getting too conceited. The mortars and ordinary artillery did, as a general thing, comparatively little injury ; it was the little whispering bullets which brought wounds and death to our ranks.

The sputtering, growling shell, travelling the air in ostentatious, curved lines, made great threatenings, and did but little damage other than frightening raw recruits and horses. Nothing can frighten the stolid veteran army mule.

The army fared better on the lines before Petersburg than at any other time in my army experience. Vegetables, sometimes fruit and other luxuries, were thoughtfully provided for us by the Sanitary Commission. The weather had become oppressively hot and dry ; the dust on the roads between our position and City Point was knee deep. No rain had fallen from the 3d of June to the 19th of July. Great clouds of fine dust were raised by the passage of troops, and caused great suffering to marching men. As the springs and surface water had dried up, we sunk wells, and got good cool water a few feet below the surface.

The *morale* of the army was good, and in this the Sanitary Commission did good service by reminding us that we were not entirely forgotten by the people of the North. We were at times in danger of believing that our people at home were becoming lukewarm and cold. When we heard of Early's raid into Pennsylvania, we thought it was a good thing, if it opened their eyes to the magnitude of the struggle in which we were engaged. We hoped this new manifestation of danger would cause them to see the necessity of coming to the front themselves, instead of sending substitutes for men. We were not sure at that period, to use a familiar expression, but we had " bit off more than we could chaw."

THE MINE.

We were on duty in the immediate vicinity of the mine which was being excavated. Our advance lines at this point were on the crest of ascending ground, a gradual ascent continued towards the enemy. Back of us was a ravine, which broadened out on the left, and curved westerly on the right into the enemy's lines. In rear of this ravine the ground gradually ascended for one hundred and fifty yards, and then sloped back to a wood. A covered way was constructed from this wood down the hill-side to where the ravine afforded protection to the men moving to the front. This enabled our men to come to the front line without needless exposure. In front of the curved way, and on the opposite side of the ravine, was the mouth of the mine in process of construction.

The mining operations were kept as secret as possible. Bushes were stuck up to conceal the soil excavated from the mine. Most members of my regiment were on friendly terms with the Forty-eighth Pennsylvania, which was engaged in its construction. That regiment was commanded by Lieutenant-Colonel Pleasants, who had been a practical coal-mining engineer, and who was said to have been the original projector of the mine. The men of his command were mostly made up of miners from the Pennsylvania coal-field. These men sometimes declared they were more at home while working under ground than on top. I make mention of this as it illustrates the material found in our army for all the varied needs of war. Artificers and engineers were found ready-made in the ranks, and needed only organization. The mine, in spite of serious impediments encountered and difficulties overcome, was ready for charging on the 23d of July.

The gallery leading under the enemy's salient was a parallelogram in form, and about one hundred and fifty yards long. When it reached the enemy's fort it branched off on either side, not unlike the top of a letter T. The miners engaged have since informed me that while at work they could hear the picks and spades of the enemy countermining. It would not have been unexpected had they encountered each other.

Our lines at this point bulged out slightly in convex form towards the enemy. From our position could be seen Cemetery Hill, not over three-fourths of a mile distant, and behind this the projecting spires of Petersburg.

The city was within reach of our ordinary artillery, and on one or two occasions buildings within its limits had been set on fire.

Our newly erected batteries were intended to keep down the fire of the enemy, in the attack which was to take place directly upon the opening of the mine. The conditions as a whole were favorable to the success of the assault to be made, but presented the disadvantage that when the salient in our front was completed, it brought an attacking column under the flank fire of the re-entrant lines of the enemy. If the ridge beyond the Elliot Salient (under which our mine was run), and about four hundred yards from it, could be seized, it would enable an attacking force not only to capture Petersburg, but a large part of the enemy's artillery and infantry.

Such was the prize to be grasped! What were the preparations for the task? As I have hitherto illustrated, our ranks had been filled with men who, to some extent, were worthless as soldiers. The first division had been reinforced with dismounted cavalry- and heavy artillery men, none of whom were over-pleased at being employed as infantry. I asked one of the soldiers of heavy artillery what branch of the service he was in. He replied, with sneering irony and stiffness, impossible to reproduce on paper, "The heavy artillery, by G—d, Calibre Forty-eight,[1] with bayonets on the end!"

In choosing troops for the assault, the expediency of using for the attack the colored division which had hitherto seen no active service, had been seriously debated. The selection was finally made by casting lots by the commanders of the white division of the corps.

The success of the attack was so desirable that it was the dictate of common sense that none but picked men should be chosen for the task. The honor of leading it fell upon the division commanded by General Ledlie. I believe, however, that if the men had been led by a man like either Warren, Hancock, or Sheridan, the success would not have been doubtful.

When the fuse was first ignited, it proved non-effective. Sergeant Harvey and Lieutenant Jacob Doughty, of the Fourth New York, volunteered to return to the mine, and examine into the causes of its failure. "I had my watch in hand," said my informant, "when

[1] The calibre of the Springfield musket.

thè mine was sprung ; it marked the time of fifteen minutes to five A.M."

A dull jarring explosion shook the ground, and then a mass of earth, through which blazed the ignited powder, was thrown into the air two hundred feet. Like a dense cloud, through which dark objects could be discovered, it hung suspended for a moment, and then fell back, and a black cloud of smoke hung over the place and floated away.

Cannon from the fort and fragments of gun-carriages were found several hundred feet inside our. lines, so terrible was the force of the concussion. The springing of the mine was the signal for the opening of our artillery, converged upon the enemy from our entire line to keep down their fire.

Every brazen throat belched and thundered. Had the assaulting column now rushed upon the enemy while they were disorganized and paralyzed, marked success must have crowned its efforts.

The crater was about twenty-five feet deep, a hundred and fifty feet long, and sixty feet wide, running across the top of the gallery leading to the fort. It was the top of the "T." Into this, after some delay, the charging column rushed pell-mell, and remained, not attempting to advance further.

General Ledlie was not leading his men ; he was in a bomb-proof, where he could neither see nor direct them. The troops in the crater were in a confused mass, and not only did not advance beyond, but hindered every other force from attempting it.

The utmost consternation had been produced upon the enemy, and they had abandoned their intrenchments for several hundred yards.

They now began to show signs of life, opening a scattering musket fire upon Ledlie's men. It was an hour before their artillery opened with any effect. A battery in the ravine then opened fire and swept the ground on our right ; another opened on the left, while a plunging fire from our front made a cross-fire from three directions.

Under this fire our division went forward by flank, and took possession of the enemy's intrenchments, which were abandoned for two or three hundred yards. Covered ways and rifle-pits were seen jumbled together. General Wilcox's brigade followed, some of the men crowding into the crater, and others, after some fighting, taking possession of the intrenchments on the left. My company formed near the rebel works, and was just on the edge of the crater, sheltered in part by its irregularities.

There was now a crowded jumble of men in the crater and around it. The heat was becoming intense. Our men were driven back every time they attempted to advance on Cemetery Ridge. At ten o'clock the colored troops moved to the attack obliquely from our left. I saw them when they charged towards the crater. At that time there was an artillery duel going on ; the shell, grape, and canister made dismal music over their heads, and they went into this vortex of death with artillery and musketry fire from front and flank.

It was scarcely seven o'clock when the colored division charged in magnificent order. I had been in the army since 1861, and had seen some hard fighting, and notwithstanding all that has been said to the prejudice of these troops on that occasion, it was a grand sight. I saw one of the color-bearers killed, and their flag go down, but it was lifted from the ground by another who was shot, but again rescued by a third, who carried it forward into the fight. Said a veteran, " A lump came up in my throat, and my eyes filled with tears at the thrilling spectacle, as is always the case when I see or read anything daring or brave." The colored troops passed beyond the crater and towards the crest, where they encountered a converging, raking fire of artillery, which drove them back in confusion, with the men who had preceded them.

The crater now became a terrible place. There was no order; confusion reigned supreme. The intense rays of the sun were converged like a burning glass into this airless hole ; a raking fire from three different directions decimated the ranks of those huddled together there.

If a shot of any kind struck into the crater, it was almost certain to kill one or more. At twelve o'clock the men were ordered to withdraw, every man for himself; it was three o'clock P.M. when they fell back. There was no formal withdrawal ; the men saved themselves as best they could.

The enemy took many prisoners, and our loss was sickening, with no results but humiliating failure. The only compensating fact was the heroism brought out in the encounter.

I cannot refrain from narrating one incident told to me. Captain Greggs, of the Forty-fifth Pennsylvania, an old Mexican soldier, was present near the edge of the crater. A rebel officer, at an embrasure on the other side near Greggs, pointed a rifle at his head, and called upon him to surrender. With a quick movement of his arm, Greggs knocked away the hand of the rebel officer, at the same time drawing his sword with the other, and running him through. The officer, impaled with the sword, fell back on the other side of the breastwork. General Bartlett, seeing the daring act, unbuckled his sword-belt, and presented it to Greggs, saying, " Captain, you are more worthy to wear it than I am." It was truly a recognition of gallantry by a brave officer.

General W. F. Bartlett, it will be remembered, was captured. His wooden leg would not permit him to get away. The brave Greggs escaped the enemy's bullets, but while on a craft going down James River, a few days afterwards, and with this sword lying across his knee, it slipped from the scabbard and was lost overboard.

We all felt blue and discouraged after the miserable affair of the crater, which, if it had been well managed, would have brought us glory with as little loss as was sustained. The casualties in this disgraceful affair, all told, are reported by Meade at forty-four hundred. We had lost where we should have won.

CHAPTER XXXVI.

IN the spring of 1865 the Confederacy was in straitened circumstances. Charleston and Savannah had fallen; Sherman had laid waste the heart of the country, and had marched his victorious army up the Atlantic coast, and established it at Goldsboro, North Carolina, 145 miles south of Petersburg, prepared to join, if need be, in Lee's destruction. Hood's army had been scattered or destroyed by Thomas; Sheridan had driven out Early, and desolated the Shenandoah Valley.

The suffering inflicted upon the South by four years of war had also produced its moral effects upon that brave people. While they desired the success of their armies, they did not so much lack men as willingness to contribute to the fighting force of the Confederacy. A number of able-bodied men, sufficient to fill up the ranks of two armies as large as that under Lee, avoided the conscription. Armed deserters were in all the mountain regions of the South. The desertions from Lee's army alone were so frequent that there were twice as many men on his rolls as in his ranks. Added to this, the grim policy promoted by Grant, of non-exchange of prisoners, kept out of the fight men enough for two armies like that which defended Richmond.

The question of supplies, always a vital one in war, had also become a very serious one for the rebel armies. All signs pointed to an early collapse of the Southern Confederacy.

The brave men under Lee, who had so long defended the Confederacy by their arms, were still capable of great deeds. Knowing that the end was near, they yet desired to struggle worthily, until their last hope should have died out.

With a view to evacuate Petersburg and Richmond, join his army with that of Johnston, and still maintain the struggle, Lee planned to compel the retirement of our left flank, so as to relieve his proposed line of retreat by the Cox road. This road follows the line of the Appomattox, above the Boydton plank road, and is the shortest line to Amelia Court-House. Here he proposed to concentrate his columns on the Danville Railroad, preparatory to moving farther south.

ATTACK ON FORT STEADMAN.

By seizing Fort Steadman and its adjacent works, Lee proposed to crown the high land with artillery, and lay hold of our railroad to City Point. He believed that this blow would compel Grant to recover his communications, and, in any event, by forcing our left flank to retire, leave free the line for the proposed concentration of his troops in retreat at Amelia Court-House.

The lines of the opposing forces at Fort Steadman were not over a hundred yards apart. This point bristled with *cheveaux de frise* and line upon line of intrenchments.

Deserters had been in the habit of leaving the Confederate lines in large numbers, and coming over to us, bringing their arms. Availing themselves of this fact, some of General Gordon's rebels walked out to the Union picket lines, on the night of the 24th, as if they were about to desert ; captured our pickets, and sent them to the rear ; charged through the gap thus made, took the main line by surprise, and captured Fort Steadman and the first division of the Ninth Corps. They then turned the guns of the captured forts upon our neighboring intrenchments, compelling the abandonment of batteries " 9," " 10," " 11," on its flank, and pushed their skirmishers towards the City Point Railroad.

The successes of the enemy were but transient ; for they not only soon found themselves under a terrible artillery fire from our flanks, but Hartranft's division of the Ninth Corps made a counter-charge, and, rather than retreat under the terrible cross-fire converged upon them, they yielded themselves prisoners of war.

The enemy lost four thousand men in their short-lived possession of Fort Steadman.

The Second and Sixth Corps were then thrown forward by General Meade, and the strongly intrenched picket line in front of these corps was captured, thus pressing more closely that portion of his line which Lee above all wished to have secure.

Thus ended in complete failure the execution of the plans on which his last hopes for successful retreat depended.

For months preceding the campaign about to open, Grant had been fearful that Lee might give him the slip, by moving out from his intrenchments, falling back into the interior, and joining his forces with those of General Joseph E. Johnston. Such a movement would compel him to follow his opponent at a great distance from his base, and thus prolong the strife.

Grant had fixed the 29th of March as the time for a general movement of all his forces against the enemy ; and Lee's initiative at Fort Steadman had neither hurried nor retarded the plans of the grim general at City Point, whose resolve was fixed, like fate, for the overthrow of Lee's army.

The disposition of troops on the 29th was as follows : Sheridan was near Dinwiddie Court-House, on our extreme left ; Weitzel was in front of Richmond, on the right ; a portion of the Army of the James was holding the works in front of Petersburg, while Ord extended his line from Hatche Run to the Vaughn road, and Warren was on the left reaching from the Vaughn road to the Boyton plank road.

The weather for several days had been good, and, when the movement began, on the extreme right flank, the roads, which in that country are usually knee deep with either dust or mud, were considered in a passable condition.

On the afternoon of the 29th the skies were overcast with clouds, and in the evening the rain poured down in torrents, stirring up the soil into a stiff batter, and making the roads decidedly difficult for pedestrian soldiers to travel.

On the 30th General Sheridan moved forward towards Five Forks, a position where a number of roads converge, about eight miles southwest of Petersburg.

A comrade of the Fifth Corps says, "On the 29th we broke camp, and marched towards Dinwiddie Court-House, over a country rendered rough with ravines and rocks, and covered with dense, tangled forests, traversed here and there by streams. About noon, encountering the enemy's pickets, we advanced through the woods at double-quick, the wild thorn bushes and vines tearing our clothes and flesh. While crossing over a field where a skirmish had taken place, I saw a boy kneeling by the side of a gray-haired, dying soldier. It was his father, who had fallen shortly before."

The Dying Confederate.

When night came, it began to rain, and the flooded roads were soon knee deep with quicksand and a reddish mud.

The next morning we built intrenchments, using the hewn logs of a barn for the purpose. It was cold, wet, and cheerless. We saw through the mist, as daylight came, the enemy's intrenched line in our front, some eighty rods distant. As we were lying on our faces, our hands and clothing were covered with red mud, and as our clothing was torn in the woods the day previous, we did not much resemble the respectable regiment that had begun the march on the 29th.

General Warren rode by our lines in the rain which deluged us, when one of our men shouted out, "Say, General, why don't you bring up the pontoons and the gun-boats?"

On the 31st Warren moved his entire corps westward from the Boydton plank road, closely pressing the intrenchments of the Confederates on the White Oak road. The position of the Fifth Corps was quite difficult, as it formed the left of the Union line, and had to protect its own flank.

Warren, not believing in long weak lines, massed his troops, so that they could be quickly reinforced, at any desirable point, and then threw forward his skirmishers in an attempt to seize the White Oak road just beyond the point where the enemy's intrenchments terminated. This movement, if successful, would have cut off Lee's direct communication with Pickett at Five Forks.

The movement had hardly begun, when the enemy attacked both from the north and west in one of their most furious sallies. Under their terrible attack Ayer's troops, overpowered, fell back upon Griffin's division which was formed *echelon* in its rear.

General Humphrey sent Miles's division to support the Fifth Corps, and then a counter-attack was made on the enemy who were driven to their intrenchments.

Chamberlain's brigade of Warren's corps especially distinguished itself in this counter-attack by capturing the Fifty-sixth Virginia and its colors.

It was four o'clock when this battle at Gravelly Run was won, but on the extreme left the distant roar of conflict told our men that Sheridan was fighting the enemy at Dinwiddie Court-House.

Slowly the tide of battle seemed to recede, which showed Warren that the enemy were driving that intrepid commander — Sheridan. Soon marching orders came to General Bartlett of the Third Brigade, and says my comrade, "We marched to the sound of the battle, over narrow roads, lined on either side with a dense growth of pines. The darkness soon came on, and we lay down to rest, when we discovered that the enemy's lines were so near us that we could not only hear their pickets talking, but could hear the conversation of soldiers in their intrenchments. The situation required us to retrace our steps, which we did quickly."

FIVE FORKS.

It was clear and cold on the morning of April 1, 1865, when the Fifth Corps took up the line of march for Five Forks. At ten o'clock the line halted. Lee had guarded the South-side Railroad with intrenchments running parallel with this road for its defences. Five Forks might be called the key point of the intrenched lines, which, if broken, opened the region that Lee was endeavoring to cover. This position we were about to attack.

The Fifth Corps, up to this time, had borne the brunt of the fighting since the army began its march on the 29th. Every veteran in rank knew that a crushing blow was about to be delivered at a vital point in the enemy's lines. The private soldiers were as anxious for its success as their commanders.

Sheridan had what he designated as "one of the liveliest times of his life," the day previous, and was now chafing with impatience to "go for them." He was seen at different parts of the line, on his powerful black horse, urging, vociferating, striking his clinched fist into the palm of his hand, and — possibly swearing. He was heard to exclaim, "My cavalry are using up their ammunition, and we've got to hurry up things!"

When, at two o'clock, the Fifth Corps was formed in double line of battle, Sheridan was heard exclaiming, "This battle must be fought on the jump! We've got to smash 'em before sundown!"

Our battle line of weather-beaten soldiers was moving into position with the steady swing of veterans, as Sheridan, accompanied by his staff and scouts (the latter wearing the Confederate uniform), came dashing along the line, uttering exclamations, and vociferating encouragement on every side. "We'll get the twist on 'em, boys! There won't be a grease spot of 'em left when we are done with 'em!" he shouted. He seemed the very impersonation of action.

Sheridan's superiority as a commander consisted not in any new application of the rules of war, but in his skilful combination in the use of cavalry with infantry.

Sheridan began this battle by the use of his cavalry as an impenetrable mask behind which to manœuvre his infantry.

First, with them, he drove the enemy from his temporary lines to his intrenchments on the White Oak road, then feinting as if to turn the Confederate right with them, he brought the pressure of his infantry to fall on the left flank of his antagonist. At the same time he protected his left flank with cavalry; defeated and drove back a small force of the enemy found advancing from Petersburg.

At four o'clock the Fifth Corps moved forward to the White Oak road, where it changed front and faced west. In this manœuvre Ayer's division, being the pivot of the movement, effected its change of front first, and encountered the enemy's skirmishers in front of a strong breastwork behind a thick veil of pines. While struggling over the boggy ground, and through the dense underbrush in front of these works, they were

Sheridan at Five Forks.

staggered by a terrible fire, which drove them back in confusion.

Sheridan, who happened to be present at this critical moment, rushed into their disordered lines, exclaiming, "Close up your ranks, boys; we'll get 'em yet! Where is my battle flag." Then, taking it from the hands of the sergeant who carried it, he waved the crimson and white banner, cheering and urging the men to close up their ranks again. The bullets pattered around him like rain, and the sergeant who had carried the flag was killed. Soon the ranks were steadied, and the veterans rushed forward with fixed bayonets upon the enemy's works, killing or capturing those who did not run.

Sheridan was soon in the captured works, and was heard to say to the prisoners, in a vein of good-natured raillery, " We want every one of you! Drop your guns, — you'll never need them again! You'll be safe now we've got you!" One thousand five hundred men were captured at this angle of the enemy's works.

The enemy was entrapped and enveloped on every side. Griffin's division was drawn towards the left to close up an interval, and fell unexpectedly on the enemy's rear. A comrade of that division says, "We had reached a hill, and looking down through the trees saw the enemy's breastworks but a little distance from us.

"We then silently formed our lines and charged on them with a wild cheer. The enemy, not aware of our presence in their rear, had not made preparations for our entertainment, and so threw down their guns without firing a shot."

Discovering, however, that they had been out-manœuvred and not out-numbered, and that they had made a blunder in surrendering, their officers rallied them, and they resumed the fight. A hand to hand encounter that baffles description then began. Men were bayoneted, brains were knocked out with muskets, and acts of individual bravery performed that would, if narrated, fill volumes. Groups of our men, who, after the Confederates had surrendered, had been separated from comrades, fought their way through the disordered mass of Confederates. Shouts and screams, curses and cheers, mingled in a babel of sounds, amid a mob of mingled contestants.

This desperate fight was raging when the cavalry bugles were heard, and from the woods, a few rods distant, there came with a cheer a squadron of cavalry rushing over the works. Sheridan soon followed, exclaiming " Smash 'em, boys! smash 'em!"

The rebel works were now in our possession, and the brave but dejected Confederates were marched to the rear.

We had too much respect for these brave men to jeer at them, but good-natured jokes passed from line to line.

"You'ns didn't outfight we'uns; you'ns played a right smart Yankee trick on we'uns."

"Don't growl, Johnnie, all is fair in war! We'll take better care of you than your Uncle Robert can!" was the good-natured response.

The fight was over, the sun had gone down, but for these veterans of the Fifth Corps, there was no rest. All night groups of men looked for wounded or dead comrades, and buried the dead. Their hearts were both glad and sad. Sad that friends and comrades had fallen; glad that victory brought to them the light of dawning peace.

CHAPTER XXXVII.

THE RACE FOR LIFE.

WHEN the news of Sheridan's successes at Five Forks reached Grant, he opened fire on the enemy from the artillery that studded the lines in front of Petersburg, thundering from the mouths of an hundred guns a pean of victory. He also ordered Wright, Park, and Ord to attack the enemy in their front on the morning of the 2d. As a result, the Confederates were pressed back into the outer defences around Petersburg.

Hard pressed, Longstreet, who had reinforced Fort Greggs, was yet able to protract a resistance, which gave time for Lee to communicate with the government at the Confederate capital his purpose of speedily abandoning the lines before Petersburg and Richmond.

Lee plainly saw that all moves but one would end in checkmate; that there was but one line of retreat that did not foreshadow disaster, and that one was the line still open on the left banks of the Appomattox. He was confident, however, of making a successful retreat, and cheerfully said, "I've got my army safely out of its breastworks, and, in order to follow me, my enemy must abandon his lines, and can derive no further benefit from the railroad on James River."

It was only the prodigous vigor of Grant, in pushing forward the pursuit, and of Sheridan's untiring ardor and energy, that foiled Lee in his purpose of uniting his army with that of Johnston.

On the morning of April 3d, the burning city of Richmond apprised Weitzel of its evacuation; that the city which for four years of war had been defended with almost superhuman energy and skill, had at last fallen.

The irony of fate was shown in its surrender, by the civil authorities, to the black troops of Weitzel.

Grant had meanwhile thoughtfully conveyed to Sheridan's soldiers intelligence of Richmond's downfall, for their encouragement.

On the 2d of April, the Fifth Corps set out on its march from Gravelly Run to Five Forks in high spirits. "As we hopefully marched forward," says a comrade, "preceded by cavalry with whom we joked, raced, and traded for chickens, an officer, riding down the road, excitedly swinging his hat, shouted that Richmond and Petersburg were evacuated! We at first were sceptical. Our hopes had been fed on fictitious victories to some extent during three years, and we shouted back derisively, 'No, you don't!' 'April fool!' 'Put him in an ice box!' 'Poultice his head with hard-tack!' and the usual slang in vogue among soldiers of that period."

Thus was received the news of the fall of Richmond by the veterans who had been largely instrumental in its accomplishment. The news, that at last there was a break in that undaunted front of the heroic army of Northern Virginia, literally seemed too good to be true. What a thrill of exultation ran through our ranks when we were satisfied of its truth! We cheered until we were hoarse, threw up our caps, shook hands with each other, and at the same time marched forward to the final battle before us.

In that terrible race for life, Lee was attempting to reach Burke-ville; for should he fail to reach this point before the Union troops, he would be forced off the direct Danville line, and could only recover it again with great difficulty.

Before leaving Richmond, he had sent forward rations for his army to Amelia Court-House. But fate, which had so often befriended him, proved treacherous at last; for, on his arrival at Amelia, he learned that the train with rations had been returned by mistake to Richmond, and his army was left unprovisioned. He could not, therefore, keep his men together, as he had planned, to defeat in detail the detached Union forces set against him. They must in part be sent out in foraging parties to gather rations for his half-starved army. This detained him until the 5th of April.

This unforeseen delay was the fatal break in Lee's plans, which enabled Sheridan and the Fifth Corps to intercept the Confederate line of retreat, and cut off the Danville Railroad, seven miles southwest from Amelia Court-House.

On the afternoon of April 5th Meade had joined his forces with those of Sheridan at Jetersville, and Lee now had no alternative but to *escape* to the mountains beyond Lynchburg. When, therefore, on the morning of the 6th, the Army of the Potomac moved forward to attack, they found Lee had departed.

Meanwhile the Army of the James had arrived by the line of the Lynchburg Railroad to Burkeville, and on the 6th it had marched towards Farmville. Its cavalry met the head of Lee's column, and so delayed his movements that the remainder of the Army of the James arrived before Lee could get away.

Sheridan, now separated from the Army of the Potomac, was pushing his way in a southerly direction, on lines parallel to the Confederate retreat, with a confidence and vigor that words cannot adequately express. On the 6th he destroyed a Confederate wagon train, accompanied by a formidable escort of infantry and artillery. Sixteen pieces of artillery and many prisoners were captured, and the four hundred wagons of the train were burned. Ewell, with his cavalry, which had been following this train, was cut off by Sheridan, who charged this force with his troopers, and otherwise delayed it until the van of the Sixth Corps had arrived. Ewell fell back, fighting; turning again and again in sudden attacks and furious sallies, showing, even in defeat and retreat, while surrounded and harassed by enemies, that his men and their commander were worthy to be named as veteran soldiers of the Army of Northern Virginia.

At last, pressed also on the right by the Second Corps of the Union Army, he surrendered all that remained of his command.

Meanwhile Lee, with the devoted followers left to him, continued the retreat and reached Farmville, on the south bank of the Appomattox, during the night.

Bleeding with wounds, fainting from fatigue, harassed by enemies, without rations, almost without hope, environed by miseries on all sides, they still continued the unequalled race. One must be lacking in the common elements of manhood, who does not feel a thrill of admiration and pity for these brave men and their great commander, in this their last struggle.

A meeting of Lee's chief officers around the bivouac fire that night counselled him that there was no alternative left to his army but surrender.

Lee, however, had not abandoned all hope, and began once more his desperate race for life. He crossed the Appomattox River, setting fire to the bridges to prevent pursuit, when the Second Corps of the Union army overtook his rear-guard at High Bridge, saved the wagon road bridge, and crossed on it in pursuit, until it found the Confederate army intrenched in a formidable position. They attacked, but were repulsed. During the night Lee continued his retreat by the narrow neck of land formed by the Appomattox and the James rivers. If Sheridan, who was hurrying with prodigous vigor to close this narrow outlet, was successful, all hope for the Confederates was lost.

In answer to a letter received from General Grant on the night of April 8th, asking for the surrender of his army, Lee, with a touch of mingled audacity and irony, had replied, "I do not think the emergency has arisen to call for the surrender of this army ; but, as the restoration of peace should be the sole object of all, I desire to know whether your proposal would lead to that end."

Grant received this note about midnight, and replied in substance, "I have no authority to treat on the subject of peace. . . . I will state, however, General, that I am equally anxious for peace with yourself, and the whole North entertain the same feeling. . . . By the South laying down their arms, they will hasten that most desirable event."

Before Lee received this letter, Sheridan had arrived at Appomattox Station on the Lynchburg Railroad, and there captured four trains of cars, loaded with supplies for Lee's starving veterans. He then encountered and drove back the Confederate vanguard, and planted himself squarely across the outlet of Lee's only path for escape.

Thus pressed, a thin line of wearied Confederates, under Gordon and Longstreet, began the attempt to cut its way through Sheridan's lines. All that now remained of Lee's army was about eight thousand men, and these, though hungry and despairing, began the fight with all their old impetuosity and vim. Sheridan directed his troopers who had dismounted, the better to carry on the fight, to fall back slowly, in order to give the Fifth Corps time to get up.

When at last the Confederate army caught sight of the gleaming bayonets and blue masses of the Union infantry advancing, they knew that all was over.

Sheridan had ordered a charge upon the Confederates, when an officer bearing a white flag, with a letter from Lee, asking for a suspension of hostilities with a view to surrendering his army, rode to our lines.

The surrender took place at a dwelling at Appomattox Court-House. All officers and men gave their paroles not to take up arms against the United States until properly exchanged. Officers were allowed their private baggage and side arms, and soldiers who owned horses were allowed to take them home to till their little farms.

More generous terms were never given to a con-

The Flag of Truce.

quered foe, — terms in keeping with the generosity of brave soldiers, to those who were no longer enemies but countrymen.

SURRENDER OF THE ARMY OF VIRGINIA. Page 350.

"LAYING DOWN THEIR ARMS."

My comrade of the Fifth Corps says, "After the battle of Five Forks, we used our legs more than we did our arms. The foraging was good, and our captures of that nature consisted of chickens, ducks, bacon, sheep, molasses, and tobacco, to which we helped ourselves, after the usual manner of soldiers.

"The roads over which we passed were crowded with artillery, baggage wagons, and cavalry, all hurrying and crowding, each claiming the right of way over its competitors. We were not very good-natured, and did not scruple to beat with the butt of our muskets anything that disputed our right of way, including cavalry.

"On the 8th of April we had a march of thirty-five miles, and that distance, when travelled over Virginia roads, was, I believe, equal at least to forty miles of marching over any other roads of any other country in the world.

"Though foraging was good, but little opportunity was given us for cooking. As night came, regiments became separated from brigades, and companies broke up into squads, so obstructed were the roads. At three o'clock in the morning I had got up with my division, from which I had for some time been separated. It was just starting out.

"Sheridan had just sent back word that Lee was at bay, and that we must hurry up and finish him. Under this incentive we marched all night with great rapidity. The morning of the 9th of April dawned, bright and balmy.

"Our wearied men had halted, and we were engaged in gathering rails and other fuel to cook our rations, when the bugle again sounded, 'Fall in! fall in!'

"Heavy firing was heard not a mile distant, and in spite of hunger and fatigue we hurried forward. We had not gone far when we met broken squads of cavalry, who told us they had been fighting all night, and said one, to emphasize the fact, 'We've had a regular nightmare, though we've not had any sleep.'

"As we marched on we came to a hill, where we saw Sheridan surrounded by his officers. Then our men, who had been in hopes that they had only a skirmish before them, and that they would soon get a chance to cook their food, on seeing Sheridan, exclaimed :

'The devil's to pay! There are no rations, nothing but fighting where he is!' That was the common opinion, and was probably the one at that time entertained by the enemy.

"The enemy's artillery opened on us as we advanced, and a shell struck and burst in a barn on the line of our advance. A cackling of hens showed us its occupants. So we took them in as we went along; and such a ridiculous squawking and fluttering of hens (as the men, in spite of orders, gathered them in) was, I think, never before seen on a line of battle.

"This charge meant, apparently, death to many in our ranks, and a soldier is not anxious to die when he is hungry, or at any other time; bosh, to the contrary, notwithstanding. That was our excuse for

Feeding the Rebs.

taking in these hens, on such a serious occasion. We descended the hill to attack the Confederates on the hill opposite, and notwithstanding the episode narrated, many of us looked serious.

"As we advanced, we saw the flutter of something white on the enemy's lines. We soon saw that it was a flag, but little did we then comprehend its meaning. Some in our ranks were even heard to growl, 'It's a signal to attack!' At a brisk gallop a mounted officer, bearing the flag, rode forward to within a few rods of our lines, and turned to the right, where Sheridan had gone an instant before. Still we went forward down the hill, to attack, when one of Sheridan's staff came from the wood, swinging his hat, and yelling at the top of his voice, 'Halt, men! Halt! Lee has surrendered!'

"At first we did not believe it (for old veterans do not believe everything they hear, like recruits), but at last, when convinced of its truth, we shouted, threw up our hats, hurrahed and hurrahed, and even cried for joy.

"Our long marches and battles and hardships were over. During the advance, the line of our late enemies was withdrawn, and later a large number of Confederates came over to see us. We gave them rations, and even divided with them our eggs and captured hens, which had been cooked. One would not have thought, to have seen us, that we had ever been enemies. We made coffee for them, and drank from the same tin cups, if not 'from the same canteens.' Some of us gave them all the rations we had and went hungry ourselves. They were most of them wearied, earnest-looking men, wearing butternut-colored and gray clothing and broad-brimmed soft hats.

"For two or three days, while preparations were being made for the formal surrender, we camped on the hill-side. To our brigade, commanded by General Chamberlain, the honor was given of receiving the formal surrender of all that remained of Lee's veterans.

"Our blue line of nine battered regiments was drawn up and stood at order arms, motionless as a blue wall tipped with steel.

"The Confederates were soon seen advancing; they approached until there was only a few yards' space between us, and then there came the order from their ranks: 'Halt! right dress! front!' and the hitherto hostile lines confronted each other for the last time. Then the order came from our general to salute: 'Shoulder arms! Present arms!' The gray line returned the salute, and the last of the Army of Northern Virginia stacked their arms, laid on them their battered equipments and bullet-riddled, weather-stained colors, and then breaking ranks, sadly turned away to seek their homes.

"Many of them tore little bits from their loved flag, now laid away forever, to keep as mementoes, and we sympathized in this expression and did not hinder them."

These war-worn men went their way, never to take up arms again for the mistaken cause they had defended so bravely, but to become citizens, with us, of one common republic.

It speaks volumes for the simplicity of Grant's greatness that he never visited the lines of the men he had beaten, or the capital they had defended.

Thus ends our story of war, of patriotism, and the surrender of those who had fought against the Union of States.

Library of Congress Cataloguing in Publication Data

Goss, Warren Lee, 1835-1925.
Recollections of a private.
(Collector's library of the Civil War)
Reprint. Originally published: New York : T.Y. Crowell, c1890
1. Goss, Warren Lee, 1835-1925.
2. United States—History—Civil War, 1861-1865—Personal narratives.
3. United States. Army of the Potomac—Biography.
4. Soldiers—United States—Biography.
I. Title. II. Series.
E601.G67   1984   973.7'3   84-2679
ISBN 0-8094-4467-4 (library)
ISBN 0-8094-4466-6 (retail)

Printed in the United States of America